PREDICTING THE PRESIDENCY

PREDICTING THE PRESIDENCY

THE POTENTIAL OF PERSUASIVE LEADERSHIP

George C. Edwards III

PRINCETON UNIVERSITY PRESS
PRINCETON AND OXFORD

Published by Princeton University Press, 41 William Street, Princeton,
New Jersey 08540

In the United Kingdom: Princeton University Press, 6 Oxford Street,
Woodstock, Oxfordshire OX20 1TW

press.princeton.edu

Library of Congress Cataloging-in-Publication Data

Names: Edwards, George C., author.

Title: Predicting the presidency : the path to effective leadership /
George C. Edwards, III.

Description: Princeton : Princeton University Press, [2016] | Includes
bibliographical references and index.

Identifiers: LCCN 2015037534 | ISBN 9780691170374 (hardcover)

Subjects: LCSH: Presidents—United States. | Executive-legislative
relations—United States. | Executive power—United States. | Political
leadership—United States. | Presidents—United States—Public
opinion. | Public opinion—Political aspects—United States.

Classification: LCC JK585 .E326 2016 | DDC 352.23/60973—dc23 LC
record available at http://lccn.loc.gov/2015037534

British Library Cataloging-in-Publication Data is available

This book has been composed in Charis

Printed on acid-free paper. ∞

Printed in the United States of America

1 3 5 7 9 10 8 6 4 2

To Carmella,
my muse and my joy

Contents

PART III CONCLUSION

Figures

Tables

Preface

ON THE MORNING of November 7, 2012, I found myself in the BBC television studio in Oxford, analyzing Barack Obama's reelection the previous evening. The anchor seemed disappointed—or at least skeptical—when I explained that despite the president's victory, he would find governing difficult in his second term. The only exception was likely to be increasing taxes on the wealthiest Americans. She persisted in asking about the president's prospects, but I could only provide the same answer: governing was going to be difficult.

I savored no schadenfreude in predicting that Obama's second term, like his first,[1] would be less transformative than either the president or his supporters hoped. Nevertheless, the prospects (or lack of them) were clear, and subsequent history has borne out my forecast. Making such predictions requires understanding how presidential leadership works and asking the right questions about it.

It was not necessary to know the rhetoric the president would employ on behalf of his initiatives, the nature of his interpersonal relations with members of Congress, the tenor of the media's coverage of the White House, or the quality of the president's public outreach efforts. Even if Obama scored very high on all these dimensions, it would not have mattered. What did matter was the president's strategic position—his opportunity structure—with the public and in Congress. Answering key questions about the president's opportunity structure allowed me to make accurate predictions about Obama's second term, even just a few hours after Mitt Romney conceded.

Political scientists have made substantial progress in their understanding of presidential leadership. My conclusion about the prospects for President Obama's second term, which ran contrary to the conventional wisdom, would be accepted by most, although not necessarily all, presidential scholars. The most visible commentators on presidential politics are not political scientists, however. Instead, they include journalists, elected officials, political activists, and pollsters. Scholars in other disciplines also make their voices heard. The vast range of social media outlets and blogs in the Internet age as well as in the traditional print and broadcast media provide these pundits broad access to the public. Unfortunately, reality checks are few and far between.

Leadership is perhaps the most commonly employed concept in politics. Politicians, pundits, journalists, and scholars critique and analyze public officials, attributing both success and failure to the quality of their leadership. When times are bad, as people often perceive them to be, the reflexive call is for new—and better—leadership. The president is the most prominent focus of political leadership in the United States, and the notion of the dominant president who moves the country and the government by means of strong, effective leadership has deep roots in American political culture.

Thus, millions of people, ranging from the general public to experienced politicos, viewed Barack Obama, and the presidency more generally, through the prism of high expectations, premised on a belief in the power of presidential persuasion. Obama would transform both politics and public policy in America. He was even awarded the Nobel Peace Prize very early in his tenure for how he would transform the world. Yet many of those who were inspired by *candidate* Obama were disappointed in *President* Obama, or at least disappointed in what he was able to accomplish. They could not understand why he often could not leverage his position and political skills to move the country and Congress to support his initiatives.

In part I of this book I apply my theory of the nature of presidential leadership to explain events that are fresh in our minds, significant issues during the first two years of Barack Obama's second term, and explain why President Obama had such difficulty in bringing about change. In doing so I show that the common view of political leadership is wrong, and I offer an alternative view, which starts with different premises and asks different questions. I also simplify the challenge of examining presidential leadership by showing how we can ask a few fundamental questions about the context of a presidency—the president's strategic position or opportunity structure—and use the answers to predict the success of a president in winning support from the public and Congress for his initiatives.

If presidential success is largely determined by the president's opportunity structure, is there any role for persuasion? Almost every president finds that a significant segment of the public and his fellow partisans in Congress are predisposed to follow his lead. Others may be inclined to support the White House because of self-interest. I explore the possibilities of the president exploiting such potential support in part II, providing a more realistic view of the potential of presidential persuasion.

Successful prediction is an indicator of successful explanation. Understanding the nature and possibilities of leadership puts us in a better position to evaluate both the performance of presidents and the opportunities for change and to set our expectations accordingly.

The stakes of understanding the potential of leadership are especially high for the White House. Raising the public's expectations based on anticipated success may inadvertently lay the foundation for later disappointment and withdrawal of support. Moreover, the adoption of a core governing strategy of changing public opinion or the positions of members of Congress based on a belief in the potential of persuasive leadership may encourage presidents to underestimate their opponents and eschew necessary compromises. Presidents—and the country—often endure self-inflicted wounds when they fail to appreciate the limits of their influence.

As has been true for several volumes over the past decade, I began this book at Oxford. I am grateful to Nigel Bowles and the Rothermere American Institute for providing me office space, intellectual exchange, and time to reflect. I am also thankful to Balliol College, an extraordinary institution that I grew to love during my tenure as Winant Professor. Finally, I greatly value my continuing relationship with Nuffield College, one of the jewels in the crown of social science, and am particularly thankful for the support of another good friend, Desmond King.

Books need to be finished as well as begun. Texas A&M University has been my institutional anchor for nearly two generations. Words are not adequate to convey how important the collegial environment and flexible schedule have been to my completing this and many other projects.

I am also grateful to Brandice Canes-Wrone, David Demarest, Matthew Dickinson, Roy Flemming, Clodagh Harrington, William Howell, Ezra Klein, Martha Kumar, Matthew Miles, Charles Walcott, Richard Waterman, and Stephen Wayne for their insightful comments on various parts of this manuscript. Eric Crahan is a talented editor who both engages analytical arguments and manages the publication process efficiently. His assistant, Ben Pokross, efficiently handled a myriad of matters. Karen Verde is a superb copyeditor, and Karen Carter an equally capable production editor. I have enjoyed working with both of these highly skilled professionals on several books.

As always, the key to any success I may have is the support of my wife, Carmella. For creating an environment in which I can focus on my work—and for just being her loving and fascinating self—I am eternally grateful.

PREDICTING THE PRESIDENCY

CHAPTER 1

Asking the Right Questions

IT IS NATURAL for new presidents, basking in the glow of an electoral victory, to focus on creating, rather than exploiting, opportunities for change. It may seem quite reasonable for leaders who have just won the biggest prize in American politics by convincing voters and party leaders to support their candidacies to conclude that they should be able to convince members of the public and the U.S. Congress to support their policies. Thus, they need not focus on evaluating existing possibilities when they think they can create their own.

Campaigning is different from governing, however. Campaigns focus on short-term victory and candidates wage them in either/or terms. To win an election, a candidate need only convince voters that he or she is a better choice than the few available alternatives. In addition, someone always wins, whether or not voters support the victor's policy positions.

Governing, on the other hand, involves deliberation, negotiation, and often compromise over an extended period. Moreover, in governing, the president's policy is just one of a wide range of alternatives. Furthermore, delay is a common objective, and a common outcome, in matters of public policy. Neither the public nor elected officials have to choose. Although stalemate may sometimes be the president's goal, the White House usually wishes to convince people to support a positive action.

In sum, we should not infer from success in winning elections that the White House can persuade members of the public and Congress to change their minds and support policies they would otherwise oppose. The American political system is not a fertile field for the exercise of presidential leadership. Most political actors, from the average citizen to members of Congress, are free to choose whether to follow the chief executive's lead; the president cannot force them to act. At the same time, the sharing of powers established by the U.S. Constitution's checks and balances not only prevents the president from acting unilaterally on most important matters but also gives other power holders different perspectives on issues and policy proposals.

PERSUASION AND PRESIDENTIAL POWER

The best-known dictum regarding the American presidency is that "presidential power is the power to persuade."[1] It is the wonderfully felicitous phrase that captures the essence of Richard Neustadt's argument in *Presidential Power*. For more than half a century, scholars and students—and many presidents—have viewed the presidency through the lens of Neustadt's core premise.

In Neustadt's words, " 'powers' are no guarantee of power"[2] *and "[t]he probabilities of power do not derive from the literary theory of the Constitution."*[3] Presidents would have to struggle to get their way. Indeed, it was the inherent weakness of the presidency that made it necessary for presidents to understand how to use their resources most effectively.

Power, then, is a function of personal politics rather than of formal authority or position. Neustadt placed people and politics in the center of research, and the core activity on which he focused was leadership. Indeed, the subtitle of *Presidential Power* is *The Politics of Leadership*. In essence, presidential leadership is the power to persuade.

To think strategically about power, we must search for generalizations. According to Neustadt:

> There are two ways to study "presidential power." One way is to focus on the tactics . . . of influencing certain men in given situations. . . . The other way is to step back from tactics . . . and to deal with influence in more strategic terms: what is its nature and what are its sources? . . . Strategically, [for example] the question is not how he masters Congress in a peculiar instance, but what he does to boost his chance for mastery in any instance.[4]

Thus, Neustadt encouraged us to focus on the strategic level of power when we examined presidential persuasion. In broad terms, persuasion refers to causing others to do something by reasoning, urging, or inducement. Influencing others is central to the conception of leadership of most political scientists. Scholars of the presidency want to know whether the chief executive can affect the output of government by influencing the actions and attitudes of others.

What did Neustadt mean by persuasion? "The essence of a President's persuasive task, with congressmen and everybody else," he argued, "is to induce them to believe that what he wants of them is what their own appraisal of their own responsibilities requires them to do in their interest, not his. . . . Persuasion deals in the coin of self-interest with men who have some freedom to reject what they find counterfeit."[5] Thus, "The power to persuade is the power to bargain."[6]

In other words, the president is not likely to change many minds among those who disagree with him on substance or have little incentive to help him succeed. Although Neustadt did not focus extensively on public opinion, we can generalize beyond public officials to their constituents. His endorsement of the findings in *On Deaf Ears*[7] that presidents rarely move the public in their direction reflects his skepticism about changing public opinion.

In his important work on the *Politics Presidents Make,* Stephen Skowronek maintains that the presidency's capacity to transform American government and politics results from its blunt and disruptive effects. Andrew Jackson forced the submission of the nullifiers and undermined the Bank of the United States, Franklin Pierce deployed the resources of his office on behalf of the Kansas Nebraska Act, and Lincoln bludgeoned the South into submission. All were transformative acts that changed the landscape of American government and politics. I agree. And Skowronek agrees that persuasion was not central to any of these actions.[8]

In addition, Skowronek argues that presidential failures can be as transformative as their successes, with retribution for failure driving political change, jarring loose governing coalitions, opening unforeseen alternatives, shifting the balance of power, and passing to successors an entirely new set of opportunities and constraints.[9] Again, I agree. My focus, however, is on presidents attempting to obtain support for policies that *they* want.

A LESS RESTRICTED VIEW

Not everyone has such restrained views of leaders, and few are blessed with the penetrating and nuanced understanding of the presidency of a Richard Neustadt. Many political commentators suggest that all the president has to do to obtain the support of the public or members of Congress is to reach into his inventory of leadership skills and employ the appropriate means of persuasion. Most presidents, at least at the beginning of their tenures, seem to believe them. In other words, these observers and participants believe presidents can *create* opportunities for change.

For example, many liberals could not understand how the White House could fail to win stricter gun control laws following the Newtown massacre on December 14, 2012. They, like the White House, thought the president could rally the public and twist enough congressional arms to achieve policy change. *New York Times* columnist Maureen Dowd complained that Obama had "not learned how to govern"—he did "not know how to work the system . . . or even hire some clever people who can tell him how to do it or do it for him." She advised her readers that the president "should have gone out to Ohio, New Hampshire and Nevada and had big rallies to get the public riled up to put pressure on Rob Portman, Kelly Ayotte and Dean Heller, giving notice that they would pay a price if they spurned him on this."[10] Thus, the president's failure was his own fault.

Presidents are not immune from the belief that they can create opportunities for change. For example, Bill Clinton's aides reported that he exhibited an "unbelievable arrogance" regarding his ability to change public opinion and felt he could "create new political capital all the time" by going public.[11] Similarly, Barack Obama believed in the power of rhetoric to rally the public on behalf of policy change. As he proclaimed while running for president in 2008,

> Don't tell me words don't matter. "I have a dream"—just words. "We hold these truths to be self-evident that all men are created equal"— just words. "We have nothing to fear but fear itself"—just words, just speeches. It's true that speeches don't solve all problems, but what is also true is that if we can't inspire our country to believe again, then it doesn't matter how many policies and plans we have, and that is why I'm running for president of the United States of America, . . . because the American people want to believe in change again. Don't tell me words don't matter![12]

It is not surprising, then, that the president dismissed the advice of his top assistants and pursued health care reform in his first year, confident that he could win the public's support.[13]

The president's own staff may also buy into the myth of presidential persuasiveness. One White House aide recalled how a few of his colleagues considered highlighting some pages of Robert Caro's book about Lyndon Johnson as Senate majority leader and leaving it on Obama's desk. "Sometimes a president just needs to knock heads," the aide declared. As he saw it, Johnson "twisted their arm, they had no choice—he was going [to] defund them, ruin 'em, support their opponent . . . and the deal was cut."[14] (I will address this misremembered history of LBJ in chapter 9.)

GETTING IT RIGHT

The underlying premise of such appraisals is that the system is responsive to presidential will, if only the White House exercises it skillfully. Such a view is naïve, however. An extensive body of research in political science has found that even the most skilled presidents have great difficulty in persuading the public[15] or members of Congress[16] to support them.

Because presidents are not in strong positions to *create* opportunities for success by persuading members of Congress or their constituents to change their minds about supporting their policies, recognizing the opportunities that already exist is particularly significant. For presidents, it may be the most important skill of all, because they typically engender change by exploiting existing opportunities rather than creating them.[17] It follows that understanding the president's opportunity structure is the key to solving the puzzle of presidential leadership.

It is important for all of us to understand how successful presidents actually lead. What are the essential presidential leadership skills? Under what conditions are they most effective? What contributions can these skills make to engendering change? The answers to these questions should influence presidents' efforts to govern, the focus of scholarly research and journalistic coverage, and the expectations and evaluations of citizens. Thus, we must seek a better understanding of presidential leadership in order to think sensibly about the role of the chief executive in the nation's political system.

LEADERSHIP

Influencing others is central to most people's conception of leadership, including those most focused on politics. In a democracy, we are particularly attuned to efforts to persuade, especially when most potentially significant policy changes require the assent of multiple power holders. Thus persuasion seems to lie at the heart of leadership.

Yet, leadership is an elusive concept. James MacGregor Burns's contention that "Leadership is one of the most observed and least understood phenomena on earth"[18] is as true now as it was when he asserted it in 1978. Writers and commentators employ the term "leadership" to mean just about everything a person who occupies what we often refer to as a position of leadership does—or should do. When we define a term so broadly, however, it loses its utility.

The Constitution and federal laws invest significant discretionary authority in the president. Making decisions and issuing commands are important, and doing them well requires courage, wisdom, and skill. At times, the exercise of unilateral authority may lead to historic changes in the politics and policy of the country. In the extreme case, the president can choose to launch a nuclear attack at his discretion. The consequences would be vast. Most people, however, would not view such an act as one of leadership. In exercising discretionary authority, the president, in effect, acts alone. He does not have to *lead* anyone to do something.

Making tough decisions, establishing an administration's priorities, and appointing able people to implement policy are core functions of the presidency. Yet these activities differ substantially from obtaining the support of the public and the Congress for the president's policies.

Similarly, an important element of a chief executive's job may be creating the organizational and personal conditions that promote innovative thinking, the frank and open presentation and analysis of alternatives, and effective implementation of decisions by advisers and members of the bureaucracy. We may reasonably view such actions as leadership, and there is no doubt that the processes of decision making and policy implementation are critical to governing. For purposes of this book, however, I focus on leadership of those who are not directly on the president's team and who are thus less obligated to support his initiatives.

DIFFERENT QUESTIONS

We have seen that there are contrasting perspectives on presidential leadership. One emphasizes creating opportunities for success through persuading others to change their minds and support the president. The other perspective is more modest and puts exploiting opportunities for success that already exist at its core. Each perspective leads analysts to ask different questions about presidential politics. We will see in chapter 4 that each perspective also leads to different answers for explaining the results of presidential leadership.

The belief that presidents not only need to persuade but that persuasion will be central to their success has encouraged journalists, commentators, some scholars, and other observers of the presidency to focus on the question of *how* presidents persuade rather than the more fundamental question of *whether they can do so*. In other words, there is more emphasis on description than analysis and too little attention given to the essential question of, what difference do efforts at leadership make?

An emphasis on the personal in politics, based on the assumption of the potential success of persuasion, has led some to overlook the importance of the context in which the president operates as well as his institutional setting. Doing so encourages ad hoc explanations and discourages generalizations about the strategic level of power. Reaching such generalizations should be central to our enterprise, however.

If the fundamental premise underlying one's approach to presidential leadership is that presidents can persuade the public or members of Congress to support of them, then it follows that certain questions will be at the core of research. One set of questions would deal with the impact of the president's characteristics on his persuasiveness. Such questions might focus on the president's personal persuasiveness, skill as a public speaker, and ability to relate to both average Americans and members of Congress. Other questions would focus on the means of persuasion such as the use of various rhetorical devices, the quality and frequency of speech making, the venues of speeches, and the investment of time in socializing with members of Congress.

If the core of presidential power is not the power to persuade, however, scholars should ask a different set of questions. Understanding the nature and possibilities of leadership puts us in a better position to evaluate both the performance of presidents and the opportunities for change. Equally important, we have a better sense of where to look for explanations of the success and consequences of presidential leadership. If there are significant limits on presidential persuasion, it follows that major changes in public policy will not necessarily turn on a president's persuasive skills or his willingness to use them.

Exploiting opportunities requires a different set of skills than creating them. If exploiting opportunities to steer true believers is more critical to engendering change than persuading the skeptical, much less converting the opposition, it follows that we should focus more on maintaining and managing coalitions and less on the verbal dexterity or interpersonal persuasiveness that is hypothetically necessary to expand coalitions and thus transform the political landscape.[19] As a result, we will ask different questions about the president's personal characteristics, focusing on how presidents actually marshal forces to bring about change. Relevant questions include the degree of the president's analytical insight regarding his opportunity structure and his skill in exploiting his opportunities. We will also want to know if he has the commitment, resolution, strength, and resiliency to persevere and take full advantage of opportunities that exist.

Moving beyond the president as an individual, we will want to study the president's strategic position, his opportunity structure. Regarding the public, we want to know where it stands independent of the president and the potential for attracting nascent support. We will see in chapter 2 that the core questions are:

- Did the public provide the president an electoral mandate for his policies?
- Does the public support the general direction of the president's policies?

- How polarized is public opinion?
- How malleable is public opinion?

By answering these questions, we are in a strong position to predict the likelihood of the president obtaining the public's support for his programs. We do not need to ask about the president's personal characteristics or means of persuasion because persuasion is not the key to the president's success. Instead, following Neustadt's recommendation to concentrate on the strategic level of power—the chances of winning in any instance—we should focus on the president's broad strategic position regarding the public.

If we wish to focus on the president's leadership on a particular issue, as I do in chapter 4, we can supplement our strategic analysis with answers to more specific questions such as:

- Is the president's initiative already popular with the public?
- If so, is it also salient to the public?
- How does the public evaluate the president's job performance?

Personalizing politics can distract our attention from factors that play a larger role in explaining presidential success in Congress as well as with the public and thus greatly oversimplify our understanding of executive-legislative relations. If presidents typically operate at the margins of coalition-building and exercise their legislative skills primarily to exploit rather than create opportunities for leadership, we should devote more effort to examining broader influences on Congress and less on personal skills. In chapter 3 I specify six key questions:

- Is there a perception in Congress that the president received an electoral mandate on behalf of specific policies?
- Does the president's party enjoy a majority in a chamber? If so, how large is it?
- What is the degree of ideological polarization in Congress?
- Are there cross-pressures among the public in constituencies held by the opposition party that would counter these members' ideological predispositions?
- How ideologically coherent is the president's party in Congress?
- Does the structure of the decision facing Congress favor the president?

In particular instances, we may also wish to know the answers to contextual questions such as:

- Are there slack resources in the budget or is the deficit a major constraint on initiatives?

- In which congressional constituencies, if any, is the president high in the job approval polls?
- Does the president's proposal deal with national security policy?
- Is the president serving during wartime or highly salient crisis?

In his sweeping and insightful analysis of presidents, Stephen Skowronek also emphasizes the context of a presidency, particularly the vitality of the dominant partisan coalition and the president's relation to it. The president's situation in "political time" establishes the parameters of the possibilities for change.[20] Thus, each president inherits a regime-based opportunity structure that he must negotiate throughout his term. Perhaps because of the comprehensive nature of his study, Skowronek discusses the opportunity structure in general terms. My analysis specifies which contextual factors matter and explains why they do so.

In addition, I view opportunity structure as dynamic. Party cohorts, public polarization, and other core features of a president's strategic position change over time. Often these changes are gradual, but sometimes there are dramatic alternations in opportunity structure within a single presidency.[21]

Finally, the model is not time-bound. Even though the values of strategic elements change over time, the variables themselves do not. They are always relevant to explaining the success of presidential leadership.

The Plan of the Book

Asking different questions produces different explanations for the success of presidential leadership. If we ask the right questions, we can predict the success of efforts of presidents to lead, increasing our confidence in the importance of those questions. In part I, I show how we can explain— and predict—presidential success in Congress by answering the right questions.

To illustrate the advantages of focusing on the president's existing opportunity structure, in chapters 2, 3, and 4, I focus on the first two years of Barack Obama's second term. In chapter 2, I examine Obama's strategic position—his opportunity structure—with the public to explain why he faced such difficulties in obtaining the public's support. In chapter 3, I focus on the president's opportunity structure in Congress, again explaining why he was not more successful.

In chapter 4, I show how adopting the strategic position perspective is considerably more useful in explaining the outcomes of important issues in these years than employing a perspective based on the potential of presidential persuasion. The strategic perspective leads us to ask different questions regarding presidential leadership—and encourages us to arrive at different, and better, answers.

If changing opinions is not central to presidential leadership, how can presidents lead? Within the parameters of the president's opportunity structure, what is the role of persuasion? If we turn our attention to exploiting opportunities, we can make headway in understanding the role of presidential leadership in American politics.

There are those in Congress and the public with a general predisposition to support the White House but who have yet to agree with a specific policy stand. Others may need to have their existing support reinforced. If persuasion is going to work, it is likely to be with such people. Others, especially members of Congress, may find it in their short-term self-interest to give the president what he wants, even if doing so is contrary to their orientations to public policy. Such conditions provide the president opportunities for success, and in part II, I analyze the possibilities of the president exploiting potential support in the public and in Congress.

Much of the president's efforts to exploit his environment focus on public opinion. The White House wants public support primarily to encourage members of Congress to back the president's proposals. Chapter 5 examines the president benefiting from motivated reasoning to reinforce and guide the opinions of those predisposed to support him. Chapter 6 looks at the president exploiting existing opinion on policies by showing the public how its views are compatible with his policies or by increasing the salience of White House initiatives that are popular with the public. I also address the president leading on issues on which opinion has yet to develop.

Chapter 7 analyzes the more complex but often important circumstance of the president cross-pressuring his co-partisans by supporting policies contrary to their predispositions. In addition, the president may cross-pressure identifiers with the opposition party by supporting policies they are inclined to favor or by offering a broad orientation to policy that encourages them to change their party identification. Chapter 8 focuses on using the technological advances of new forms of media to reach and potentially mobilize supporters.

Chapter 9 turns to Congress. Presidents are unlikely to change many congressional minds, but they can take advantage of members' ideological predispositions or their proclivities to support their party leader. Sometimes the structure of the decision before Congress favors the president's position. The key to successful leadership for the president is understanding his strategic position and then making the most out of it.

In the concluding chapter I take a broad view of presidential leadership. First, I stress the importance of strategic assessments in presidential leadership and the leverage they give us in evaluating the likely success of strategies for governing. I also explore how what we have learned about presidential leadership should affect presidents' attempts to govern. Before a president can fashion a strategy for accomplishing his goals, he must rigorously analyze the most significant features of his environment to understand the opportunity structure of his administration. Ideally, such appraisals will influence how much and what types of change presidents seek and the strategies they choose for achieving it. Finally, I suggest that the mistaken belief in the potential of persuasion undermines the potential for compromise necessary for governing in America.

PART I

Predicting the Presidency

CHAPTER 2

Strategic Position with the Public

PUBLIC SUPPORT IS a key political resource, and modern presidents have typically sought it for themselves and their policies. Their goal is to leverage public opinion to obtain backing for their proposals in Congress. Because presidents have typically enjoyed impressive electoral success, it is not surprising that they often focus on creating opportunities for change. Why focus on evaluating existing possibilities when you can fashion new ones?

Yet it is a mistake for presidents to assume they can change public opinion. There is nothing in the historical record to support such a belief, and there are long-term forces that work against presidential leadership of the public.[1] Adopting strategies for governing that are prone to failure waste rather than create opportunities,[2] so it is critically important for presidents to assess accurately the potential for obtaining public support.

All presidents wishing to make important changes in public policy— and that includes most presidents—should seek to answer the following questions about their strategic position with public opinion:

- Does the president have an electoral mandate from the voters for his policies?
- Does the public support the general direction of the president's policies?
- How polarized is public opinion?
- How malleable is public opinion?

In this chapter I illustrate the utility of asking—and answering—these questions by analyzing the first two years of Barack Obama's second term.

Analysts of presidential leadership operate under the same imperatives as the White House. If they are going to understand presidential politics and predict the likely outcomes of the president's efforts to win changes in policy, they have to understand the potential of presidential leadership of the public, the opportunities that he or she may have. To reveal the president's strategic position with the public requires asking the right questions.

THE PRESIDENT'S VIEW

The Obama White House believed in the power of the presidential pulpit. More importantly, it believed that the president was an irresistible persuader. According to David Axelrod, the president's top counselor in his first term, "I don't think there's been a President since Kennedy whose ability to move issues and people through a speech has been comparable."[3] This faith in presidential persuasion was the foundational premise of the administration's decision to try to move a large agenda simultaneously and explains its response to political problems.

Barack Obama entered the presidency with an impressive record of political success, at the center of which were his rhetorical skills. In college, he concluded that words had the power to transform: "with the right words everything could change—South Africa, the lives of ghetto kids just a few miles away, my own tenuous place in the world."[4] It is no surprise, then, that Obama followed the pattern of presidents seeking public support for themselves and their policies that they could leverage to obtain backing for their proposals in Congress.

The president often said that he learned during his first term that enacting legislation that was not well understood or supported by the public carried a political price. According to White House press secretary Jay Carney, the president believed he had to keep explaining "what his vision is, what his policy proposals are, what the nature of the debates are." Moreover, the president concluded that negotiations with the opposition would not work unless he turned up the public heat on lawmakers,[5] so his only option on debt talks, immigration, climate change, and gun control was to appeal to the public from the presidential pulpit, and through his political network.[6]

Obama told Charlie Rose in 2012 that his biggest regret was that he had not developed a consistent message in his first two years. "The mistake of my first couple years was thinking that this job was just about getting the policy right, and that's important. But, you know, the nature of this office is also to tell a story to the American people that gives them a sense of unity and purpose and optimism, especially during tough times."[7]

Convinced that the most essential aspect of his job, given the divisions in Washington, was rallying public opinion to his side, he planned to remain in a campaign mode in his second term. As he told David Axelrod, "From here on out, I have to take my case to the American people."[8] According to one White House official, "Republicans in Congress are not going to make these decisions because they are suddenly persuaded by the president. They are going to make these decisions because they've decided it's in their political interest to do so."[9]

The adoption of this strategy stemmed from what the White House saw as successful public campaigns to press Congress to renew a temporary payroll tax cut in 2011 and to extend lower federal student loan rates in the summer of 2012. Although Republicans complained that the president was more interested in campaigning than negotiating, he ended up getting what he wanted and, in his aides' view, he gained politically as well.[10] The White House did not emphasize or perhaps even recognize that the president was making a case for policies that enjoyed broad public support *before* he went public.[11]

On the other hand, experience had chastened the president. There is not much evidence that Barack Obama could depend on creating opportunities for change by obtaining public support and leveraging it to gain support for his proposals in Congress. In general, public opinion moved against the president over time. Andrew Kohut, president of the Pew Research Center, summarized these trends well when he declared at the end of 2009, the year in which Obama enjoyed his highest approval levels,

> What's really exceptional at this stage of Obama's presidency is the extent to which the public has moved in a conservative direction on a range of issues. These trends have emanated as much from the middle of the electorate as from the highly energized conservative right.[12]

The president knew that he had not succeeded in rallying the public to support his primary initiatives, such as health care and immigration reform and steps to combat climate change. According to Jonathan Alter, the president was much taken with an article by Ezra Klein in the *New Yorker*, which discussed research by me that showed the failure not only of himself but also of all recent presidents to move the public in their direction. These findings made the president a fatalist about how his words would be received.[13] Others in the administration also had learned the limits of going public. Discussing the president's efforts to obtain congressional support for immigration reform, Press Secretary Jay Carney declared in July 2013, "There are limits to the powers of the bully pulpit on every issue."[14]

Thus, the president had developed conflicting impulses. Nevertheless, he persisted in a strategy of attempting to create opportunities for change by mobilizing the public behind his initiatives. What were the prospects of success in such a strategy? What was the president's strategic position with the public in his second term? The rest of this chapter answers these questions.

MANDATE

New presidents traditionally claim a mandate from the people, because the most effective means of setting the terms of debate and overcoming opposition is the perception of an electoral mandate, an impression that the voters want to see the winner's programs implemented. Indeed, major changes in policy, as in 1933, 1965, and 1981, rarely occur in the absence of such perceptions.

Mandates can be powerful symbols in American politics. They accord added legitimacy and credibility to the newly elected president's proposals. Concerns for representation and political survival encourage members of Congress to support the president if they feel the people have spoken.[15] As a result, mandates change the premises of decisions. Perceptions of a mandate in 1980, for example, placed a stigma on big government and exalted the unregulated marketplace and large defense budgets, providing Ronald Reagan a favorable strategic position for dealing with Congress.

When asked about his mandate in his first press conference following his reelection in 2012, President Obama displayed no note of triumphalism. Instead, he replied in modest and general terms, "I've got a mandate to help middle-class families and families that are working hard to try to get into the middle class. That's my mandate." He also noted that the "clear message" from the campaign was to put our partisan differences aside.[16]

The president had it about right. A *Washington Post*-ABC News poll in December 2012 found that only a third of Americans saw him as having won a broad-based mandate in the November election.[17]

The basic ingredients for encouraging perceptions of a mandate were missing. Winning 51 percent of the vote is hardly a landslide. Moreover, Obama was reelected with a smaller percentage of the vote than he received in his first election, the first president to do so since Andrew Jackson in 1832. Republicans increased their share of the presidential vote among a number of important demographic groups, including whites and men (four percentage points), younger voters (six points), white Catholics (seven points), and Jews (nine points). He lost the Independent vote by five percentage points (50 percent to 45 percent),[18] which he won 52 percent to 44 percent in 2008.

More broadly, Obama ran a hard-edged negative campaign focused on convincing voters that Mitt Romney was unworthy of becoming president.

He gave lip service to an agenda, publishing scaled-back and repackaged ideas from his first term in a 20-page pamphlet and often micro-targeting his policy views to elements of the Democratic coalition rather than addressing the broad electorate.

Perhaps equally important, the Republicans retained their majority in the House. Clearly they did not interpret their success as a mandate for the president, and it was their perceptions that mattered most. "Pretty much everyone in our conference is returning with a bigger margin of victory than the president of the United States," said House Republican Tim Huelskamp. "He certainly doesn't have a mandate."[19] Paul Ryan of Wisconsin agreed that the president won no mandate. "They also reelected the House Republicans," he noted.[20] (It was convenient for Republicans to ignore the fact that Democrats actually won more votes for House seats than did Republicans.)

There was one specific policy on which the president could reasonably claim a mandate, however: increased taxes on the wealthy. As he noted shortly after the election, he spoke incessantly during the campaign about his insistence on eliminating the Bush tax cuts for the wealthiest Americans.

> If there was one thing that everybody understood was a big difference between myself and Mr. Romney, it was when it comes to how we reduce our deficit, I argued for a balanced, responsible approach, and part of that included making sure that the wealthiest Americans pay a little bit more.
>
> I think every voter out there understood that that was an important debate, and the majority of voters agreed with me.[21]

Similarly, in a press conference a week before his inauguration, Obama proclaimed his intent "to carry out the agenda that I campaigned on," reminding listeners of his campaigning on the question of tax fairness and a "balanced" approach to deficit reduction. "Turns out," he said pointedly, "the American people agree with me. They listened to an entire year's debate over this issue, and they made a clear decision about the approach they prefer."[22] In chapter 4, I discuss the consequences of this preference.

SUPPORT FOR THE DIRECTION OF THE PRESIDENT'S PROGRAM

To bring about change, presidents generally require broad public support for the general direction of their initiatives. Democrats, including Barack Obama, wish to move policy in a liberal direction. However, in Obama's second term, more Americans viewed themselves as conservative than as

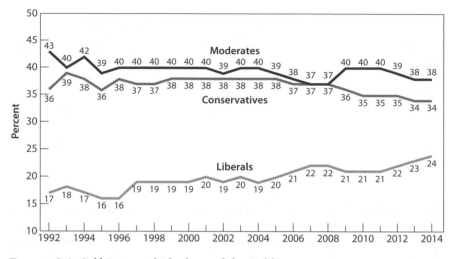

FIGURE 2.1. Self-Reported Ideology of the Public

liberal (figure 2.1). In 2013, conservatives outnumbered liberals 38 percent to 23 percent. A significantly higher percentage of Americans in most states, even some solidly Democratic ones, called themselves conservative rather than liberal. No state had a majority of people who called themselves liberal, and only Hawaii, Massachusetts, and Vermont (and Washington, DC) had pluralities of liberals.[23] Americans were more than twice as likely to identify themselves as conservative rather than liberal on economic issues, 41 percent to 19 percent. The gap was narrower on social issues, but conservatives still outnumbered liberals, 35 percent to 32 percent.[24]

We can also see the dominance of conservatism if we disaggregate opinion by political party (table 2.1). While 68 percent of Republicans in 2012 called themselves conservative, only 38 percent of Democrats identified as liberal. Thirty-eight percent of Democrats said they were moderates and another 20 percent saw themselves as conservative. Among Independents, 30 percent said they were conservative and only 22 percent identified as liberal.[25]

Ideological identification is not determinative, of course, and there is a well-known paradox of the incongruity between ideological identification and issue attitudes.[26] Scholars have long known that only a fraction of the public exhibits the requisite traits of an "ideologue."[27] Nevertheless, many more Americans are able to choose an ideological label and use it to guide their political judgments than in previous decades.[28] Scholars have found that ideological self-placements are influential determinants of vote choice,[29] issue attitudes,[30] and views toward government spending.[31]

TABLE 2.1. Ideological Self-Identification of Party Groups

Party Group	% Conservative	% Moderate	% Liberal
Republicans	68	26	5
Independents	30	43	22
Democrats	20	38	38

Source: Pew Research Center, 2012 Values Survey, April 4–15, 2012.

Question: "Do you think of yourself as___?"

Many liberal policies require public support for, or at least toleration of, government activism in the form of new programs, increased spending, and additional taxes. When asked whether government should do more to solve problems or was doing too many things better left to businesses and individuals, 43 percent of voters in 2012 chose the former, but 51 percent chose the less active government option.[32]

Scholars have found that policymakers are more likely to be attentive to the public's general mood toward policy than to frequently ill-informed views on specific policies.[33] James Stimson developed a well-known measure of the public's mood toward support for government programs. He found that in 2012, as Obama was ready to begin his second term, the American public was more conservative than at any point since 2001 and moved further in that direction in 2013 and 2014.[34] Moreover, this turn toward the right occurred in every state.[35]

Showing the difficulty of obtaining support for liberal policy, in April 2013, three years after its passage, only 37 percent of Americans approved of the Affordable Care Act.[36] Forty-one percent did not know the ACA was in place, with many thinking Congress had repealed it or the Supreme Court had found it unconstitutional.[37] In March 2013, 67 percent of the uninsured who were younger than age 65—and 57 percent of the overall population—said they did not understand how the ACA would impact them. Many also continued to hold false impressions of the law: 57 percent incorrectly believed that the ACA included a public insurance option. Nearly half believed the law provides financial assistance for illegal immigrants to buy insurance. And 40 percent—including 35 percent of seniors—still believed that the government would have "death panels" to make decisions about end-of-life care for Medicare beneficiaries.[38] In perhaps the unkindest cut of all, Gallup found that in 2012, 2013, and 2014, more than half the public felt that it was not government's responsibility to provide health care coverage for all Americans.[39]

When asked whether it preferred smaller government offering fewer public services or larger government offering more services, the public

TABLE 2.2. Public Support for Larger Government

	%		
Poll Date	Smaller Government, Fewer Services	Larger Government, More Services	No Opinion/ Depends
June 12–15, 2008	50	45	5
January 13–16, 2009	53	43	4
June 18–21, 2009	54	41	4
January 12–15, 2010	58	38	4
April 22–25, 2010	56	40	4
August 29–September 1, 2011	56	38	6
August 22–25, 2012	54	41	5
September 4–8, 2013*	51	40	9
July 29–August 4, 2014*	56	35	9

Source: ABC News-*Washington Post* Poll; Pew Research Center/*USA Today* Poll (2013); CBS News Poll (2014).

Questions:
"Generally speaking, would you say you favor (smaller government with fewer services), or (larger government with more services)?"
*(CBS News Poll; Pew Research Center/*USA Today* Poll): "If you had to choose, would you rather have a smaller government providing fewer services, or a bigger government providing more services?"

chose the former. Support for larger government was modest when Obama took office, and decreased during his tenure (table 2.2). Similarly, in September 2012, Gallup found that 54 percent of the public felt the government was doing too much, while 39 percent thought it should do more to solve the nation's problems.[40] A year later, 60 percent of the public felt the federal government had too much power, the highest level Gallup had ever found.[41]

The public's resistance to government activism should not be surprising. In their sweeping "macro" view of public opinion, Robert Erikson, Michael MacKuen, and James Stimson show that opinion always moves contrary to the president's position. They argue that a moderate public always gets too much liberalism from Democrats and too much conservatism from Republicans. Because public officials have policy beliefs as well as an interest in reelection, they are not likely to calibrate their policy stances exactly to match those of the public. Therefore, opinion movement is typically contrary to the ideological persuasion of presidents. Liberal presidents produce movement in the conservative direction and conservatives generate public support for more liberal policies.[42]

The public continuously adjusts its views of current policy in the direction of a long-run equilibrium path as it compares its preferences for ideal policy with its views of current policy.[43] Thus, the conservative policy period of the 1950s produced a liberal mood that resulted in the liberal policy changes of the mid-1960s. These policies, in turn, helped elect conservative Richard Nixon. In the late 1970s, Jimmy Carter's liberal policies paved the way for Ronald Reagan's conservative tenure, which in turn laid the foundation for Bill Clinton's more liberal stances. Negative reaction to the conservatism of George W. Bush encouraged the election of the more liberal Barack Obama. Stuart Soroka and Christopher Wlezien have reached similar conclusions with their thermostatic model of public opinion.[44]

PUBLIC POLARIZATION

Presidents rarely enjoy consensual public support, and opinion is naturally divided when the White House advocates controversial policies. In the absence of large majorities in both houses of Congress, however, enacting major changes in public policy usually requires expanding public support beyond those who identify with the president's party. The degree of partisan polarization will strongly influence the prospects of doing so.

In recent decades, there has been an increase in partisan-ideological polarization as Americans increasingly base their party loyalties on their ideological beliefs rather than on membership in social groups,[45] and they align their policy preferences more closely with their core political predispositions.[46] Partisans are more likely to apply ideological labels to themselves, a declining number of them call themselves moderate, and the differences in the ideological self-placements of Republicans and Democrats have grown dramatically since the 1980s. This polarization of partisans has contributed to much more ideological voting behavior.[47] Moreover, the most ideologically oriented Americans make their voices heard through greater participation in every stage of the political process.[48] They are the likeliest to vote, contribute to political campaigns, and discuss politics with others. They are also less likely to support compromise.

The policy divide between the Democratic and Republican electoral coalitions now encompasses a wide variety of issues, including both economic and social concerns. Pew found that in 2012 the average difference between the parties on 15 issues was 18 percentage points, the highest in the time series, which began in 1987. The greatest difference, 41 percentage points, was on the social safety net, followed by the environment (39

TABLE 2.3. The Policy Divide in Public Opinion, 2012

	% Favor	
Issue	Democratic Voters	Republican Voters
Activist Government	74	17
Keeping Health Care Law	81	14
Raising Income Taxes	83	44
Same-Sex Marriage	73	29
Legal Abortion	82	43

Source: Alan I. Abramowitz, "The Electoral Roots of America's Dysfunctional Government," Paper delivered at the Conference on Governing in Polarized Politics, Rothermere American Institute, University of Oxford, April 16–17, 2013, p. 38. Based on 2012 National Exit Poll.

percentage points), and equal opportunity and the scope and performance of government (33 percentage point each). These issues are at the heart of policymaking in Washington.[49] The median Republican is now more conservative than 94 percent of Democrats, and the median Democrat is more liberal than 92 percent of Republicans.[50]

Table 2.3 compares the preferences of Democratic and Republican congressional voters in the 2012 national exit poll on the proper role of government along with four specific policy issues—health care reform, taxes, abortion and same-sex marriage. On each issue, a majority of Democratic voters was on the liberal side while a majority of Republican voters was on the conservative side. The divide between supporters of the two parties was especially stark on the issue of health care where the question was whether the Affordable Care Act should be preserved or repealed. The great majority of Democratic voters wanted the law to be preserved or expanded while nearly all Republican voters wanted it to be partially or completely repealed.

Party affiliation strongly affected the views of the public about the ACA. In more than six months of tracking polls in 2013 and 2014, Gallup found that Republicans were up to 17 times more likely to disapprove than were Democrats, even when controlling for the respondents' health insurance status or ratings of their own health.[51] Similarly, Democrats among the public were twice as likely as Republicans to say they would comply with the Act's individual mandate.[52]

Partisan polarization extends behind policy disagreements. Republicans and Republican-leaning Independents not only did not support Obama when he initially ran for the presidency. By Election Day 2008, they perceived a huge ideological gulf between themselves and the new president and viewed him as an untrustworthy radical leftist with a socialist agenda. Forty-one percent of McCain voters judged Obama to be an "extreme liberal," further left than Republican voters had placed any previous Democratic candidate. Moreover, they placed him further to the left of their own ideologies than they had placed any previous Democratic candidate.[53]

Thus, the Republicans' campaign to brand Obama as a radical socialist out of touch with American values resonated with many McCain voters.[54] An African American candidate was also likely to exacerbate right-wing opposition,[55] as was his Ivy League education and somewhat detached manner. The fact that he spent part of his childhood in Muslim Indonesia and that his middle name was "Hussein" provided additional fodder for those willing or even eager to believe that he was outside the mainstream. Republican voters did not simply oppose Obama; they despised and feared him.

The polarization of the 2008 campaign and the nature of the opposition to Obama laid the groundwork for the intense aversion to Obama and his policies that appeared shortly after he took office. His initial actions of seeking the release of additional TARP funds and promoting an historic economic stimulus bill confirmed for conservatives that he was indeed a left-wing radical who needed to be stopped at all costs and, along with the president's support of health care reform, fueled the emergence of the Tea Party movement.

Partisan polarization reached record levels during Obama's first term.[56] Early on in the Obama presidency, the Democratic political organization Democracy Corps concluded from its focus groups that those in the conservative GOP base believed that Obama "is ruthlessly advancing a secret agenda to bankrupt the United States and dramatically expand government control to an extent nothing short of socialism."[57] In August 2010, a national poll found that 52 percent of the Republican respondents said it was definitely (14 percent) or probably (38 percent) true that "Barack Obama sympathizes with the goals of Islamic fundamentalists who want to impose Islamic law around the world."[58] It is not surprising, then, that the differences in evaluations of the president between partisans reached record levels in the Obama administration (table 2.4).

The 2012 election was even more polarized than the election in 2008. Seventy-seven percent of Republicans characterized Obama as "very liberal." Only 7 percent of Democrats viewed him that way.[59] More than half the Republican voters interviewed in the American National Election Studies study termed him an "extreme liberal," an historically high percentage (figure 2.2). These perceptions contrasted starkly with objective measures that found the president's stances to be rather moderate.[60]

An examination of states that deviated from Obama's share of the nationwide vote (about 51 percent) by 10 percentage points or more reveals

TABLE 2.4. Party Differences in Presidential Public Approval

Year of Obama's Tenure	Party Difference*	Next Largest Gap	Party Difference*
1st, 2009–2010	65	Clinton, 1992–1993	52
2nd, 2010–2011	68	Reagan, 1982–1983	56
3rd, 2011–2012	68	G. W. Bush, 2003–2004	59
4th, 2012–2013	76	G. W. Bush, 2004–2005	76
5th, 2013–2014	71	G. W. Bush, 2005–2006	72+
6th, 2014–2015	70	G. W. Bush, 2006–2007	70

Source: Gallup Poll.
* Differences expressed as percentage points.
+ Bush's gap exceeded Obama's by one percentage point

Question: "Do you approve or disapprove of the job ___ is doing as president?"

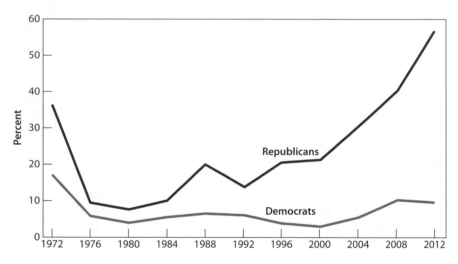

FIGURE 2.2. Perceptions of Democratic Presidential Candidates as "Extremely Liberal"

that there were more "polarized" states than in any election in generations. A few states (figure 2.3)—Vermont, Rhode Island, Massachusetts, New York, Maryland, and Hawaii, and the District of Columbia—were polarized in favor of Obama. Most of the polarized states, however, voted for Republican Mitt Romney. The majority of these 16 states form a belt stretching from West Virginia, Kentucky, and Tennessee through Ala-

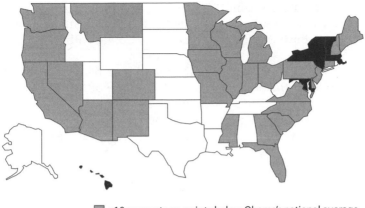

≤10 percentage points below Obama's national average
≥10 percentage points above Obama's national average

FIGURE 2.3. Polarized States in 2012 Presidential Election. White = ≤ 10 percentage points below Obama's national average. Black = ≥ 10 percentage points above Obama's national average

bama, Louisiana, and Arkansas west to the states occupying the center of the country: Texas, Oklahoma, Kansas, Nebraska, and North and South Dakota. In addition, Wyoming, Idaho, Utah, and Alaska were strongly in the Republican camp. Given these results, it is not surprising that there were only 35 House districts where the presidential vote was within five percentage points of the national presidential popular vote margin.[61]

Party loyalty in voting hit a record high in 2012. The ANES found that 93 percent of Democrats voted for Obama and 91 percent of Republicans voted for Romney. Among Independent leaners, 85 percent voted for the candidate of the party toward which they leaned.[62] There was a 26-percentage-point difference in the underlying partisanship of the districts won by Republicans and Democrats in 2012 (as measured by the presidential vote), the highest ever. States are generally more diverse and thus more politically competitive than House districts, but the gap between the Senate parties' electoral constituencies reached a record level of 15 percentage points.[63]

As Obama began his second term, this polarization persisted in the underlying partisan and ideological divisions of the country. Many Republicans continued to exhibit a strong antipathy toward the president. Even after nearly four years in office, many Republicans clung to the views that he was foreign born (and in their eyes ineligible to be president), a Muslim (which they saw in negative terms), or both.[64] Indeed, in early 2013 a majority of Republicans supported impeaching the president.[65] Thus, the president entered his second term with the widest partisan gap in approval of any newly reelected president ever, 80 percentage points (91 to 11). George W. Bush was the previous record holder with a 76-percentage-point difference.[66]

In 2014, the Pew Research Center found that partisan antipathy had risen sharply over the past generation. The share of Republicans and Republican leaners who had *very* unfavorable opinions of the Democratic Party had jumped from 17 percent to 43 percent since 1994. Similarly, the share of Democrats and Democratic leaners with very negative opinions of the Republican Party more than doubled, from 16 percent to 38 percent. Among Republicans and Democrats who had a very unfavorable impression of the other party, the great majority said the opposing party's policies represented a *threat* to the nation's well-being. In all, 27 percent of Democrats and Democratic leaners and 36 percent of Republicans and Republican leaners held such views. Consistent liberals and consistent conservatives, those who held nearly uniform liberal or conservative beliefs, were even more alarmed: 50 percent of consistent liberals and 66 percent of consistent conservatives saw the other party as a threat to the nation.[67]

There is other evidence that some important elements of polarized politics arise from the grass roots.[68] Did the Tea Party beget Rand Paul or did Rand Paul beget the Tea Party? Most would agree with the former. One author concluded that the Tea Party was born only three weeks after Obama took office, when Rick Santelli, a libertarian business reporter for CNBC, criticized the administration for making Americans pay for their neighbors' mortgages.[69] Similarly, did MoveOn.org take its lead from Barack Obama? Not necessarily, as its efforts to counter the president's policy regarding Syria illustrate. Elites might co-opt grassroots movements, but they can only do so if their messages resonate with the general public.

Helping to maintain ideological purity is the reinforcement of views through increasing social isolation. Sixty-three percent of consistent conservatives and 49 percent of consistent liberals say most of their close friends share their political views, compared with just 35 percent among the public as a whole.[70]

Race has also been a polarizing factor in opinion about the president's policies, starting with the 2008 election.[71] There is evidence that predispositions to opposing the president combined with the salience of race contributed to the acceptance of smearing labels such as that Obama was Muslim or a socialist.[72] There is also reason to believe that negative stereotypes about blacks significantly eroded white support for the president,[73] as did racial resentment.[74] The race of the president (and thus racism) influenced partisan preferences[75] and support for health care reform.[76]

Also contributing to the high levels of polarization is the fragmented nature of the media, which helps to insulate the public and thus contribute to its polarization.[77] Sixty-three percent of Republicans and Republican leaners reported that they received most of their news from Fox News, which is known for its conservative reporting and commentators.[78] Forty percent of Republicans said they watched Fox regularly.[79] The president's initial actions were grist for commentators on the right, especially those on radio and cable television. They aggressively reinforced the fears of their audiences and encouraged active opposition to the White House.

Constraints on Opinion Change

The contexts of individual presidencies vary, but there are some features of the political landscape that every president faces. Just how malleable is public opinion? What obstacles do all presidents have to overcome in their attempts to move the public to support their policies?[80]

Lack of Attention

The first step in the president's efforts to lead the public is focusing its attention, and it is likely that reaching the public will require frequent repetition of the president's views.[81] As former White House public relations counselor David Gergen put it, "History teaches that almost nothing a leader says is heard if spoken only once."[82] According to George W. Bush, "In my line of work you got to keep repeating things over and over and over again for the truth to sink in, to kind of catapult the propaganda."[83] Moreover, the impact of communications tends to decay rapidly, and people tend to rely on the most recent message (and the most recent events) when forming their attitudes.[84]

Given the protracted nature of the legislative process, and the president's need for public support at all stages of it, sustaining a message can be equally as important as sending it in the first place. Nevertheless, despite the enormous total volume of presidential public statements, they are dispersed over a broad range of policies, and wide audiences hear only a small portion of the president's remarks. The president rarely concentrates a televised address on an issue before Congress and actually makes few statements on even significant legislation. In addition, the president faces strong competition for the public's attention from previous commitments of government, congressional initiatives, opposing elites, and the mass media. Of equal consequence, the president often provides competition for himself as he addresses other issues, some of which are on his own agenda and others that events and others force upon him.

Reception and Understanding of Messages

If the president is going to lead the public successfully, it must *receive* and *understand* his messages. Yet the White House finds it increasingly difficult to obtain an audience for its views—or even airtime on television to express them. Those who are unaware of a message are unlikely to know the president's positions. Moreover, many people who do pay attention miss the president's points. Because the president rarely speaks directly to the American people as a whole, the White House is dependent on the press to transmit its messages. The media are unlikely to adopt consistently either the White House's priorities or its framing of issues.

Presidents make a substantial effort to frame issues in ways that will favor their preferred policy options and to place their own performance in a favorable light. However, as we will see in chapter 6, there are many limitations on successful framing, including the presence of competing frames and the fact that different people perceive the same message differently. With all his personal, ideological, and partisan baggage, no president can assume that all citizens hear the same thing when he speaks.

A related matter of perception is the credibility of the source (discussed in chapter 5). Experimental evidence supports the view that perceived source credibility is a prerequisite for successful framing. The president is likely to be more credible to some people (those predisposed to support him) than to others. Many people are unlikely to find him a credible source on most issues, especially those on which opinion is divided and on which he is the leader of one side of the debate. High levels of polarization point toward severe credibility problems for the chief executive.

Predispositions

Perhaps the most difficult task for the president in leading the public is overcoming the predispositions of his audience if he is to change people's minds about his policies or his performance. Yet a series of related psychological mechanisms often bias perceptions of both facts and evaluations of them. Most people seek out information confirming their preexisting opinions and ignore or reject arguments contrary to their predispositions. When exposed to competing arguments, they typically uncritically accept the confirming ones and dismiss or argue against the opposing ones. Partisanship is especially likely to bias processing perceptions, interpretations, and responses to the political world. I address predispositions, perceptions, and partisanship in detail in chapter 5.

Those who pay close attention to politics and policy, the very people who might be attentive to the president, are likely to have well-developed views and strong partisan attachments and thus be less susceptible to persuasion. Better-informed citizens possess the information and sophistication necessary to identify the implications of messages. They are best able to construct ostensibly reasonable counterarguments and rebuttals to evidence that they are emotionally inclined to resist and thus reject communications inconsistent with their values. In the typical situation of competing frames offered by elites, reinforcement and polarization of views are more likely than conversion among attentive citizens.[85]

It may seem that those with less interest and knowledge present the most potential for presidential persuasion. Such people cannot resist arguments if they do not possess information about the implications of those arguments for their values, interests, and other predispositions. However, these people are also less likely to be aware of the president's messages, limiting the president's influence. To the extent that they do receive the messages, they will also hear from the opposition how the president's views are inconsistent with their predispositions.

Even if their predispositions make them sympathetic to the president's arguments, people may lack the understanding to make the connection between the president's arguments and their own underlying values. Moreover, the more abstract the link between message and value, the fewer people who will make the connection.[86]

Misinformation

In addition, people are frequently *misinformed* (as opposed to uninformed) about policy, and the less they know, the more confidence they have in their beliefs. Thus, they resist correct factual information. Even when others present them with factual information, they resist changing their opinions.[87] The increasing array of media choices means that individuals are less likely to encounter information that would correct misperceptions. Moreover, the tendency to process information with a bias toward their preexisting views means that those who are most susceptible to misinformation may reject the corrections that they receive.[88] Interestingly, misperceptions are often most prevalent among those who are generally well informed about politics. Political knowledge neither corrects nor mitigates partisan bias in perception of objective conditions. Instead, it enhances it.

Other psychological factors also increase the likelihood that corrections will fail to undo the effects of misperceptions. Negations (i.e., "I am not a crook") often reinforce the perception they are intended to counter.[89] In addition, even if people initially accept corrections debunking a false statement, they may eventually fall victim to an "illusion of truth" effect in which people misremember false statements as true over time.[90] Finally, misleading statements about politics continue to influence subjects' beliefs even after these statements have been discredited.[91]

Loss Aversion

Research in psychology has found that people have a broad predisposition to avoid loss and place more emphasis on avoiding potential losses than on obtaining potential gains.[92] In their decision making, they place more weight on information that has negative, as opposed to positive, implications for their interests. Similarly, when individuals form impressions of situations or other people, they weigh negative information more heavily than positive. Impressions formed on the basis of negative information, moreover, tend to be more lasting and more resistant to change.[93]

Risk and loss aversion and distrust of government make people wary of policy initiatives, especially when they are complex and their consequences are uncertain. Since uncertainty accompanies virtually every proposal for a major shift in public policy, it is not surprising that people are naturally inclined against change.[94] Further encouraging this predisposition is the media's focus on political conflict and strategy, which elevates the prominence of political wheeling and dealing in individuals' evaluations of political leaders and policy proposals. The resulting increase in public cynicism highlights the risk of altering the status quo.

The predisposition for loss aversion is an obstacle for presidential leadership of the public. Most presidents want to leave some substantial change at the core of their legacies. Yet those proposing new directions in policy—and Barack Obama was all about change—encounter a more formidable task than do advocates of the status quo. Those opposing change have a more modest task of emphasizing the negative to increase the public's uncertainty and anxiety to avoid risk.[95]

Michael Cobb and James Kuklinski found in an experimental study of opinion change on NAFTA and health care that arguments against both worked especially well. They found people to be both risk- and loss-averse, and arguments against change, which accentuate the unpleasant consequences of a proposed policy, easily resonated with the average person. In addition, they suggest that fear and anger, which negative arguments presumably evoke, are among the strongest emotions and serve as readily available shortcuts for decision making when people evaluate an impending policy initiative.[96] Kevin Arceneaux found a similar bias toward loss aversion.[97]

CONCLUSION

Facing a Republican-controlled House of Representatives, President Obama would need strong backing from the public to break the legislative gridlock that had characterized the last two years of his first term. Yet in the first years of his second term, his strategic position with public opinion was not strong and provided him little in the way of opportunity for passing major legislation. The public was highly polarized, less than enthusiastic about activist government, and did not provide him with a mandate for governing. Many in the public always were inclined to support his policies, of course, but the prospects of expanding his coalition and sending a strong signal to Congress were dim. Despite criticism from some ill-informed liberal commentators that he was failing to exploit the potential of the bully pulpit,[98] the reasonable prediction was that public opinion would not respond positively to the president's leadership. Instead, it would continue to present an obstacle to obtaining support from members of Congress not already inclined to support him. As we will see, this prediction accurately describes the battles to come.

CHAPTER 3

Strategic Position with Congress

EVERY PRESIDENT NEEDS support in Congress to pass his legislative proposals. It is not surprising that someone who has emerged victorious after a long campaign for the presidency would conclude that he can persuade members of Congress to support his policies. As with leading the public, then, presidents may not focus on evaluating existing possibilities when they think they can create their own. Yet assuming party support in Congress or success in reaching across the aisle to obtain bipartisan support is fraught with danger. Not a single systematic study demonstrates that presidents can reliably move members of Congress, especially members of the opposition party, to support them.

The best evidence is that presidential persuasion is at the margins of congressional decision making. Even presidents who appeared to dominate Congress were actually facilitators rather than directors of change. They understood their own limitations and quite explicitly took advantage of opportunities in their environments. Working at the margins, they successfully guided legislation through Congress. When these resources diminished, they reverted to the more typical stalemate that usually characterizes presidential-congressional relations.[1]

There are several components of the opportunity for obtaining congressional support, aside from existing public support for the president's initiatives. First is the presence or absence of the perception of a mandate for change. Do members of Congress think the public has spoken clearly in favor of the president's proposals? We have already seen that Republicans saw no mandate for President Obama in the results of the 2012 election. They saw no need to defer to the public's decision to return him to the White House.

Members of the president's party are much more likely to support his policies than are members of the opposition. Moreover, controlling the agenda is critical to enacting legislation. Thus, party control of Congress is a key to legislative success. Because party unity is imperfect and because of the need for extraordinary majorities in the Senate, the size of the president's party's cohort is also critical. Another crucial element is the ideological distribution of members of Congress, especially of the opposition. The ideological cohesion of his party and its compatibility with the president's policies tell us the size of his core of support. The number of opposition party members who are moderates will determine the likelihood of the president successfully expanding his coalition on a bill. The orientation of opposition party identifiers in the public is also crucial. Are they likely to be responsive to White House calls for support?

Another important aspect of the president's strategic position with Congress is the structure of the choice facing the legislature. What is the default position if Congress fails to pass legislation? In a typical situation, in which the White House advocates passage, the president loses if Congress fails to act. However, the opposition party may propose legislation the president opposes. In such a case, the default position favors the president. The president has a special advantage when the opposition party wants to avoid the reversion to a policy state it wishes to avoid if Congress does not take positive action. This situation provides the president significant leverage in negotiating new legislation.

Despite the evidence that the president's personal legislative skills have little influence on members of Congress, critics often called on President Obama to develop closer personal relations with members from both sides of the aisle. Would an emphasis on improving interpersonal relations between the president and individual members of Congress alter the balance of power?

DIVIDED GOVERNMENT

The presence or absence of unified government is critical to presidential success in Congress. The president's initiatives are much less likely to pass under divided government,[2] and control of the agenda can facilitate or obstruct their progress in the legislative process.

The House is the chamber where majority control is most important, because the rules allow the majority to control the agenda and many of the alternatives on which members vote. Republicans controlled the House in the 113th Congress. Political necessity sometimes forced Republican leaders to allow votes on issues not supported by a majority of the party. In 2013–2014, Speaker John Boehner allowed four important bills to come to the floor that were opposed by most Republicans but passed with a majority of Democratic votes. The issues were extending the Bush tax cuts but with higher taxes on the wealthiest taxpayers, federal relief funds for victims of Hurricane Sandy in the Northeast, the Violence Against Women Act, and the February 2014 increase in the debt limit. The public supported these bills, and party leaders felt blocking them would be worse for the party's reputation than allowing them to go forward. The president could not expect many other bills to meet this criterion, however. To retain his credibility with his members, many of whom shuddered at the idea of finding middle ground with Democrats, the Speaker had to present a unified front, holding that the House was the last line of defense against the president's progressive agenda.

A Democratic majority in the Senate meant there would be fewer hearings harassing the administration and, more important, that his proposals would arrive on the floor. However, the Democratic majority was not large enough to overcome the persistent threat of filibusters, forcing the president to seek Republican support even in a chamber controlled by his party. As we will see, the prospects of such support were severely limited.

IDEOLOGY

An important aspect of the president's opportunity structure is the ideological division of members of Congress. Are they likely to agree with the president's initiatives? Under divided government, is there potential to reach across the aisle and obtain support from the opposition party?

The ideological gap between the parties in the House reached a record high in the 112th Congress (2011–2012), and the 2012 election did nothing to mitigate the ideological differences between the congressional parties. Seven of the sixteen Republican incumbents who lost had been among the 48 members of the Republican Main Street Partnership, a caucus of moderate conservatives. Keith Poole predicted that the ideological gap between the House party coalitions would be about the same for the 113th Congress (2013–2014) as in the 112th Congress.[3]

The Senate did gain some likely moderate Democrats (Heidi Heitkamp of North Dakota, Joe Donnelly of Indiana, and Angus King, a Maine independent who organizes with the Democrats), but lost an equal number through retirements (Kent Conrad of North Dakota, Ben Nelson of Nebraska, and James Webb of Virginia). Republican departures included three of the party's more moderate members (Scott Brown, Olympia Snowe, and Richard Lugar), and all three of its newcomers, Deb Fischer (Nebraska), Ted Cruz (Texas), and Jeff Flake (Arizona) belonged to the

TABLE 3.1. Presidential Support in the House, 1953–2014

President		% Support*		
	President's Party	President's Party	Opposition Party	Difference in Support†
Eisenhower	Republican	63	42	21
Kennedy	Democrat	73	26	47
Johnson	Democrat	71	27	44
Nixon/Ford	Republican	64	39	25
Carter	Democrat	63	31	32
Reagan	Republican	70	29	51
G. Bush	Republican	73	27	44
Clinton	Democrat	75	24	51
G. W. Bush	Republican	84	20	64
Obama‡	Democrat	85	15	70

* On roll-call votes on which the winning side was supported by fewer than 80 percent of those voting.
† Differences expressed as percentage points.
‡ 2009–2014.

Tea Party faction. In all, seven of the incoming senators were likely to be more extreme than the incumbents they replaced, and none of the remaining four were likely to be significantly more moderate than their predecessors. Thus, there was good reason to expect the Senate to be even more ideologically polarized than it was in the 112th Congress.[4]

The polarization of party elites has been asymmetrical, with most of it the result of the rightward movement of the Republicans.[5] According to Mann and Ornstein, the Republicans have become ideologically extreme, scornful of compromise, contemptuous of facts, evidence, and science, dismissive of the legitimacy of the opposition, and at war with government.[6] When House Republican Majority Leader Eric Cantor proposed a plan to address the problem of those Americans with preexisting health conditions who either lose their insurance or cannot obtain it, his colleagues rebuffed him. Instead of dealing with the problem, they chose to vote to repeal the Affordable Care Act for the thirty-seventh time. It is little wonder that President Obama told aides that a sizable mistake at the start of his administration was his naiveté in thinking he could work with Republicans on weighty issues.[7]

The president was correct. Tables 3.1 and 3.2 show the average levels of support on contested votes on which the president took a stand. In both

TABLE 3.2. Presidential Support in the Senate, 1953–2014

	% Support*			
President	President's Party	President's Party	Opposition Party	Difference in Support†
Eisenhower	Republican	69	36	33
Kennedy	Democrat	65	33	32
Johnson	Democrat	56	44	12
Nixon/Ford	Republican	63	33	30
Carter	Democrat	63	37	36
Reagan	Republican	74	31	43
G. Bush	Republican	75	29	46
Clinton	Democrat	83	22	61
G. W. Bush	Republican	86	18	68
Obama‡	Democrat	94	19	75

* On roll-call votes on which the winning side was supported by fewer than 80 percent of those voting.
† Differences expressed as percentage points.
‡ 2009–2014.

the House and the Senate, the differences between the support of Democrats and Republicans during the Obama presidency were the greatest in the past 60 years. The president obtained very little support from Republicans in either chamber, and there was no reason to expect change in that level of success.

With 173 members in 2014, the Republican Study Committee was the largest caucus in Congress. Its philosophy of governance would vex any Speaker: Members consider themselves conservatives first and Republicans second. They did not come to Washington to play for the Republican team; they came to fight for conservative principles. If that meant voting against party interests, so be it. For core RSC believers, ideological purity trumped legislative accomplishment.[8]

As we have seen, in the months following the 2012 elections, Speaker John Boehner brought a few bills to the floor that lacked majority support among House Republicans. Upset at the Speaker's effort to position the party more favorably with the public, conservatives outside of Congress—including leaders of Heritage Action for America, the Club for Growth, Phyllis Schlafly, L. Brent Bozell, the Tea Party Express, Morton Blackwell, Richard Viguerie, Citizens United, the Family Research Council, and the Traditional Values Coalition—signed a letter seeking to constrain his discretion in bringing matters to the floor. They urged the passage of a rule that would bind the House Republican Conference to bring legislation to the floor only if a majority of House Republicans support it (the so-called Hastert Rule). In effect, the signers wanted the most conservative elements in the House to have a guaranteed veto over the chamber's agenda.

REPUBLICANS AND THEIR CONSTITUENCIES

The president often requires opposition party support to pass his legislative proposals. Are there constituency cross-pressures to cooperate with the White House to counter the ideological predispositions of opposition party members of Congress to oppose him?

One of the most important political trends in the past half century has been the polarization of the congressional parties' respective electoral bases. The partisan realignment of the South[9] and the sorting of conservatives and liberals outside the South into the Republican and Democratic parties, respectively, has increased the level of consistency between party identification and ideology. In the 2012 election, more than 90 percent of self-identified liberals and conservatives identified with the "appropriate" party. Moreover, the relationship between ideology and voting has become much stronger. In 2012, about 89 percent of self-identified liberals voted for Democrats in the House and Senate elections, while 85 percent of conservatives voted for Republicans.[10] As a consequence, Democratic and Republican elected officials today represent electoral coalitions with strongly diverging policy preferences across a wide range of issues.

Gary Jacobson reports that the 2012 House elections were "highly nationalized, partisan, and president-centered events." The consistency between opinions of the president and the House vote—approving of Obama and voting Democratic, or disapproving and voting Republican—at 90 percent, was the highest on record.[11] It is not surprising, then, that the electoral constituencies of the House Republicans contain relatively few Obama supporters. Not a single Republican won in a Democratic-leaning district. Of the 234 Republicans elected to the House in 2012, just 17 represented congressional districts that Obama also won. Only six states elected senators from different parties than the candidate they supported for president. Among the House Republicans' electoral constituents— those respondents who said they had voted for a winning Republican— only 15 percent reported also voting for Obama. The comparable figure for Senate Republican voters was only 10 percent, the lowest on record. By contrast, the overlap between the electoral constituencies of the president and his partisans in Congress exceeded 90 percent.[12]

Most members of the House come from districts where they face little threat of losing their seat to the other party. Charlie Cook calculated that there are only 90 swing seats (districts that fall into the range of five percentage points above the national average for a party).[13] According to Jacobson, only 29 representatives serve districts without a clear partisan tilt.[14] More than 80 percent of those elected to the House in 2012 won with at least 55 percent of the vote. Fifty-seven percent of House Republicans won with 60 percent of the vote or more. Another 28 percent won with between 55 and 60 percent of the vote.[15]

In 2012 only one Republican senator (Dean Heller of Nevada) was elected in a state Obama carried. The 26 states that voted for Obama in 2012 sent 43 Democrats and just 9 Republicans to the Senate. Only four Republican senators represented states that had voted Democrat in each presidential election since 2000: Susan Collins of Maine, Mark Kirk of Illinois, Pat Toomey of Pennsylvania, and Ron Johnson of Wisconsin. Of the 13 states where the 14 Republican senators would stand for reelection in 2014 (South Carolina had two, Lindsey O. Graham and Tim Scott), Obama won just one in 2012—Maine. In the remaining dozen states, he lost all but Georgia by double digits. Indeed, the average margin of victory for Romney across the 13 states was 20 percentage points.

The decline in shared constituencies between the president and Republican members of Congress reflects an increase in party loyalty and thus a falloff in ticket-splitting among voters. Party-line voting reached its highest level ever for House and Senate elections in 2012, with defection rates of 10 percent in House elections and 11 percent in Senate elections. Similarly, 2012 witnessed the lowest incidence ever of ticket-splitting—voting for a Democrat for president and a Republican for U.S. representative or senator, or vice versa—12 percent for the House and 11 percent for the Senate.[16]

As a result of this individual-level behavior, the proportion of House districts delivering split verdicts—preferring the president of one party and the House candidate of the other—reached a low of only 6 percent in 2012. Split outcomes are more common in Senate elections because states tend to be more politically heterogeneous and more evenly partisan balanced than congressional districts. Nevertheless, in 2012, only six states delivered split verdicts. In 2013–2014, only 21 senators represented states lost by their presidential candidate, a modern-day low.

The electoral coalitions of the two parties are increasingly divided by race as well as by party and ideology. In the 113th Congress, 80 percent of the House Republicans represented districts in which the white share of the voting-age population exceeded the national average, while 64 percent of House Democrats represented districts in which the minority share of the voting-age population exceeded the national average.[17] Although the most salient demographic fact about America is that it is becoming more diverse, Republican districts actually became on average two percentage points more white in 2012. More than 60 percent of House Republicans represented congressional districts where Latinos made up less than 10 percent of the population. Differences in cultural values and attitudes toward government accompany these differences in the racial composition of constituencies, making it more difficult to achieve bipartisan compromises. Few House Republicans have much experience in courting nonwhite voters—or much electoral incentive to do so.

As a consequence of these differences in constituencies, most congressional Republicans are far more afraid of losing a primary to a more conservative challenger than a general election to a Democrat. The right's demonstrated capacity to punish incumbent Republicans in primaries discourages straying from party orthodoxy. For them, a deal is often more dangerous than no deal.

The potential for such challenges is real, as the Republican primary electorate is very conservative (a majority of Republican voters want their party's leaders to move *further to the right*),[18] and the Tea Party has been active in challenging Republican incumbents.[19]

Pew found that among Republican and Republican-leaning registered voters, 86 percent of those who agree with the Tea Party always or nearly always voted in primary elections. Among other Republicans and Republican leaners, only 67 percent gave the same responses. As a result, Tea Party Republicans make up nearly half of those in the GOP who always vote in primaries (49 percent), despite being a minority of Republicans and Republican leaners overall (37 percent).[20]

Republicans in the public, especially activist Tea Party Republicans, are much less likely than Democrats or Independents to support compromise on policy issues.[21] We experienced a taste of this inflexibility during a Republican presidential primary debate in Ames, Iowa, on August 11, 2011, when every candidate rejected the notion of a budget deal that would include tax increases even if accompanied by spending cuts ten times as large.

Researchers have found those affiliated with the Tea Party are simply different from other conservatives. For example, 71 percent of Tea Party conservatives agreed that President Obama was "destroying the country," an opinion shared by only 6 percent of conservatives who did not identify with the Tea Party. They fear that the country is changing in fundamental ways and are conspiratorial in their interpretation of politics. Thus, they view politics as a struggle for survival rather than a negotiation among opposing views.[22] Representatives and senators associated with the Tea Party do not necessarily consider their primary function to be making government work, contrary to long-held views of many Americans.[23]

In perhaps the most extreme expression of conservative rigidity, the Utah Republican Party denied longtime conservative Senator Robert Bennett its nomination for reelection in 2010. Republican governor Charlie Crist had to leave his party and run for the Senate as an Independent in Florida because he was unlikely to win the Republican nomination against conservative Marco Rubio. Senator Lisa Murkowski lost her renomination in Alaska to a largely unknown candidate on the far right of the political spectrum. The previous year, Republican senator Arlen Specter of Pennsylvania switched parties, believing there was little chance he could win a Republican primary against conservative Pat Toomey.

In 2012, Senator Richard Lugar lost the Republican primary in Indiana to a candidate supported by the Tea Party. The Arizona Republican Party formally reprimanded Sen. John McCain in January 2014, censuring him for a liberal voting record and working with Democrats in Washington and condemning the five-term senator for a record that was "disastrous and harmful" to the nation. Most dramatically, House Majority Leader Eric Cantor lost his primary to Tea Party challenger David Brat.

Although well-heeled donors and other activists among the Republican "establishment" made substantial efforts to influence the selection of Republican candidates in the 2014 midterm elections, they were not seeking moderate candidates. Instead, their goal was to weed out fringe figures prone to making incendiary comments and thus likely to lose the general election. The candidates they backed were strongly conservative.

Equally important as a curb on compromise is the fact that when elected officials interact with the more politically engaged voters within their reelection constituencies—the voters who are the most attentive to what they are doing, the most likely to influence their friends and neighbors, the most likely to donate money to their campaigns, and the most likely to vote in primary elections—the divide between their supporters and their opponents is even greater than it is among rank-and-file voters. Active supporters of Republican elected officials, especially those associated with the Tea Party, are generally very conservative.[24]

Although only 27 percent of the public wanted Congress to shut down the government rather than pass a budget that funded the Affordable Care Act—the goal of Tea Party–affiliated members of Congress—50 percent of Republicans, and 57 percent of conservative Republicans, would shut down the government before they would fund the president's signature health care law.[25] At the same time, Republican congressional leaders faced mounting disapproval among Tea Party Republicans. In September 2013, just 27 percent of Republicans and Republican leaners who agreed with the Tea Party approved of the job Republican leaders in Congress were doing, compared with 71 percent who disapproved.[26]

When the House did vote to raise the debt limit in early 2014, only 28 members—12 percent—of the Republican majority voted for the bill, although many more privately knew the bill needed to pass. As one close observer put it, "The implications for governing are obvious. If many lawmakers are unwilling or refuse to vote for legislation that they understand to be necessary, and even beneficial, out of fear of retribution from an empowered and outspoken wing of their party, reaching agreement on major policy like immigration becomes difficult if not impossible." "The incentives are not aligned," one House Republican acknowledged.[27]

Compounding the pressure to stay to the right were conservative radio and television commentators who relentlessly incited the Republican base against the president, questioned his legitimacy, and aggressively encouraged active opposition to the White House.

Party differences in electoral bases are strongly related to party differences in presidential support and roll call voting.[28] Congressional Republicans are responding rationally to their incentives for reelection when they oppose the president. Thus, for example, the number of Republicans in the 113th Congress who saw cutting a deal with the president as politically advantageous was close to zero.

The debt limit battle in early 2014 illustrates the problem. Eighty House Republicans sent Speaker John Boehner a letter demanding he use the threat of a government shutdown to defund Obamacare. The average district of these members was 75 percent white (compared to 63 percent for the House as a whole). Latinos made up an average of 9 percent of the 80 district's residents, while the overall average for Congress was 17 percent. The districts also had slightly lower levels of education (25 percent of the population in their districts had college degrees, while that number was 29 percent for the average district). The members themselves represented this lack of diversity. Seventy-six of the members were male, and 79 of them were white.[29]

Obama defeated Romney by four points nationally. But in these 80 districts, Obama lost to Romney by an average of 23 percentage points. The Republican members themselves did even better, averaging a 34-percentage-point margin of victory. In short, these 80 members represented an America where the population was getting whiter, where there were few major cities, where Obama lost the 2012 election in a landslide, and where the Republican Party was becoming more dominant and more popular, contrary to national trends.[30]

IMPACT OF REPUBLICAN ANTIPATHY

Given the broad influences of ideology and constituency, it is not surprising that presidential leadership itself demarcates and deepens cleavages in Congress. As Frances Lee has shown, the differences between the parties and the cohesion within them on floor votes are typically greater when the president takes a stand on issues. When the president adopts a position, members of his party have a stake in his success, while opposition party members have a stake in the president losing. Moreover, both parties take cues from the president that help define their policy views, especially when the lines of party cleavage are not clearly at stake or already well established. In early 2010, Republican senators, including the Minority Leader Senator Mitch McConnell, demanded that Obama endorse bipartisan legislation to create a deficit reduction commission. When he did so, they voted against the bill, killing it. When the president supported a deficit reduction plan from the Gang of Six in 2011, Republicans turned to oppose it.[31]

After his reelection victory in 2012, the president optimistically proclaimed that his victory "might break the fever" with congressional Republicans, who had declared their top goal was to deny him a second term. "They might say to themselves, 'You know what, we've lost our way here. We need to refocus on trying to get things done for the American people'."[32] Nevertheless, the relentless confrontation of some Republicans continued.[33] This dynamic of presidential leadership further complicated Obama's efforts to win Republican support.

One example of this challenge was presidential nominations. After Democrats changed the rules to make it easier to end filibusters on nominations, Republicans continued partisan warfare. For example, there were party-line votes on nearly every cloture vote taken on judicial nominations in the 113th Congress. After forcing Democrats to secure cloture, Republicans then typically refused to yield post-cloture consideration time for the nominees (2 hours for trial judges, 30 for appellate judges). When confirmation votes eventually did occur, however, most judicial nominees were confirmed with GOP support—often with no dissent.[34]

The unremitting opposition of Republicans is most clear regarding the Affordable Care Act. First, it passed with only Democratic votes, thus undermining its acceptance. Republican opposition also meant that Democrats could not pass legislation to smooth out some rough language in the bill, forcing the administration to fill far more gaps through regulation than it otherwise would have had to do.

Next, most Republican governors declined to create their own state insurance exchanges, compelling the federal government to take at least partial responsibility for creating marketplaces serving 36 states—far more than ever intended. Republicans also refused to appropriate dedicated funds to do that extra work, leaving the Health and Human Services Department and other agencies to cobble together HealthCare.gov by redirecting funds from existing programs.

In addition, nearly half of the states declined to expand their Medicaid programs using federal funds. Moreover, some states refused to do anything at all to educate the public about the law. Congressional Republicans sent so many burdensome queries to local hospitals and nonprofits gearing up to help consumers navigate the new system face-to-face that at least two such groups returned their federal grants and gave up the effort. When the White House let it be known that it was in talks with the National Football League to enlist star athletes to help promote the law, the Senate's top two Republicans sent the league an ominous letter wondering why it would "risk damaging its inclusive and apolitical brand." As a result, the NFL backed off.

On the eve of the open enrollment date of October 1, congressional Republicans shut down the government, disrupting last-minute planning and limiting the administration's ability to prepare the public for the likelihood of potential problems, because it was battling to defend the Affordable Care Act itself.

Reflecting James Q. Wilson's adage that American politics is a bar fight, not a prize fight, and thus does not end with a single victory, conservatives continued to sabotage the law. For example, Rush Limbaugh advised his listeners that they could avoid penalties for failing to buy mandated insurance by arranging to avoid federal income tax refunds, since the IRS can only levy fines by withholding refunds, not by liens or criminal sanctions.

Opponents of the president's health care reform also took to the courts to challenge the law. First, opponents of the ACA charged that the mandate for individuals to have health insurance exceeded the power of Congress. The Court rejected this argument in *National Federation of Independent Business et al v. Sebelius et al* (2012). Three years later, in *King v. Burwell* (2015), the conservatives argued, cynically in the minds of many observers, that the law did not provide for federal subsidies to persons in states that had not established their own health insurance exchanges. However, the Court upheld the law in June.

Immigration was a key policy area in which Republican antipathy for Obama fatally complicated policymaking. As I discuss in chapter 5, any immigration bill identified as Obama's made it more difficult for Republican members of Congress to support it. Because Republicans in Congress come from solidly Republican states or districts, it was easier for them to support an immigration bill that had broad-based support in the business and farming communities (and that also happened to be supported by Obama and the Democratic leadership) than to back a bill so popularly identified with the other side.

Similarly, in 2014 both the president and Congress agreed on the need to pass a new authorization for the president to take military action against the Islamic State. The White House resisted proposing its own wording, however. It feared that any language the president suggested would immediately become a target for partisan disagreement.[35]

Democrats and Their Constituencies

As he began his second term, the president found his party in the House was more ideologically coherent than in the immediate past. However, this coherence occurred through the resignations, retirements, and primary and general election defeats of moderates, who are the first to go under in the tides of nationalized elections. In 2013 there were only 15 members of the moderate Blue Dog coalition. As recently as 2010, there had been 54 members.[36] Most of the centrist Democrats who had been elected to the House in 2006 and 2008 could not hang on until 2013. Thirty-four House Democrats voted against the Affordable Care Act when it passed in 2010. By the 2014 midterm election, only four of those lawmakers were still in office and running for reelection.

After their party's losses in competitive and Republican-leaning seats, the remaining House Democrats, like their Republican counterparts, represented secure seats. In 2013, 96 percent of House Democrats held seats in districts Obama won in 2012; only 9 represented districts won by Romney. Only 10 Democrats won Republican-leaning districts in 2012.[37]

Ten Democratic senators represented states Republican presidential candidates won in each election since 2000. Seven of the 21 Senate Democrats who would stand for reelection in 2014 represented states that Romney won, by double digits in six of them. Thus, there was a notable group of Senate Democrats who had an incentive to display some independence from the president.

Equally important, by trying to negotiate with Republicans, the president would face resistance from identifiers with his own party. Cuts to education and other major domestic policies including big-ticket items such as Social Security, Medicare, and Medicaid benefits and eligibility for the middle class were not popular with the public or Democratic leaders in Congress.[38] House Minority Leader Nancy Pelosi warned against raising the eligibility age for Medicare from 65 to 67 as a way to shrink federal spending. "We are not throwing America's seniors over the cliff to give a tax cut to the wealthiest people in America. We have clarity on that," she declared.[39] In response to the president's proposal to make cuts in the growth of Medicare expenditures and change the cost-of-living measure for Social Security increases, 107 House Democrats—more than half the caucus—signed a letter declaring their "vigorous opposition to cutting Social Security, Medicare or Medicaid benefits."[40] A number of Democratic senators, especially those from Republican-leaning states, actively opposed the president's proposals regarding entitlement spending.[41]

Liberals complained that Obama was too slow to withdraw troops from Iraq and wrong to increase the troop presence in Afghanistan. They were frustrated by his failure to persuade Congress to close the detention facility at Guantanamo Bay, Cuba. By 2013, they were criticizing his expansive use of drone warfare and his strong support for surveillance programs. Possible U.S. military strikes in Syria caused a number of left-leaning groups, including MoveOn.org, to publicly oppose the president, and many Democrats in Congress threatened to oppose a resolution authorizing such action.

By 2014 and with the midterm elections on the horizon, many Democrats began publicly breaking with the White House on free trade, sanctions on Iran, the Keystone XL pipeline, the Affordable Care Act, the National Security Agency's electronic surveillance programs, and energy policy. For some, but not all, of these lawmakers, the opposition was the predictable effort to position themselves for reelection.

In response, the White House reopened the Office of Political Affairs and promoted David Simas, a top communications aide, to be its new director. The president wanted to show that he was serious about defending Democratic control of the Senate and taking back the House from Republicans and attending to candidate needs, including fundraising. There was not much the Office could do, however, as the Democrats lost nine Senate seats and 13 House seats in the 2014 midterm elections.

THE STRUCTURE OF CONGRESSIONAL CHOICE

The structure of the choices facing Congress can also help or hinder the president's legislative agenda. Congress can take no vote, vote down, or pass a presidential initiative. Because Congress cannot act on every proposal and because there are many ways to prevent action in the U.S. system of separation of powers, most proposals flounder. The default position is for Congress to take no action. Although White House initiatives are likely to receive some congressional attention, many never come to a vote.[42]

From the standpoint of the president seeking support for a presidential initiative, there are two critical components of these choices. The first is the presence or absence of broad political incentives to act on an issue. More specifically, are there political incentives for the opposition to act? Typically, there are not. Indeed, the opposition party usually opposes presidential initiatives.

There are times, however, when at least some members of the opposition see benefits to legislating on a matter on the president's agenda. One example was immigration reform. With Mitt Romney winning an anemic 27 percent of the Latino vote in the 2012 presidential election, and the demographic trend of Hispanics composing an increasing percentage of

the electorate, many Republican party leaders advocated appealing to Latinos with action on immigration reform. Such a situation was an advantage for a White House that wished to pass an immigration bill, and it is
not surprising that the Senate passed a bipartisan immigration reform bill
in 2013. Unfortunately for the president, House Republicans, representing
overwhelmingly white districts, did not see the same incentives as their
Senate brethren and took no action on immigration reform except supporting a modest increase in funding for border control.

The second component of the structure of congressional choice is the
beneficiary of a failure to act. If the president opposes congressional initiatives, he benefits from the default position. However, if he wishes Congress to pass legislation, and all contemporary presidents do, the advantage usually shifts to the opposition. Most policies, from gun control to
efforts to combat global warming, do not take effect without positive action from Congress. In the Obama administration, Republicans usually
lacked incentives to act.

Nevertheless, there are some instances when not acting on expiring
legislation can be to the disadvantage of the opposition. There can be little
doubt that a unique aspect of the "fiscal cliff" issue was of invaluable aid
to the president. The default position, the broad tax increases that would
occur if no new policy was enacted after the expiration of the Bush tax
cuts, was unacceptable and highly salient to Republicans. Thus, they had
incentives to negotiate and pass a bill to avoid being blamed for tax increases and undermining their long held economic beliefs.

Sequestration was a different story. Once again, policy changes would
occur if Congress failed to act. In this case, $85 billion of automatic bud-
get cuts would go into effect for both defense and domestic discretionary
(not entitlement) programs unless the Congress and the president could
agree on a budget bill. The default position was more acceptable to Republican deficit hawks than was seeking revenue to pay for discretionary
programs.

Calculating political advantage on budgetary issues is difficult. Making
progress toward their goal of limiting the size of government provided
Republicans an incentive to strike a bargain with the president. Moreover,
such a deal would also offer a measure of political cover because both
parties would share responsibility for the pain of cuts to entitlements. On
the other hand, resisting the tax increases that would be part of a bargain
with the White House would shield Republican incumbents from primary
challenges, and deferring unpopular cuts on entitlements would be advantageous in the elections of 2014 and 2016. In theory, the most effective
budgetary leverage the Republicans had was a refusal to raise the debt
limit. Obama promised not to negotiate on the debt limit, however, view-

ing Republicans as having more to lose politically if the public held them responsible for plunging the country into an economic crisis.

SCHMOOZING

The president's strategic position with the public and Congress represents the broad parameters within which he attempts to govern. It dominates his efforts to lead Congress. What about more particularistic aspects of relations with the legislature? Would an emphasis on improving interpersonal relations between the president and individual members of Congress alter the balance of power?

Obama had a distaste for socializing with lawmakers and nurturing personal relationships with Washington insiders. He rarely included anyone other than his close friends and aides in his golf foursome and did not host members of Congress at Camp David. The president preferred to spend social time with family and close friends. A number of analysts complained that this tendency may have made it more difficult to establish a rapport with Republican leaders.[43]

For example, political analyst Charlie Cook advised Obama in print that he would recommend the president start his second term by "engaging Congress, maybe even getting to know members a little and starting a dialogue." Such activities would enhance the "wheeling and dealing, cajoling, seduction, and threatening that is required to move heaven and earth to be a successful president." Thus, Lyndon Johnson "listened to the concerns, objections, and demands of key members to ascertain what he needed to do to get their support or, failing that, secure a pledge not to actively oppose his agenda."[44]

The president was skeptical that the back-slapping politics employed by some of his predecessors could overcome the deep divides in Washington.[45] According to David Remnick,

> Obama and his aides regard all such talk of breaking bread and breaking legs as wishful fantasy. They maintain that they could invite every Republican in Congress to play golf until the end of time, could deliver punishments with ruthless regularity—and never cut the Gordian knot of contemporary Washington.[46]

The president suggested he felt burned in his first term after playing a round of golf with House Speaker John Boehner and spending months trying to negotiate a grand bargain on the debt, only to be "left at the altar."[47] During his first year, Obama held occasional Wednesday-night receptions for members of Congress. "But he stopped those niceties because they didn't make a difference when Republicans' only goal was defeating him," an adviser explained.[48] White House press secretary Jay Carney added that there was not much the president could do to sway members of Congress. "You're imagining leverage here."[49]

The White House knows Lyndon Johnson cannot be the model for Obama. A landslide victory in 1964, huge Democratic majorities in each house of Congress, and the moderate stances of many Republicans were invaluable assets for Johnson. So were the slack resources in the budget and the president's freedom to use them to trade for votes. As White House chief of staff William Daley said of LBJ's famous deal-making tactics, these days "you'd go to jail for what Johnson did."[50]

Thus, Obama correctly concluded about Johnson,

> When he lost that historic majority, and the glow of that landslide victory faded, he had the same problems with Congress that most Presidents at one point or another have. I say that not to suggest that I'm a master wheeler-dealer but, rather, to suggest that there are some structural institutional realities to our political system that don't have much to do with schmoozing.[51]

When Obama did ask Republicans to a social occasion, he was sometimes rebuffed. In the fall of 2012, he organized a screening at the White House of Steven Spielberg's film *Lincoln*. Spielberg, the cast, and the Democratic leadership found the time to come. Mitch McConnell, John Boehner, and three other Republicans declined their invitations, pleading the press of congressional business.[52]

Threats of primary challenges from the Republican right based on the sin of conferring with the president trump any ride on *Air Force One* or trip to Camp David.[53] For example, Republican Representative Scott Rigell of Virginia reported that he hesitated when the White House invited him to travel to his district with the president aboard *Air Force One*, knowing he would come under attack from conservatives for having a private talk with the president.[54]

The president understood these dynamics. When challenged at a White House news conference in January 2013 about criticism of his infrequent outreach, the president responded, "I promise you, we invite folks from Congress over here all the time. Sometimes they don't choose to come, and that has to do with the fact that I think they don't consider the optics useful for them politically."[55]

Nevertheless, early in his second term Obama began a "charm offensive" with Republicans. These efforts included calls to and dinners with Republicans, inclusion in golf games, and meetings with the House and Senate Republican caucuses.[56] Although the president received positive reviews from the opposition, Republicans remained skeptical. In the words of one close observer "very, very, *very* skeptical."[57] In the end, the White House faced the same implacable Republican opposition as it had during the president's first term.

There were also complaints that the president had failed to establish close relations with members of his own party. Yet even those raising the issue provided no evidence that this social distance had negatively affected the president's legislative success. Moreover, the White House maintained that the president held frequent meetings with groups of law-makers and many one-on-one phone calls or meetings, and he routinely consulted Democrats when crafting policy on a wide range of issues.[58]

It is possible that the lack of personal relationships made some Democrats less likely to fight for the president's priorities or defend him when times were tough. There is no systematic evidence to support such an argument, however, and the most rigorous research on the impact of the president's personal legislative skills has found that, at best, they are at the margins of coalition-building.[59] Strategic position dominates presidential leadership of Congress.

Summary

On the evening of Obama's first inauguration, Frank Luntz hosted a dinner for senior Republicans to plot their opposition to the new president. They agreed that it was necessary to engage in implacable opposition to Obama at every turn.[60] Congressional Republicans vowed to start hammering vulnerable Democrats immediately and stand united against the president's economic plan, no matter what was in it. They would rebuff any effort to meet their concerns. On his way to talk to Republicans on Capitol Hill during his first week in office, Obama learned that Speaker John Boehner and Majority Leader Eric Cantor had instructed their caucus to listen politely but take no part in the president's efforts to try to save economy.[61]

Despite Obama's reelection in 2012, little had changed. As he began his second term, the president faced a Republican majority in the House and a substantial Republican block in the Senate with little or no inclination to support his initiatives. With the exception of a few issues that served their interests independent of the White House's efforts, the ideology and constituencies of Republicans encouraged vigorous opposition. Moreover, cutting a deal with Republicans would complicate his efforts to keep the Democrats in the fold. Thus, it is no surprise that within the first 100 days of his second term the president had lost on gun control and sequestration. Ultimately, he would not make progress on immigration reform, environmental protection, and other priorities. Donna Hoffman and Alison Howard studied the success of presidents in winning congressional support for their proposals made in their State of the Union messages over the period of 1965–2014. The lowest level of success occurred in the 113th Congress (2013–2014).[62]

Knowing the president's strategic position with Congress allows us to explain and predict the challenges Obama would face. In the next chapter, I explicitly contrast the explanations offered by the strategic position and persuasion perspectives.

CHAPTER 4

Different Questions, Different Answers

WE HAVE SEEN that presidential leadership is highly dependent on the context—the opportunity structure—in which the president finds himself. Moreover, we can discern the impact of that context by asking a few key questions. The answers to these queries allow us to predict the level of success the president is likely to experience in achieving his legislative goals.

If the president's strategic position is dominant in explaining the potential of presidential leadership, what is the role of presidential persuasion? Can the president convince others to change their minds and thus create opportunities for change? In this chapter, I investigate the relative utility of the strategic position and persuasion perspectives. I do so by contrasting the conclusions they lead us to reach about the nature and consequences of presidential leadership. To illustrate the point, I focus on several prominent issues arising since Barack Obama's reelection.

The significance of asking different questions is that they yield different answers. If we assume the president has a high probability of succeeding in persuading others to support his initiatives, we are led in one direction for an explanation of his successes and failures. If we do not make such an assumption, we are led to seek other explanations and make different predictions of ultimate outcomes.

When we examine the president's successes, we want to know the contribution of persuasion and whether other factors offer more powerful explanations. For his failures, we want to investigate whether a dependency on persuasion contributed to them, whether aspects of his strategic position were critical to the outcome, and whether we can gain analytical leverage by asking if the president understood and effectively exploited his strategic position.

Each of the cases that follow shares some key aspects of the president's opportunity structure. These elements vary little over the course of a Congress. Except in rare instances, such as in 2001, a change in the majority party in a chamber does not occur during a Congress. Similarly rare is the perception of a mandate for certain policy changes. If there is such a perception, its impact dissipates over the first few months of a new term.[1] The ideologies and core constituencies of members of Congress are essentially constant over the two years of a Congress. The basic thrust of public opinion toward government activism also changes little during a Congress.

As we discussed in chapters 2 and 3, in the Obama presidency these factors, along with highly polarized partisan politics, determined the basic parameters of the battles over public policy and do not require reprising here. Because the president's strategic position regarding both the public and Congress was not strong, we would expect him to have difficulty achieving his legislative goals.

There was some variability in Obama's opportunity structure, however. Public approval of the president and support for specific proposals before his public relations efforts began varied. So did the willingness of at least some Republicans to address issues such as immigration reform. Finally, the structure of the decision facing Congress—the nature of the default position of not acting—varied by policy.

Fiscal Cliff, 2012

The first issue the president faced following his reelection was an urgent one: impending tax increases as the Bush-era tax cuts were set to expire on December 31, 2012. Obama wished to maintain the tax cuts for most Americans, but to increase taxes on families with more than $250,000 of taxable income. In the end, the president obtained some of what he wanted. Congress agreed to tax increases on families with more than $450,000 of taxable income. How can we explain this outcome?

Persuasion

One possibility is that the White House's success was the product of the president taking his case to the public and winning widespread support for his policy. Similarly, he may have persuaded congressional Republicans that his proposal was worth supporting.

MOVING THE PUBLIC

It is not surprising that the president initially emphasized public pressure over closed-door negotiations after he felt burned by failed debt talks in 2011.[2] On November 27, 2012, the president met at the White House with 15 small-business owners to argue that his tax proposals would help such firms. The next day, he hosted an event in which middle-class Americans talked about how the automatic tax increases slated for the end of the year would negatively affect them. He also met separately that day with corporate leaders. On November 30, the president flew to Pennsylvania to tour a toy manufacturing facility that he argued would be hurt if automatic tax increases took effect at the end of the year.

The president did a number of television interviews, his preferred form of interaction with the press. The White House focused these interviews in media markets in heavily urban areas that included House districts that elected Republicans to the House but were competitive for Obama in 2012 and who might therefore be vulnerable to pressure from the president's supporters in their districts.[3] In addition, Obama and White House aide David Plouffe asked supporters to engage in the tax fight directly by sending emails and beginning a social-media campaign on Twitter and Facebook.

Did public opinion change as a result of the president's public relations efforts? The time Congress considered the fiscal cliff was quite short, so there is not a long time series data set to examine. We do know that major poll organizations had shown majority public support for the substance of the president's proposal for some time, and before the president's public relations offensive.[4] Indeed, the public had generally been supportive of increasing taxes on the wealthy, a policy on which Bill Clinton campaigned in 1992. Although it is possible that in the afterglow of his reelection victory opinion may have shifted a bit in the president's direction,[5] the public supported the thrust of the president's proposal from the beginning of his legislative effort.

We can also obtain a sense of public opinion on taxing the wealthy by examining table 4.1. The data show there has been little variation in the public's view on whether the wealthy are paying their fair share of taxes over the entire Obama administration.

TABLE 4.1. Are the Wealthy Paying Too Little in Taxes?

Poll Date	% Fair Share	% Too Much	% Too Little	% Unsure
April 6–9, 2009	23	11	61	2
April 8–11, 2010	26	10	62	3
April 7–11, 2011	25	13	59	2
April 9–12, 2012	25	15	55	4
April 4–7, 2013	26	13	60	3

Source: Gallup Poll.

Question: "As I read off some different groups, please tell me if you think they are paying their fair share in federal taxes, paying too much, or paying too little. How about upper-income people?"

Despite the general public support for taxing the wealthy, the White House could not win the ultimate battle for public opinion. Gallup found that only 46 percent of the public approved of the president's handling of the negotiations while 48 percent disapproved, and only 43 percent approved of the result while 45 percent disapproved.[6]

CONVINCING CONGRESS

In the House, Democrats voted 172–16 in favor of the tax agreement while nearly two-thirds of Republicans (151) voted against it and only 85 supported it. The measure passed the Senate by a lopsided 89–8 vote; only three Democrats and five Republicans voted against the agreement. There is no evidence, however, that Republicans welcomed the opportunity to increase taxes on high-income families. Indeed, one will look in vain for a congressional Republican arguing that increasing taxes was a good idea. On the other hand, there is plenty of testimony that Republicans held their noses to support the agreement and thus avoid falling off the fiscal cliff— and being blamed for it. As we will see, the structure of the choice before Congress encouraged Republicans to do so.

If we focus on the president's ability to change public opinion during the consideration of the bill, we will conclude that the president was a failure, giving us little leverage in explaining his success. If we attempt to explain congressional action as a result of presidential persuasion, we will be in error and miss the real source of the president's success. Examining the president's strategic position and his exploitation of it offers us a better explanation for his winning a tax increase.

Exploiting Opportunities

Persuasion cannot explain the outcome of the fiscal cliff deliberations. Instead, features of the strategic landscape dominated. The president took public opinion as he found it and took advantage of the structure of the choice before Congress, resulting in many Republicans voting against their wishes to preserve some of their previous gains in tax rates.

INCREASING THE SALIENCE OF ISSUES

Even if the president cannot change the public's views on issues, he may be able to influence *what* it is thinking about. Instead of seeking to change public opinion regarding an issue, presidents may make appeals on policies that already have public support in an attempt to make them more salient to the public and thus encourage members of Congress to support White House initiatives to please the public.

Brandice Canes-Wrone has pioneered in exploring this aspect of the presidential leadership area. She found that presidents "almost never appeal to the public about an initiative likely to mobilize popular opposition." "Only on popular domestic proposals can presidents increase their prospects for legislative success by going public." Presidents are also more likely to publicize foreign policy initiatives if a majority of the public favors them and will generally avoid going public on initiatives that face mass opposition.[7]

The conditions for successfully employing such a strategy were favorable in the matter of the fiscal cliff.

- The public was following the negotiations over the fiscal cliff issue closely.[8]
- The public felt it was important to resolve the problem to prevent tax increases for the middle class.[9]
- The public wanted to do so through a compromise between the parties.[10]
- The public wanted this compromise to include increasing taxes on the wealthy.[11]
- Even many of the nation's leading chief executives dropped their opposition to tax increases on the wealthiest Americans.[12]
- Equally important, the public was more likely to assign blame to the Republicans than to the Democrats if the two sides failed to reach an agreement.[13]
- Throughout the negotiations, the president held an advantage over House Speaker John Boehner in the public's evaluations of their performance on them.[14]

The president had a winning hand in arguing that Republicans were holding hostage a tax cut for the middle class to preserve tax cuts for the wealthy. Thus, his basic strategy was not to persuade the public that something needed to be done and that it was important to raise taxes on the wealthy as part of the resolution of the issue. The public already agreed to this, by substantial margins. His goal was to make the issue more salient and thus pressure Republicans to respond. At the same time, cuts to domestic policies were not popular.[15] It should not be surprising that Obama studiously avoided discussing details of spending cuts, the other part of the budgetary equation.

DEFAULT POSITION: ADVANTAGE OBAMA

The default position in Congress is almost always the failure to pass legislation. If congressional inaction is more acceptable to one side of a dispute, then the other side has an incentive to compromise in order to avoid the results of the failure to act, especially if avoiding the default position is particularly salient to them and their constituents.

There can be little doubt that a unique aspect of the "fiscal cliff" issue was of invaluable advantage to the president. The default position, the broad tax increases that would occur if no new policy was enacted, was unacceptable and highly salient to Republicans. Thus, they had incentives to negotiate and pass a bill in order to avoid being blamed for tax increases and undermining their long held economic beliefs. Knowing the bill would pass because of support from some of their colleagues, the remaining House Republicans could vote consistent with their ideologies and constituencies and oppose any tax increase. In other words, these Republicans could "vote no but hope yes."

If the only thing an analyst knew about the entire fiscal cliff issue was the default position, she would predict correctly that many Republicans would have to support a tax increase on the wealthy.

THE RESILIENCE OF STRATEGIC POSITION

Despite his advantages on the issue, the president could obtain increased taxes only on families with more than $450,000 of taxable income—not $250,000 as he wished. Republican ideology, constituency pressure, and antipathy toward Obama were not immovable objects, but they certainly posed serious obstacles for the White House. For many conservatives, these considerations discouraged any compromise. The president's reelection, the reasonable claim of a mandate on tax increases, broad public support, and the risk of across-the-board tax cuts could not trump the implacable opposition of many House Republicans to tax increases.

SEQUESTRATION

The next major issue for the White House was sequestration. As a result of the 2011 budget deal between the president and Congress, $85 billion in automatic budget cuts would go into effect for both defense and domestic discretionary (non-entitlement) programs unless the two branches could agree on a new budget bill. The administration thought that Republicans would compromise on the budget to avoid large cuts to defense and public complaints about cuts in public services.

Persuasion

From the perspective of the Obama White House, in an ideal world the president would have persuaded the public and some Republicans in Congress to support a new budget that would include increased revenues and a different distribution of expenditures than that found in the sequestration bill. The environment is rarely so accommodating, however, and the president found he could convince neither the public nor congressional Republicans to support a new budget.

MOVING THE PUBLIC

The president hoped to spark a public revolt against Republicans over sequester-induced budget cuts. On February 20, 2013, he conducted interviews with eight local television stations in an attempt to intensify pressure on congressional Republicans. He and his aides played hardball, warning of a parade of horrors such as long waits at airports, public teacher dismissals, and private sector job losses resulting from voided federal contracts.

Although pluralities favored avoiding the sequestration as a general principle, the president could not obtain majority support for avoiding spending cuts, much less mobilize the public on his behalf.[16] His dire warnings of the consequences of the spending cuts had little impact. By March 1, Obama acknowledged that his campaign of highlighting fallout from the cuts had failed to persuade Republicans to consider tax increases as part of a package to avert the reductions resulting from the sequester.[17] Even five months following the sequestration, Gallup found that a majority of the public, including majorities of both Democrats and Independents, did not know enough to say whether it was good or bad for themselves or the country.[18]

If we assume that the president had the potential to rally the public to his side, we would blame the president for failing to do so. Such a conclusion would be incorrect. In response to a question from the press, Obama playfully replied, "Well, I'd like to think I've still got some persuasive power left. Let me check. [Laughter.] Look, the issue is not my persuasive power."[19] He was right. Persuasion was not the issue.

Conversely, if we understand that going public rarely succeeds, we would have predicted that the president would not convince the public to support his policy of raising additional revenue to avoid a sequester. The problem was not the president's lack of persuasiveness. No president has it. The problem for Obama was his dependence on persuasiveness as his core strategy.

CONVINCING CONGRESS

Republicans were in no mood for tax increases after they were forced to accept some hikes to resolve the fiscal cliff issue. Opposition to tax increases had long been the key unifying force for Republicans. Both their ideology and their constituents pointed them toward opposition to the president. They had no incentive to negotiate or compromise with the White House, and there was no way the president could change these views or incentives.

It did not take long for the White House to understand the weakness of its position. For example, in April the president and congressional Democrats abandoned their once-firm stand that they would address growing airport bottlenecks only in a broader fix to the across-the-board spending cuts triggered by sequestration. They supported bipartisan legislation to increase the nation's air traffic control system to full strength, losing them leverage of avoiding flight delays they had hoped would force Republicans into a larger agreement.[20]

Exploiting Opportunities

The president's strategic position presented him with few opportunities to exploit. He lacked the public's support, and, as we have seen, he could not change it. Moreover, most Republicans in Congress saw no reason to engage with Obama.

DEFAULT POSITION: ADVANTAGE DEFICIT HAWKS

The White House thought the automatic cuts to defense spending would help it to gain leverage to obtain Republican support for more revenues and thus prevent the sequestration. Actually, the president's strategic position was weak because the default position was more acceptable to Republican deficit hawks than seeking revenue to pay for discretionary programs. Much to the White House's surprise, the Republicans called the president's bluff, and the budget cuts occurred. Moreover, the White House could not fully employ its leverage. The president would not risk a government shutdown by demanding a sequester fix out of fear the public would blame Democrats for the shutdown.[21] In attempting to ignite public support, the president misunderstood his strategic position.

GUN CONTROL

On a Friday night in December 2012, after 20 schoolchildren and 6 adults were gunned down at Sandy Hook Elementary School in Newtown, Connecticut, President Obama convened his top aides in the Oval Office and weighed whether he should make a big push on new gun control laws, even though he had planned to start the second term focused on new immigration laws. No one thought it would be easy, but aides counseled that Obama had little choice but to try. They said that it would rightly be seen as a failure of leadership if he did not and that a grieving nation, especially his supporters, would demand action. Obama edited the speech he would give that Sunday at the memorial for the Newtown victims and inserted a phrase promising to use "whatever power this office holds" to confront gun violence with new legislation, locking in his commitment.[22]

Persuasion

Gun control is a well-established issue. People have long-term and reasonably fixed views about guns. The anti-gun control lobby, headed by the National Rifle Association, is legendary for its aggressiveness, electoral resources, political savvy, and support among the public. Any president would have found it extremely difficult to win against such obstacles.

MOVING THE PUBLIC

On January 16, 2013, at a White House event advocating gun control, the president proclaimed that his proposal would not pass "unless the people demand it." Shortly before the event, former White House press secretary Robert Gibbs told MSNBC, "The president has the most exciting campaign apparatus ever built. It's time to turn that loose." "If the NRA has a list," Gibbs declared, "then Obama for America [OFA] has a bigger list." (OFA was the president's personal political operation, affiliated with the Democratic National Committee.)[23]

Thus, President Obama vowed to rally public opinion to press a reluctant Congress to ban military-style assault weapons and high-capacity magazines, expand background checks, and toughen gun-trafficking laws. "I will put everything I've got into this," Obama said, "and so will Joe [Biden]." The White House believed the massacre had changed the dynamics on gun control. "I have never seen the nation's conscience so shaken by what happened at Sandy Hook," Biden said. "The world has changed and is demanding action."[24]

To exploit the opportunity he perceived to exist, the president kept his word and aggressively took his case to the public. Table 4.2 provides examples of his efforts. In addition, the vice president and other administration officials were active in promoting the president's proposals.

In the immediate aftermath of the shooting, the public favored stricter gun control laws in general (table 4.3). Despite the president's efforts, this support *diminished* in the period leading up to the Senate's votes on gun control provisions. The most widely supported form of gun control was background checks on potential purchasers of guns. Ninety percent or more of the public supported such checks (table 4.4). This percentage remained unchanged during the gun control debate. Opinion on more controversial proposals such as banning assault rifles and large magazines for automatic weapons displayed a similar immobility (tables 4.5 and

TABLE 4.2. President Obama's Going Public on Gun Control

Type of Communication	Date	Location
State of the Union Message	February 12, 2013	Joint Session of Congress
Weekly Radio Address	January 19, 2013	White House
	March 23, 2013	White House
	April 13, 2013*	White House
Press Conferences	December 19, 2012	White House
	March 1, 2013	White House
	April 16, 2013**	White House
Unveiling of Gun Control Proposals	January 16, 2013	White House
Meeting with Police Chiefs and Sheriffs	January 28, 2013	White House
Speech in East Room	March 28, 2013	White House
Statements	March 14, 2013	White House
	April 10, 2013	White House
	April 17, 2013	White House
Speeches Outside DC	February 4, 2013	Minneapolis
	April 3, 2013	Denver
	April 8, 2013	Hartford

Source: www.whitehouse.gov.

* Delivered by the mother of a Newtown shooting victim.
**Joint press conference with president of Mexico.

TABLE 4.3. Support for Stricter Gun Control Laws

	% Responding			
Poll Date	More Strict	Less Strict	Kept As They Are	Unsure/NA
December 14–16, 2012	57	9	30	4
January 11–15, 2013	54	9	34	3
February 6–10, 2013	53	10	34	3
March 20–24, 2013	47	11	39	3
April 24–28, 2013	54	10	33	3

Source: CBS News Poll and CBS News/*New York Times* Poll.

Question: "In general, do you think gun control laws should be made more strict, less strict, or kept as they are now?"

TABLE 4.4. Support for Background for Gun Purchases

Poll Date	% Favor	% Oppose	% Unsure/NA
January 11–15, 2013	92	7	1
February 6–10, 2013	91	7	2
March 20–24, 2013	90	8	2
April 24–28, 2013	88	11	1

Source: CBS News Poll and CBS News/New York Times Poll.

Question: "Do you favor or oppose a federal law requiring background checks on all potential gun buyers?"

TABLE 4.5. Support for Banning Assault Weapons

Poll Date	% Favor	% Oppose	% Unsure/NA
January 10–13, 2013	58	39	3
March 7–10, 2013	57	41	2
April 11–14, 2013	56	42	2

Source: ABC News/Washington Post Poll.

Question: "Would you support or oppose a law requiring a nationwide ban on the sale of assault weapons?"

TABLE 4.6. Support for Banning Large Ammunition Clips

Poll Date	% Favor	% Oppose	% Unsure/NA
December 14–16, 2012	59	38	2
January 10–13, 2013	65	32	3
April 14–16, 2013	56	41	3

Source: ABC News/Washington Post Poll.

Question: "Would you support or oppose a law requiring a nationwide ban on high-capacity ammunition clips, meaning those containing more than 10 bullets?"

4.6). To the extent there was any movement in public opinion, it was not in the president's direction.

Although the president could not move opinion, a majority of the public supported many proposals for stricter gun control, in some instances dating from previous years and in all of them before the president began his public relations efforts. A bigger problem for the president was the heavily partisan tilt to opinion on gun control. It was his inability to per-

TABLE 4.7. Party Support for Stricter Gun Laws

Party Group	More Strict	Less Strict	Kept As They Are	Unsure/NA
	% Responding			
All	47	11	39	3
Democrats	66	2	30	2
Independents	43	15	39	3
Republicans	29	16	52	3

Source: CBS News Poll, March 20–24, 2013.

Question: "In general, do you think gun control laws should be made more strict, less strict, or kept as they are now?"

suade Republicans—the core constituency of Republican members of Congress—that undermined his ability to win stricter gun controls. Actually, it was a lost cause.

In January, Gallup surveyed the public as to its satisfaction with 17 policy areas. Guns sparked the greatest difference between Republicans and Democrats. Fifty-nine percent of Republicans and 28 percent of Democrats were satisfied with U.S. gun laws, a difference of 31 percentage points.[25] It is not surprising, then, that there were great differences between party identifiers in their support for stricter gun control. Gallup's initial surveying of the president's proposals elicited 53 percent support overall as opposed to 41 percent in opposition. Eighty-two percent of Democrats supported Obama's initiative, but only 22 percent of Republicans did so.[26] Table 4.7 presents results from the March 20–24 CBS poll on support for the general notion of stricter gun laws, disaggregated by party identification. The gap in support for stricter gun laws was 37 percentage points.

In addition, polls showing 90 percent or more support for background checks were somewhat misleading. Republicans were decidedly less supportive of the legislation than of the general idea of making private gun sales subject to background checks; 57 percent supported the Senate bill, while 81 percent favored expanding background checks. Many of those who had reservations about the bill expressed concerns that it included other restrictions beyond background checks, or that it introduced a "slippery slope" toward more government power. Republicans—particularly conservatives and those who agreed with the Tea Party—were most likely to see a distinction between the concept and the Senate bill. Only 50 percent wanted Congress to pass the Senate bill, and only 28 percent of Republicans and Republican-leaning independents who agreed with the Tea Party wanted the Senate to pass the bill.[27]

TABLE 4.8. Public Responses to Senate Votes on Gun Control

Party Group	% Responding			
	Very Happy	Relieved	Disappointed	Angry
All	20	19	32	15
Republicans	29	23	26	8
Independents	26	22	28	13
Democrats	9	13	41	26

Source: Pew Research Center poll, April 18–21, 2013.

Question: "What word best describes how you feel about the Senate voting down new gun control legislation that included background checks on gun purchases?"

Following the Senate's votes, the Pew Research Center asked a national sample whether they were "very happy," "relieved," "disappointed," or "angry" at the outcome, specifically mentioning background checks (table 4.8). Forty-seven percent expressed negative feelings about the vote (15 percent were angry and 32 percent were disappointed) while 39 percent had a positive reaction (20 percent were happy and 19 percent were relieved) to the Senate's actions. Only Democrats had a majority of negative reactions (67 percent to 22 percent). Republicans had positive reactions by 51 to 34 percent, and Independents had positive reactions by 48 to 41 percent.[28] Thus, the overall balance of positive and negative reactions to the Senate votes tracked more closely to measures of the public's broad views on gun control than to attitudes toward background checks.

In the 16 states where both senators voted against the president's proposals, 46 percent of the public were very happy or relieved that the bill did not pass; 37 percent said they were angry or disappointed. By contrast, in the 21 states where both senators supported the legislation, 51 percent responded they were either angry or disappointed that the legislation failed, while 38 percent were very happy or relieved about the outcome. Just 16 percent of people in these states said they were angry the legislation was voted down, while 35 percent were simply disappointed.[29] In addition, in a poll taken the month following the Senate votes, only 40 percent of Republicans (as opposed to 73 percent of Democrats) listed curbing gun violence as a high priority.[30]

CONVINCING CONGRESS

The White House reported that the president talked to 43 senators on behalf of gun control reform and made last-ditch appeals to several senators, including Republicans Dean Heller of Nevada, and Kelly Ayotte of

New Hampshire. Both rejected his entreaties.[31] It is possible that Obama simply lacked persuasiveness and that someone else could have expanded the gun control coalition. An examination of more fundamental aspects of the president's environment leads us to reject such a conclusion.

All but four Republican senators voted against more rigorous background checks. Three of them (Susan Collins of Maine, Ronald Kirk of Illinois, and Patrick Toomey of Pennsylvania) represented blue states. The four Democrats who voted against the background check proposal were from red states with high rates of gun ownership: Max Baucus of Montana, Mark Pryor of Arkansas, Mark Begich of Alaska, and Heidi Heitkamp of North Dakota.

Republicans in the public are much more likely than Democrats to own guns,[32] and those who place a high priority on maintaining gun rights are more likely to be active politically than those who do not.[33] In May 2013, a plurality of conservative Republicans (47 percent) said they would refuse to vote for a candidate with whom they agreed on most issues but disagreed with on gun control.[34] Thus, the senators who voted against the president, all but four of whom were Republicans, acted pragmatically and did not risk alienating their constituents.

Just how would a president twist congressional Republicans' arms to insist that they vote against the wishes of their constituents and their own long-held views on gun control? With what could he threaten them, given his lack of support in their constituencies and their fear of a challenge from the right? How could he buy their votes in an era of extraordinarily scarce resources and divided government? Suggestions of the potential of presidential pressure were illusory.

Exploiting Opportunities

Exploiting opportunities requires that there be opportunities in the first place. The president's strategic position was stronger on gun control than it was on sequestration—the public supported more rigorous gun control, at least in the abstract. Nevertheless, the distribution of public opinion simply reinforced the inclinations of Republicans and a few Democrats to oppose gun control.

Believing victory was near, many commentators who supported gun control were horrified at the president's failure to obtain stricter laws.[35] They, like the White House, thought the president could rally the public and twist enough congressional arms to achieve policy change. Thus, his critics declared that Obama's failure to persuade those opposed to gun control—Republicans—in either the public or Congress must be his own fault.

The critics—and the White House—misread the president's opportunity structure on gun control. There were few opportunities for the president to exploit. There was very little possibility that the president, any president, could change opinion among those in the public and Congress with long commitments to gun rights, especially when those positions were widely held. The president's strategic position dominated the consideration of gun control.

THE DEFAULT POSITION: ADVANTAGE TO GUNS RIGHTS

In the case of gun control, as with most policy initiatives, the default position favored those opposed to change. All the president's opponents had to do was secure 41 votes in the Senate and gun control proposals were dead. They had little difficulty winning these votes.

GOVERNMENT SHUTDOWN

On October 1, 2013, parts of the federal government shut down after Congress and the president could not agree on a budget. Many Republicans attempted to leverage the pressure of deadlines involving the start of the fiscal year and reaching the limits of federal borrowing on October 17 to force Democrats to swallow unpalatable measures. Repealing the Affordable Care Act (ACA) as part of a deal to fund the government and raise the debt limit was the GOP's highest priority. After the Democratic-controlled Senate and the president rejected such efforts, the shutdown occurred. Sixteen days later, the shutdown ended in the early hours of October 17—just before the United States was set to reach its borrowing limit—when the president signed a bill that extended government funding until January 15, 2014, and suspended the debt ceiling until February 7, 2014.

One could term this a victory for the president because the Republicans did not succeed in gutting the Affordable Care Act, the government was funded, and the public blamed the GOP for what many of them saw as a fiasco.

Persuasion

Once again, we must consider the possibility that the White House's success was the product of the president taking his case to the public and winning widespread support for his policy. Similarly, he may have persuaded congressional Republicans that his proposal was worth supporting.

MOVING THE PUBLIC

Before the shutdown, most Americans wanted members of Congress to compromise and reach agreement on a spending plan. Fifty percent of the public opposed the House Republicans' proposal to cut off funding for the ACA as part of any budget agreement, while only 38 percent favored this proposal. Unsurprisingly, 87 percent of Tea Party Republicans and 61 percent of non–Tea Party Republicans supported defunding ACA. However, there was a substantial divide in the Republican base over how far to go to achieve the goal of defunding the ACA. By 54 percent to 38 percent, non–Tea Party Republicans wanted to see a compromise on the budget, even if it was one with which they did not particularly agree. Conversely, 71 percent of Tea Party Republicans wanted lawmakers who shared their views to stand by their principles and demand the repeal of ACA, even if that led to a government shutdown.[36]

Once the shutdown began, fully 72 percent of Americans disapproved of shutting down the federal government over differences on the ACA; just 25 percent approved of this action. Republicans were divided: 48 percent approved, while 49 percent disapproved. Most Tea Party supporters approved of the government shutdown, however.[37] By the end of the shutdown, 81 percent of the public disapproved of it,[38] and 75 percent felt Congress should deal separately with the ACA rather than use it as leverage in a fight over the budget.[39] By a 2-to-1 margin, Americans wanted Congress to agree to a compromise plan on increasing the debt limit, even one with which they disagreed, rather than holding out for the plan they might prefer.[40]

Before the shutdown, the public said it was more likely to blame congressional Republicans than President Obama and the Democrats if a shutdown occurred.[41] After the shutdown, blame shifted only slightly, if at all, to reinforce the direction of opinion.[42] At this point, nearly half the public viewed the Democratic Party unfavorably, but even more—62 percent—held that view about Republicans, a record high in the Gallup Poll. The favorability ratings of Republican leaders John Boehner and Mitch McConnell hit all-time lows.[43]

However, it does not take presidential coaxing to persuade voters that they like government services and do not want to risk ruining the economy by defaulting on the national debt. We can see how little room there was for the president to convince voters to support his stance. The public's reactions were essentially unchanged from what Americans told pollsters in late September about who they *expected* to blame in the event of a shutdown. Table 4.9 shows the results of three polls, which used a similar question before and after the shutdown. The stability in opinion is striking. There was essentially no change at all during the month.

More important, a willingness to assign blame correlated strongly with partisanship. Democrats overwhelmingly blamed Republicans, and Republicans returned the favor by overwhelmingly blaming Obama and the Democrats (table 4.10). Independents were split. Opinion seems to have been locked in before the shutdown occurred. Republicans received a higher percentage of blame largely because more Americans identified as Democrats than as Republicans.

TABLE 4.9. Blame for Government Shutdown, Before and After

| | | % Blame | | |
| | | | | |
Poll Date	Republicans	Obama and Democrats	Both Equally	Unsure/No Answer
September 19–23, 2013[1]	44	35	16	4
October 1–2, 2013[2]	44	35	17	4
October 18–21, 2013[3]	46	35	14	4

Source: CBS News Poll and CBS News/New York Times Poll.

Questions:
[1] "As you many know, if a budget agreement in Washington is not reached by the end of the month, the federal government could partially shut down. Who would you blame more if there is a partial shutdown of the federal government: the Republicans in Congress, or Barack Obama and the Democrats in Congress?" [options rotated]
[2] "Who do you blame more for the partial government shutdown: the Republicans in Congress, or Barack Obama and the Democrats in Congress?"
[3] "Who do you blame more for the partial government shutdown and the difficulties in reaching an agreement on the debt ceiling: the Republicans in Congress, or Barack Obama and the Democrats in Congress?" [options rotated]

TABLE 4.10. Blame for Government Shutdown

| | | % Blame | | |
| | | | | |
Party Group	Republicans	Obama and Democrats	Both Equally	Unsure/No Answer
All	44	35	17	4
Republicans	10	73	15	2
Democrats	76	9	11	3
Independents	40	30	24	7

Source: CBS News poll, October 1–2, 2013.

Question: "Who do you blame more for the partial government shutdown: the Republicans in Congress, or Barack Obama and the Democrats in Congress?"

This stability is what we should expect. Table 4.11 shows the results of asking the public who was to blame for the government shutdowns in 1995–1996. We find very little change in attributions of blame from before until well after the shutdowns. Moreover, we find the same advantage for the Democratic president over the Republican Congress. The public does not like government shutdowns. More recently, it has shown that it also does not care for legislatively induced debt crises.

TABLE 4.11. Responsibility for Government Shutdowns, 1995–1996

Responsibility	Poll N	Dates of Poll	Republicans (%)	Clinton (%)	Both (%)	No Opinion (%)
NBC[1]	1465	10/27–31/ 1995	43	32	18	7
Gallup[2]	652	11/14/1995	49	26	19	6
Gallup[3]	615	11/17–18/1995	47	25	21	7
CBS[4]	819	11/19/1995	51	28	15	6
NBC[5]	805	11/19/1995	47	27	20	6
ABC[6]	852	1/6–7/1996	50	27	20	3
CBS[7]	1479	10/17–20/1996	53	28	11	8

Questions:
[1] "If President [Bill] Clinton and the Republican Congress do not reach a budget agreement in time to avoid a major shutdown of the federal government, who do you think will be more to blame—President Clinton or the Republican Congress?"
[2] "Overall, who do you blame more for the recent shutdown of the federal government— President (Bill) Clinton or the Republican leaders in Congress?"
[3] "(As you may know, the Republicans in Congress and President (Bill) Clinton have not reached an agreement on the federal budget. As a result, the federal government has shut down all non-essential services.) Overall, who do you blame more for the recent shutdown of the federal government . . . President (Bill) Clinton, or the Republican leaders in Congress?"
[4] "Monday night, the federal government was partially shut down when President (Bill) Clinton and the Republican leaders in Congress could not agree on a resolution to keep the government running while they debated the federal budget. Who do you blame more for the partial government shutdown—the Republicans in Congress or Bill Clinton?"
[5] "As you know, President (Bill) Clinton and the Republican Congress have not reached a budget agreement, and this has led to a shutdown of the federal government. Who do you think is more to blame for this shutdown— President Clinton or the Republican Congress?"
[6] "As you may know, the Clinton administration and the Republicans have agreed to temporarily reopen the government offices that were closed for nearly three weeks while they worked on a new budget. Whose fault do you think this partial government shutdown mainly was—(President Bill) Clinton's or the Republicans' in Congress?"
[7] "Who do you think was more responsible for the government shutdowns (last winter because of disagreements between Congress and the president over the budget)—the Republicans in Congress or President (Bill) Clinton?"

We also cannot credit the public's response to the shutdown to the president's ability to persuade it to take a more favorable view of the ACA. As table 4.12 shows, there was no change at all in disapproval from September until Congress passed the budget. The next month, disapproval increased substantially in the wake of the problematic start of enrollment

TABLE 4.12. Support for the Affordable Care Act around the Government Shutdown

Poll Date	% Approve	% Disapprove	% Unsure/No Answer
September 9–23, 2013	39	51	10
October 1–2, 2013	43	51	6
October 18–21, 2013	43	51	6
November 15–18, 2013	31	61	8

Source: CBS News Poll.

Question: "From what you've heard or read, do you approve or disapprove of the health care law that was enacted in 2010?"

in the federal and state insurance exchanges. Similarly, approval of the ACA remained the same throughout the shutdown and then diminished notably by the next month.

CONVINCING CONGRESS

The president's strategic position regarding Congress is what precipitated the shutdown. Conservative Republican members, buoyed by Tea Party supporters in their districts and their strong antipathy for the president, voted their consciences and represented their constituents in opposing the Affordable Care Act and pushing the government to the brink of default.

Passing a budget required Republican votes, and ultimately some in the GOP did vote for the agreement. In the House, Democrats voted 198-0 for the budget agreement while 62 percent of Republicans (144) voted against it. Still, 87 Republicans supported the bill. The president did about the same in the Senate, winning all 54 Democratic votes and 18 (40 percent) of the 45 Republicans.

Were these Republican votes the result of the president's persuasiveness? Hardly. Even the urgings of Speaker John Boehner, Majority Leader Eric Cantor, and Majority Whip Kevin McCarthy could not bring most House Republicans into the fold. Most Republican senators sided with Ted Cruz and his Tea Party stalwarts.

Those Republicans who did support the budget agreement were angry at being placed in the position of defending a strategy that was bound to fail and that was clearly alienating the public. By the end of the shutdown, 51 percent of Republicans along with 72 percent of Democrats wanted their representatives to compromise rather than hold out.[44] Even then, it was only when facing a deadline over the government's ability to borrow money to pay past bills that House Republicans found a way out of their dilemma.

Exploiting Opportunities

Persuasion cannot explain the outcome of the battle over the government shutdown. As usual, the president's strategic position dominated. The president began with favorable public opinion, which remained stable throughout the deliberations over the budget and the debt limit. This public support turned out to be an invaluable asset, as Republicans saw their favorability ratings sinking to all-time lows, encouraging them to put an end to their self-inflicted wounds and fund the government. The president had another advantage to his strategic position: the prospect of defaulting on the national debt.

DEFAULT POSITION: ADVANTAGE OBAMA

The structure of the issue before Congress was of considerable advantage to the president. If the legislature failed to pass a budget, the government would remain partially shuttered, causing hardships for many Americans. Similarly, most financial experts predicted that a financial crisis would result if Congress failed to increase the debt ceiling. No one wished for another financial crisis. As in the case of the fiscal cliff, many Republicans ended up voting against their wishes. The nature of the choices they faced forced them to act.

CONCLUSION

The lens through which we examine presidential leadership matters. If we base our analysis of White House efforts to enact legislation on the premise that a skilled president can reshape the political landscape to pave the way for change, we are likely to make several types of errors.

We make the first type of error when we incorrectly attribute presidential success to persuasion. The president did not persuade the public to support higher taxes on the wealthy or to oppose a government shutdown, for example. It already held those views. Similarly, he did not persuade members of Congress to change their views about taxation or the budget. Democrats were already on board, and Republicans were trying to avoid policy disasters for which they would be blamed.

We make another type of error when we fault the president for failing to convince the public or Congress to back him, inaccurately assuming the potential of persuasion. On both gun control and sequestration, there were ideological and constituency pressures that far outweighed any possible influence of presidential persuasion. In these cases, the default position of inaction also favored the president's opponents.

Yet other errors occur if we fail to discern the impact of the nonpersuasive factors of strategic position. Exploiting the opportunity provided by both existing public opinion and the default position of inaction was critical for the president's success in both the taxation and government shutdown issues. Understanding the role of strategic position also helps us to understand that failure was likely when the president and his aides miscalculated the opportunity structure on gun control.

In sum, the evidence seems clear. It makes a difference which perspective we adopt to view presidential leadership. Different perspectives lead us to ask different questions—and arrive at different conclusions. By highlighting the critical aspects of the president's strategic position, we are best positioned to understand events and predict the likely consequences of the president's efforts to achieve his goals.

The president's dependency on existing opportunities implies a critical interdependence between leaders and followers, which we miss when we focus only on the pinnacle of power. Moreover, there are many influences on followers and potential followers and many obstacles to influencing them. The president is an important agenda setter,[45] for example, but there are other key influences on the agenda as well.[46] Thus, we need to devote more attention to thinking about politics from the bottom up as well as the top down and to the context in which the president seeks to lead.

Because presidential power is not the power to create opportunities through persuasion, successful presidents facilitate change by recognizing opportunities in their environments and fashioning strategies and tactics to exploit them. Because the president will persuade few opposition party adherents to support him and his initiatives, most of our attention should be directed toward those predisposed to support his initiatives, which is the focus of part II. Nevertheless, we need to be attentive to the potential for exploiting opportunities such as the opposition's preexisting agreement with the president's proposals or the structure of a decision facing Congress favoring the president.

PART II

Exploiting Opportunities

CHAPTER 5

Reinforcing Opinion

PRESIDENTS INVEST HEAVILY in leading the public in the hope of leveraging public support to win backing in Congress. Nevertheless, there is overwhelming evidence that presidents rarely move the public in their direction. Most observers view Ronald Reagan and Bill Clinton as excellent communicators. Yet pluralities, and often majorities, of the public opposed them on most of their policy initiatives. Moreover, public opinion typically moved away from the positions they favored rather than toward them.[1]

Despite the favorable context of the national trauma resulting from the 9/11 terrorist attacks, the long-term disdain of the public for Saddam Hussein, and the lack of organized opposition, George W. Bush made little headway in moving the public to support the war in Iraq, and once the war was over, the rally resulting from the quick U.S. victory rapidly dissipated.[2] Notwithstanding his eloquence, Barack Obama could not obtain the public's support for his initiatives that were not already popular. His health care reform lacked majority support even years after it passed, for example.[3]

Even Franklin D. Roosevelt, the president often considered the greatest politician of the twentieth century, faced constant frustration in his efforts to move the public to prepare for entry into World War II, and his failure to persuade the public regarding his plan to pack the Supreme Court effectively marked the end of the New Deal.[4] George Washington, who was better positioned than any of his successors to dominate American politics because of the widespread view of his possessing exceptional personal qualities, did not find the public particularly deferential.[5]

Occasionally an experiment finds a positive impact of presidential leadership on the public. Unfortunately, the environment in which the president usually operates differs fundamentally from that found in experiments done to date. The president's world is inhabited by committed, well-organized, and well-funded opponents. Experiments that only offer respondents one view and only seek their immediate reactions to presidential stimuli are simply irrelevant to presidential leadership.[6]

In the much more typical case, intense disagreement among elites generates conflicting messages. John Zaller argues that attitudes on major issues change in response to changes in the intensity of competing streams of political communication. When there is elite consensus, and thus only one set of cues offered to the public, opinion change may be substantial. However, when elite discourse is divided, people respond to the issue according to their predispositions, especially their core partisan and ideological views.[7] Thus, when Paul Sniderman and Sean Theriault offered people competing frames, as in the real world, they adopted positions consistent with their preexisting values.[8] Similarly, when people can choose their sources of information, as they can in everyday life, they are unresponsive to opinion leadership that differs from their preexisting views.[9]

Occasions in which elite commentary is one-sided are rare. Consensual issues tend to be new, with few people having committed themselves to a view about them. Most issues that generate consensual elite discourse arise from external events, like surprise attacks on the United States such as the terrorist assaults on September 11, 2001, or its allies, such as the invasion of Kuwait in 1990. Thus, the president's greatest chance of influencing public opinion is in a crisis (which attracts the public's attention) in which elites articulate a unified message. At other times, most people are too inattentive or too committed to views to be strongly influenced by elite efforts at persuasion.[10]

If presidents cannot change the public's predispositions, they still may be able to exploit them in their continual quest for support. Perhaps the White House can win the support of those predisposed to support them—their fellow partisans—by sending signals as to the appropriate stance of a party identifier.

MOTIVATED REASONING

Motivated reasoning is a central concept in the study of political behavior. It refers to the confirmation bias (seeking out information that confirms prior beliefs), a prior attitude effect (viewing evidence consistent with prior opinions as more compelling than evidence that is inconsistent with them), and the disconfirmation bias (challenging and dismissing evidence inconsistent with prior opinions, regardless of their objective accuracy). Motivated reasoning may distort a person's perception of new information and the conclusions she reaches about it. Most people seek out information confirming their preexisting opinions and ignore or reject arguments contrary to their predispositions. When exposed to competing arguments, they typically accept the confirming ones and dismiss or argue against the opposing ones.[11]

Partisan identification is a primary anchor of political behavior and the basis for much motivated reasoning.[12] Partisan leanings significantly influence perceptions of conditions and policies and interpretations and responses to politics. Partisans display a selective pattern of learning in which they have higher levels of knowledge for facts that confirm their worldview and lower levels of knowledge for facts that challenge them.[13] Even the most basic facts are often in contention between adherents of the parties, such as whether inflation, tax rates, or the budget deficit had risen or fallen or whether there were weapons of mass destruction in Iraq.[14] In 2015, a national poll found that only 43 percent of Republicans thought the number of people with health insurance had increased despite clear evidence that millions of people gained health insurance as a result of the Affordable Care Act.[15] Similarly, partisans frequently credit a president of their own political party for perceived policy successes and blame a president of the opposite party for perceived failures.[16]

As Adam Berinsky states, "In the battle between facts and partisanship, partisanship always wins."[17] Partisan bias and the misperceptions it causes are often most prevalent among those who are generally well informed about politics.[18] Political knowledge neither corrects nor mitigates partisan bias in perception of objective conditions. Instead, it enhances it.

The impact of elite discourse is important, as it clarifies where parties stand. Members of the public use the cues of elites to align their partisanship and ideology, usually bringing their issue attitudes in line with the stances of their party's elites.[19] Thus, "when partisan elites debate an issue and the news media cover it, partisan predispositions are activated in the minds of citizens and subsequently constrain their policy preferences."[20] In times of highly polarized politics, the incentive to be loyal to one's own group and maximize differences with the opposition group is likely to be especially strong.[21]

It is not surprising that research has found that party cues influence opinion.[22] James Druckman, Erik Peterson, and Rune Slothuus found that polarized environments intensify the impact of party endorsements on opinions, decrease the impact of substantive information, and, ironically, stimulate greater confidence in those—less substantively grounded— opinions. Under conditions of high polarization and when presented with opposing frames, partisans' opinions move only in the direction of the frame endorsed by their party, regardless of strength of the frames.[23] Moreover, increased confidence in their opinions makes people less likely to consider alternative positions and more likely to take action based on their opinions, such as attempting to persuade others.[24]

Signaling does not encourage people to change their minds by reasoning about an issue. Instead, signaling provides cues to people that serve to short-circuit their reasoning processes, trigger motivated reasoning, and thus shape how they process information provided by different sides, including largely ignoring arguments from the opposition.[25] Some work has found that party cues encourage motivated reasoning to produce arguments supporting the correctness of their party's position.[26] Either way, the signaler is showing supporters where their predispositions should take them on a particular matter. Persuasion begins *after* people have expressed their predispositions.

MOTIVATED REASONING AND PRESIDENTIAL SIGNALING

Individuals interpret a policy, ranging from war to the budget deficit, in light of their opinions concerning the policy's sponsor.[27] The president typically enjoys high levels of approval from his co-partisans—and much lower levels from identifiers with the opposition party. Because the president's credibility mediates his impact as a cue giver,[28] the chief executive is likely to be more credible to those predisposed to support him than to adherents of the opposition party.[29]

Motivated reasoning may provide an opportunity for the president as leader of his party. When the president signals his views on issues, identifiers with his party should be responsive to those signals. These cues help his co-partisans cut through the complexity of policy debates and reach a conclusion. Of course, the strength of a person's partisanship should moderate partisan-motivated reasoning.[30]

People must also receive the president's signals and view them as authoritative if they are to be influenced by them. In addition, the impact of presidential signaling should vary with the extent the signals reinforce or challenge party identifiers' existing views or address new issues on which opinion is not yet formed.

As by far the most visible political figure in the country, the president is well-positioned to signal his policy stances. Although the public is not likely to be attuned to the full range of issues with which the president deals, there is ample opportunity for the White House to inform citizens about the broad outlines of the president's positions on the most salient issues. These issues are generally high on the White House's policy agenda.

The president's signals are not only visible but also authoritative. Who can speak with more authority than the chief executive and the leader of his party? The president has no peers, no squabbling colleagues such as one finds in debates in Congress. It is not that the president lacks critics. Far from it. It is that no one else can as credibly claim to speak for the

Partisan's Opinion in Relation to President's Stance

Co-partisans	Support	Oppose	No opinion
Opposition	Support	Oppose	No opinion

▢ Cross-pressured public
▮ The public has not formed opinions on an issue

FIGURE 5.1. Consistency of President's Stance with Partisans'. Medium-shaded cells indicate cross-pressured public. Dark-shaded cells indicate the public has not formed opinions on an issue.

whole nation and present statements in the context of the symbolic trappings of the White House.

Existing opinions about the issues on which the president signals his views should also influence the public's responsiveness to White House signals. The president's signals can be consistent with the opinions or predispositions typically held by identifiers with his party, contrary to those opinions, or on new issues on which most citizens have yet to develop opinions. Figure 5.1 portrays these situations.

The two unshaded cells represent the typical condition in which the president's stances are consistent with those of his fellow partisans and opposed to the views of opposition party identifiers. The darker cells indicate the less common circumstance in which the public has not developed specific views or general predispositions regarding an issue. The medium-shaded cells indicate instances in which the views of the White House and identifiers with the president's party are not congruent or when the president takes stands that are consistent with the views of opposition party identifiers. As a result, partisans of both parties may be cross-pressured.

In this chapter I focus on the president sending his co-partisans signals to reinforce their predispositions regarding White House policy initiatives. In the following chapter, I analyze the president exploiting existing favorable opinion and on leading in the unusual instances in which there is no opinion on an issue. In chapter 7 I discuss the president leading his co-partisans in cross-pressured situations and channeling of cross-pressured opposition party identifiers to reconsider their party identification.

REINFORCEMENT

Preaching to the converted has limited potential to change opinions and is not what most political commentators have in mind when they advocate that the White House employ the bully pulpit. Nevertheless, the audience for much presidential rhetoric is those who already agree with the White House. When presidents take stands with which their co-partisans already agree, they reinforce those views. When Barack Obama proposed to expand health care, maintain food stamp payments, or combat climate change, he was acting consistently with the views of most Democrats. He did not need to convince them that they should change their views.

Reinforcement is important in politics. Perhaps the most important function of a coalition-builder, in an election or in dealing with a legislature, is consolidating core supporters. Maintaining preexisting support or activating those predisposed to back him can be crucial to a president's success. Important policies usually face substantial opposition. Often opponents are virulent in their criticism. Presidents quite naturally believe they must engage in a permanent campaign just to maintain the status quo. Such efforts may require reassuring supporters as to one's fundamental principles, strengthening their resolve to persist in a political battle, or encouraging them to become more active on behalf of a candidacy or policy proposal.

Reinforcement by definition does not change opinions. Those whose views the president reinforces already agree with the White House. Thus it is difficult to identify an impact of reinforcement when it occurs. Nevertheless, if the opinions of opposition party identifiers and Independents turn increasingly against a president's policy, and those of his co-partisans—those whose views have been reinforced—do not, we may conclude that this steadfastness is evidence of reinforcement. Similarly, reinforcement might explain co-partisans increasing their support in the face of opposition party attacks while other groups hold fast in their opposition.

Although White House signaling may attract the support of the president's co-partisans, signaling is a two-edged sword. We have seen that individuals interpret policies in light of their opinions concerning the policy's sponsor and that the president is not likely to enjoy a high level of approval from identifiers with the opposition party. Motivated reasoning should encourage those predisposed to oppose the president also to oppose his policies.

For policies that are long-established and at the core of differences among the parties, signaling should have little negative effect. Partisans are already sorted into the appropriate camps. For issues on which opinion is not well established, signals from the White House may move identifiers with the opposition party to oppose the president's policies. One of the ironies of polarized politics is that proposals such as a mandate for health insurance or a cap-and-trade proposal to limit greenhouse gases once proposed by one party become anathema to it when they are adopted by the president of another party.

The contribution of signaling to increasing overall public support for the president's policies depends also on the size of the two groups of partisan identifiers. If those identifying with the president's party compose a larger group than those identifying with the opposition, the White House may receive a net benefit from signaling. However, if the reverse is true, the president is likely to be worse off as a result of signaling. In other words, signaling might actually *decrease* the nation's support for an initiative.

HEALTH CARE REFORM

The turbulent history of the Affordable Health Care Act, the signature policy of the Obama presidency, provides an opportunity to examine public opinion about an issue over an extended period of time. The battle to pass the ACA heated up in mid-2009 and lasted through March 2010 when the House voted for final passage. At that time it was the least popular major piece of legislation when passed in at least a century. Moreover, conflict continued as individual states made decisions about whether to expand coverage in their Medicaid programs. After taking control of the House in 2011, Republicans repeatedly voted to repeal all or parts of the act. On July 30, 2012, the Supreme Court weighed in with a split decision upholding the constitutionality of the individual mandate provision of the law in *National Federation of Independent Business v. Sebelius*. The disastrous rollout of the website for enrollments in health care exchanges in the fall of 2013 kept the issue in the public eye and extended the controversy into 2014, when Republicans made it an issue in the midterm elections.

The Kaiser Family Foundation has conducted tracking polls in most months since Congress passed the ACA. Table 5.1 presents the public's favorability toward the law since April 2010. The questions make no reference to any person or party associated with health care reform. At a glance, we see that overall public opinion on the ACA is quite stable. In 2013–2014, for example, overall favorable opinion ranged only from 33 to 39 percent. It is also readily apparent that, in general, support for the law was low. Only in July 2010 did even half the public hold a favorable view of the ACA.

Figure 5.2 displays in graphic form the data for partisan affiliation provided in table 5.1. For all groups, there are occasional anomalies in the time series, but most of the variance is well within the error range of comparing the results of two polls. The standard deviation for Republicans and Independents is only 4 percentage points. Democrats' standard deviation was 6 percentage points, 50 percent greater than the other groups. An indicator that the Democrats may be responding to a unique influence is that Democratic support correlates (r) with Republican support only at .12.

TABLE 5.1. Support for the Affordable Care Act

Poll Date	% Favorable			
	All	Democrat	Independent	Republican
April 9–14, 2010	46	78	36	13
May 11–16, 2010	41	72	36	8
June 17–22, 2010	48	69	37	23
July 8–13, 2010	50	73	49	21
August 16–22, 2010	43	68	48	16
September 14–19, 2010	49	75	41	21
October 5–10, 2010	44	69	42	11
November 3–6, 2010	42	68	34	15
December 1–6, 2010	42	69	37	12
January 4–14, 2011	41	73	37	12
February 8–13, 2011	43	66	34	11
March 8–13, 2011	42	71	43	9
April 7–12, 2011	41	64	37	12
May 12–17, 2011	42	72	41	17
June 9–14, 2011	42	65	35	20
July 13–18, 2011	42	64	33	16
August 10–15, 2011	39	60	38	24
September 7–12, 2011	41	65	33	14
October 13–18, 2011	34	52	36	11
November 10–15, 2011	37	62	32	12
December 8–13, 2011	41	64	34	19
January 12–17, 2012	37	62	33	12
February 13–19, 2012	42	64	30	16
February 29–March 5, 2012	41	66	40	12
April 4–10, 2012	42	70	40	7
May 8–14, 2012	37	62	39	8
June 28–30, 2012	41	71	34	7
July 17–23, 2012	38	69	38	12
August 7–12, 2012	38	64	35	8
September 13–19, 2012	45	72	34	16
October 18–23, 2012	38	64	41	10
November 7–10, 2012	43	72	32	12
February 14–19, 2013	36	57	37	12

TABLE 5.1. (*continued*)

Poll Date	All	Democrat	Independent	Republican
		% *Favorable*		
March 5–10, 2013	37	58	32	18
April 15–20, 2013	35	57	31	15
June 4–9, 2013	35	58	36	12
August 13–19, 2013	37	59	32	15
September 12–18, 2013	39	67	34	11
October 17–23, 2013	38	70	34	12
November 13–18, 2013	33	55	33	7
December 10–15, 2013	34	68	33	7
January 14–21, 2014	34	58	28	9
February 11–17, 2014	35	59	32	11
March 11–17, 2014	38	66	35	15
April 15–21, 2014	38	68	32	11
May 13–19, 2014	38	64	37	14
June 12–18, 2014	39	66	31	15
July 15–21, 2014	37	62	31	12
August 25–September 2, 2014	35	57	30	11
October 8–14, 2014	36	59	35	10
November 5–13, 2014	37	67	35	13
December 2–9, 2014	41	69	40	10
January 15–21, 2015	40	64	38	11
March 6–12, 2015	41	65	37	14
April 8–14, 2015	43	70	42	16
June 2–9, 2015	39	65	37	16
June 25–29, 2015	43	61	41	17
August 6–11, 2015	44	76	39	20

Source: Kaiser Family Foundation.

Questions:
"As you may know, a health reform bill was signed into law in 2010. Given what you know about the health reform law, do you have a generally favorable or generally unfavorable opinion of it?" [options rotated]
2010: "As you may know, a new health reform bill was signed into law earlier this year. Given what you know about the new health reform law, do you have a generally favorable or generally unfavorable opinion of it?"

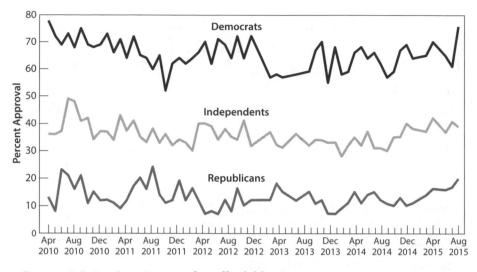

FIGURE 5.2. Partisan Support for Affordable Care Act

Republican identifiers formed negative evaluations early and never changed their views. Sometimes their support dipped into the single digits. Only three times between the bill's passage in 2010 and August 2015 did even one-fifth of Republicans view the law favorably. Typically their support was below 15 percent, and they averaged only 13 percent support. Independents displayed higher levels of support, but in general their support remained in the mid-30s, averaging 36 percent. Reflecting deep partisan divisions of opinion, only Democrats viewed the law favorably, averaging 66 percent approval. Even among the president's co-partisans, however, more than a third typically did not support the law.

What should we conclude about the impact of presidential signaling? Focusing on the period between August 2013 and July 2014 is useful in exploring this question and in illustrating the difficulties of isolating the impact of signaling. This period included the rollout of individual enrollment in health insurance through the federal government's health exchange. Preceding the rollout, there was a great deal of publicity extolling the benefits of health care reform as the government encouraged people to enroll. Then the White House went into a defensive mode as the website malfunctioned, frustrating potential enrollees and providing the media and Republicans endless stories of governmental failure. House Republicans were quick to schedule hearings, generating even more negative headlines.

On December 3, 2013, after two months of intense coverage of the botched HealthCare.gov rollout, the president hosted a White House event launching a three-week coordinated campaign to refocus the public on the

Affordable Care Act's benefits. The White House took the lead in emphasizing a different benefit each day until the December 23 enrollment deadline for January 1 coverage. For example, on December 4, the White House and Democratic allies focused on how Americans were paying less for preventative care under Obamacare. The next day they highlighted that people with preexisting conditions could no longer be charged more or denied coverage. The day after that, they emphasized the slowing growth in health care costs. The daily message was amplified through press events and social media by Democratic members of Congress, the Democratic National Committee, congressional campaign committees, and advocacy organizations.[31]

Republicans, of course, engaged in active opposition to the White House. Near the end of November 2013, a memo distributed to House Republicans provided talking points and marching orders regarding Obamacare: "Because of Obamacare, I Lost My Insurance"; "Obamacare Increases Health Care Costs"; "The Exchanges May Not Be Secure, Putting Personal Information at Risk"; "Continue Collecting Constituent Stories." This document was part of an increasingly organized Republican attack on the ACA. Republican strategists said that over the next several months they intended to keep Democrats on their heels through a multilayered, sequenced assault. The idea was to gather stories of people affected by the health care law—through social media, letters from constituents, or meetings during visits back home—and use them to open a line of attack, keep it going until it entered the public discourse and forced a response, then quickly pivot to the next topic.[32]

Not only did Republicans in Congress continually try to repeal the president's signature policy, but the ACA also faced the most lopsided negative political ad onslaught in history. From March 23, 2010 through late April 2014, Kantar Media CMAG tracked $445 million in total estimated broadcast and national cable TV ad spending about the law. The organization found a negative-to-positive ratio of more than $15 to $1, or $418 million to $27 million.[33]

There was plenty of signaling going on, most of it not helpful to the White House. Did the president's efforts to reinforce Democratic opinion matter? Did Democrats hold steadfast or even increase their support for the ACA in the face of the onslaught of Republican criticism?

Complicating the analysis of this question is the plethora of highly visible issues on the governmental and media agenda during this same period. For example, the civil war in Syria reached a peak of attention in the last half of September 2013. Then, the battle over the budget caused the federal government to shut down on October 1, the same day HealthCare.gov opened to the public. This highly salient conflict continued until October 17. The dilemma of isolating the impact of efforts to lead the public is omnipresent. The best we can do is maintain our sensitivity to alternative explanations and not over interpret findings.

Examining the data in table 5.1, we find that Independent opinion hardly changed at all during the period, except for a small decline in January. Republican opinion also was stable, although there was a slight decline into single-digit support in the three months after the rollout, no doubt reflecting the negative news about the government's performance, reinforcing negative views. All the public relations efforts of both sides did little to change opinion among these groups.

On the other hand, Democratic opinion was much more volatile. Support nosedived in November, declining by 15 percentage points. It then nearly regained its October level in December, declining again for the next two months and then increasing yet again in the spring. Democrats were not as stable in their opinions as the other partisan groups, but they were resilient. This resilience of Democratic opinion may be a product of presidential reinforcement. It is unlikely that the rebound of support for the ACA would have been as impressive if the White House had not countered the Republican assault on it.

Those who lean toward the president's party should be less supportive of the president than identifiers with the party and be less resolute in their support for his policies. Conversely, opposition party leaners should show higher support and less steadfast opposition than identifiers with the opposition party. Table 5.2 shows the percentage of Independents leaning Democrat and Independents leaning Republican holding favorable opinions of the ACA. The results are from the same polls as used to obtain the results in table 5.1, except that the time series does not begin until August 2010 and data are not available in December 2010 and August 2011 and after April 2015. I display the data graphically in figure 5.3.

The data for Democratic leaners show roughly the same pattern as we found for Democrats in table 5.1. As we expected, Democratic leaners offer lower support for the ACA than do Democrats, averaging 59 percent favorability (in contrast to the 66 percent favorability of Democratic identifiers). However, Democratic leaners displayed less variance in their support, with a standard deviation of 5 percentage points (Democratic identifiers had a standard deviation of 6 percentage points). At this time, it is not possible to determine whether these leaners were less supportive and less responsive to the president than Democratic identifiers because of diminished partisan-motivated reasoning because of their more tenuous association with the Democratic party or whether they identified less strongly with the party because they had more qualms about its policies in the first place.

Republican leaners averaged 14 percent favorability, only 1 percentage point higher than Republican identifiers. Their standard deviation was 3

TABLE 5.2. Partisan Leaners' Support for Health Care Plan

Poll Date	% Favorable	
	Leaning Democrat	Leaning Republican
August 16–22, 2010	66	12
September 14–19, 2010	64	18
October 5–10, 2010	60	16
November 3–6, 2010	66	18
January 4–14, 2011	61	19
February 8–13, 2011	64	17
March 8–13, 2011	61	17
April 7–12, 2011	65	15
May 12–17, 2011	56	15
June 9–14, 2011	60	13
July 13–18, 2011	53	14
September 7–12, 2011	65	11
October 13–18, 2011	59	13
November 10–15, 2011	56	12
December 8–13, 2011	59	11
January 12–17, 2012	59	8
February 13–19, 2012	62	21
February 29–March 5, 2012	62	20
April 4–10, 2012	67	15
May 8–14, 2012	58	9
June 28–30, 2012	67	9
July 17–23, 2012	64	8
August 7–12, 2012	55	17
September 13–19, 2012	68	13
October 18–23, 2012	55	17
November 7–10, 2012	62	10
February 14–19, 2013	59	13
March 5–10, 2013	54	7
April 15–20, 2013	56	14
June 4–9, 2013	58	16
August 13–19, 2013	68	11
September 12–18, 2013	61	15
October 17–23, 2013	59	10

TABLE 5.2. (*continued*)

	% Favorable	
Poll Date	Leaning Democrat	Leaning Republican
November 13–18, 2013	49	13
December 10–15, 2013	49	12
January 14–21, 2014	53	16
February 11–17, 2014	57	12
March 11–17, 2014	52	14
April 15–21, 2014	59	17
May 13–19, 2014	61	16
June 12–18, 2014	54	16
July 15–21, 2014	57	11
August 25–September 2, 2014	51	19
October 8–14, 2014	51	16
November 5–13, 2014	55	18
December 2–9, 2014	61	15
January 15–21, 2015	55	15
March 6–12, 2015	66	11
April 8–14, 2015	67	21

Source: Kaiser Family Foundation.

Questions:
2010: "As you may know, a new health reform bill was signed into law earlier this year. Given what you know about the new health reform law, do you have a generally favorable or generally unfavorable opinion of it?"
2011–2015: "As you may know, a health reform bill was signed into law in 2010. Given what you know about the health reform law, do you have a generally favorable or generally unfavorable opinion of it?" [options rotated]

percentage points, as opposed to 4 for Republican identifiers. Thus, the Republican leaners did differ from Republican identifiers in the ways we theorized, but the differences were very small. In essence, anyone identifying in any way with Republicans steadfastly opposed the president's signature policy.

The RAND Health Reform Opinion Study is unique in that it followed the same group of respondents, beginning in the fall of 2013. It covered more than 5,500 individuals, and one-fourth were surveyed each week of each month. Each individual was contacted once per month. This method allows us to observe the evolution of opinion over time.

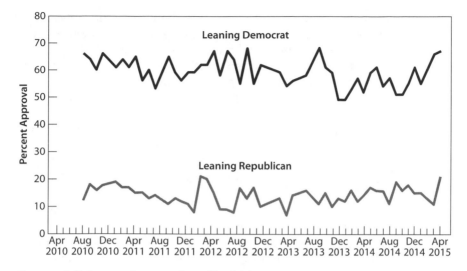

FIGURE 5.3. Leaner Support for Affordable Care Act

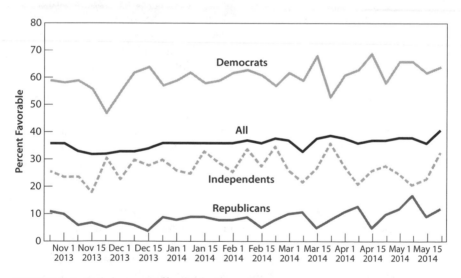

FIGURE 5.4. Opinion on Affordable Care Act

Figure 5.4 shows the favorability of various partisan groups toward the ACA for the period between the fall of 2013 and May 2014. Overall opinion tracked closely with that found in the Kaiser Family Foundation surveys. Support for the ACA was generally low, and opinion was relatively stable, despite the turmoil of the period.

Table 5.3 shows the results of comparing the favorability toward the ACA of each panel with its views in the survey one month earlier. The overall pattern is one of stability, with most opinion changes of 3 percentage points or less. Only once (December 22) did overall support change as much as 4 percentage points. Republican opinion changed by 5 percentage points on January 15, but then lost 4 percentage points a month later.

Lacking partisan moorings, Independent opinion was more volatile. Much of this instability appears to be the result of sampling error, however. For example, favorability increased by 9 percentage points on February 8 but fell by 12 points on March 8. Similarly, the November 15 reading was unusually low, so the large December 15 increase simply moved favorability among Independents back to its typical level. Otherwise, Independent opinion varied in a narrow range.

Democratic opinion also showed some variance, but, again, most of it seems to be the result of sampling error. The December 15 change was large but the favorability was unusually low on November 15, and most of the increase was gone by January 15. Similarly, the December 22 increase was in comparison to an unusually low November 22 reading.

To this point, we have found that Democratic opinion, the opinion that should be most responsive to the White House's signaling, was not steadfast in support of the ACA, but it was resilient. Democrats did decrease their support for the law in the face of the debacle of the website rollout, but they quickly rebounded to support.

We have to be cautious in attributing Democratic resilience to the president's actions. We can confidently stipulate that the White House sent clear signals of its support for the ACA, of course, but we have no way to know what poll respondents actually heard. Moreover, we cannot employ controls as we would in a less complex analysis. For example, the rollout of HealthCare.gov was, in effect, a constant, especially when we look at opinion in 2014.

In addition, we are not simply looking for a one-time statistically significant increase in approval. (In comparing aggregate survey results of two samples of the size employed by most of the polling firms cited in this volume, differences between the results must be about 6 percentage points before there is a 95 percent chance that the differences are not the result of sampling error. Comparing changes in the results of subgroups of the samples, such as Democrats or Republicans, the differences must be larger to reach the 95 percent confidence level.) Instead, our theorizing alerts us to look for stability or resilience in the face of partisan opposition as well as possible increases in support for the president's initiatives.

On balance, our theorizing about the impact of motivated reasoning provides a basis for concluding that presidential reinforcement contrib-

TABLE 5.3. Opinion Movement on ACA

Beginning Poll Date	All[1]	Democrats	Independents	Republicans
	Percentage Point Change from Previous Month in Favorability to ACA			
December 1, 2013	−3	−3	−1	−3
December 8, 2013	0	3	−1	0
December 15, 2013	2	8	10	−3
December 22, 2013	4	10	−1	4
January 1, 2014	3	4	3	1
January 8, 2014	3	0	−5	3
January 15, 2014	2	−6	5	5
January 22, 2014	0	2	−1	−1
February 1, 2014	0	3	0	0
February 8, 2014	1	1	9	0
February 15, 2014	0	3	−5	−4
February 22, 2014	2	−2	6	0
March 1, 2014	1	0	0	2
March 8, 2014	−3	−4	−12	2
March 15, 2014	2	7	−1	0
March 22, 2014	1	−4	1	0
April 1, 2014	1	−1	2	1
April 8, 2014	3	1	−1	2
April 15, 2014	−1	1	−1	0
April 22, 2014	−2	5	−8	2
May 1, 2014	0	5	−3	1
May 8, 2014	2	5	0	4
May 15, 2014	−1	−7	−3	4
May 22, 2014	4	6	5	2

Source: RAND Health Reform Opinion Study.

Question: "As you may know, a health reform bill (the Affordable Care Act or Obamacare) will take effect in 2014. Given what you know about the reform law, do you have a generally favorable or unfavorable opinion of it?"

[1] Each line represents the change for the panel group from one month earlier.

uted to Democrats' resilience in their support for the ACA in the face of opposition party attacks while other groups held fast in their opposition.

The Pew Research Center also polled the public's views of the ACA regularly since its passage (although there are significant gaps in the time series). Its questions, unlike the questions asked by the Kaiser and RAND studies, explicitly mentioned the president's name. The results appear in table 5.4 and show results for Republicans and Independents similar to those found in the Kaiser Family Foundation and RAND studies. Support is low and stable.

The results for Democrats show higher levels of support than found in the Kaiser and RAND polls, however, perhaps because the president's name provided an important signal as to the appropriate opinion. When primed with the president's name, Democrats slowly increased their support for the ACA until it was reliably in the 70s by 2012. The change was not dramatic, but it was statistically significant and helped counter the steady stream of attacks on the policy.

Such findings of sustained and even increasing support are what we would expect if signaling co-partisans reinforced their support for the president's initiatives. It is important to note that the increase in Democratic support occurred despite the disastrous rollout of the individual enrollment website in October 2013. Indeed, Democratic opinion seemed to be immune to the bad news when the president's name was in the question.

It is unusual to see a statistically significant increase in support for a policy that is otherwise controversial. It appears that when the president's name was included in the question about ACA, some previously recalcitrant Democrats changed their minds about the policy and switched to approval. Given that we see no evidence of such change in evaluating the ACA in the results from the other polling organizations, we should be cautious in our interpretation. There is also a gap in the Pew data from February 2011 until March 2012, the period when the sustained change occurred. Nevertheless, it is suggestive that the increase in support for the ACA when Obama's name was in the question mirrors a similar increase in Democratic overall approval of Obama's job performance, probably strengthening the impact of motivated reasoning.

GEORGE W. BUSH AND SOCIAL SECURITY REFORM

The George W. Bush White House began the president's second term as it began his first—by launching an extensive public relations effort, in this case to convince the public to support the president's reform of Social Security. Even before the inauguration, the White House announced plans

TABLE 5.4. Partisan Support for Health Care Plan

Poll Date	% Favor/Approve		
	Democrat	Independent	Republican
July 22–26, 2009	61	34	12
August 20–27, 2009	64	37	13
September 10–15, 2009	68	37	17
September 30–October 4, 2009	59	26	14
November 12–15, 2009	61	33	15
December 9–13, 2009	59	32	11
January 6–10, 2010	63	34	12
February 3–9, 2010	65	33	14
March 10–14, 2010	64	32	11
April 1–5, 2010	71	36	11
July 8–11, 2010	65	30	10
September 9–12, 2010	69	34	11
January 5–9, 2011	69	38	15
March 7–11, 2012	76	44	11
April 4–15, 2012	74	36	9
June 7–17, 2012	73	36	13
June 28–July 9, 2012	80	43	12
September 4–8, 2013	75	36	11
October 9–13, 2013	75	35	8
December 3–8, 2013	73	34	9
February 27–March 16, 2014	72	37	8
April 3–6, 2014	73	34	10
April 23–27, 2014	73	39	10
September 2–9, 2014	72	41	11
October 15–20, 2014	74	40	10
November 6–9, 2014	78	42	10
February 18–22, 2015	78	39	11
July 14–20, 2015	77	45	18

Source: Pew Research Center for the People and the Press Poll.

Question: "As of right now, do you generally favor or generally oppose the health care proposals being discussed in Congress?"
Question for April 2010: "Do you approve or disapprove of the health care legislation passed by Barack Obama and Congress last month?"
Question for July and September 2010: "Do you approve or disapprove of the health care legislation passed by Barack Obama and Congress in March?"
Question for January 2011: "Do you approve or disapprove of the health care legislation passed by Barack Obama and Congress last year?"
Question for February 2011–2012: "Do you approve or disapprove of the health care legislation passed by Barack Obama and Congress in 2010?
Question for 2013–2015: Do you approve or disapprove of the health care law passed by Barack Obama and Congress in 2010?

to reactivate Bush's reelection campaign's network of donors and activists to build pressure on lawmakers to allow workers to invest part of their Social Security taxes in the stock market. As Treasury Secretary John W. Snow put it, the "scope and scale goes way beyond anything we have done."[34] The same architects of Bush's political victories would be masterminding the new campaign, principally political strategists Karl Rove at the White House and Ken Mehlman, who was the Bush-Cheney campaign manager, at the Republican National Committee.

Mehlman declared that he would use the campaign apparatus—from a national database of 7.5 million email activists, 1.6 million volunteers, and hundreds of thousands of neighborhood precinct captains—to build congressional support for Bush's plans, starting with Social Security. "There are a lot of tools we used in the '04 campaign, from regional media to research to rapid response to having surrogates on television," he said. "That whole effort will be focused on the legislative agenda."[35] In addition to their own efforts, White House and RNC officials worked closely with the same outside groups that helped Bush win reelection in 2004, especially Progress for America.

White House allies also launched a market research project to determine how to sell the plan in the most comprehensible and appealing way, and Republican marketing and public relations gurus built teams of consultants to promote it. The campaign used Bush's campaign-honed techniques of mass repetition, sticking closely to the script, and using the politics of fear to build support—contending that a Social Security financial crisis was imminent. There were campaign-style events to win support and precision targeting of districts where lawmakers could face reelection difficulties. The White House also used hard-hitting television ads to discredit its opponents and build support for the president's plan.[36]

In his February 2, 2005, State of the Union message, President Bush proposed that Congress make Social Security "a better deal" for younger workers by establishing provisions for voluntary personal retirement accounts. These would work by allowing everyone younger than 55 to divert as much as 4 percent of their income subject to Social Security taxation into individual accounts. The president argued that this money would grow over time at a greater rate than anything the current system could deliver. In addition, these workers would be able to pass along the money that accumulated in their personal accounts to their children or grandchildren. The money would be theirs "and the government can never take it away."

Democrats immediately pointed out that private accounts (as they insisted on calling them) would actually make Social Security's financial problems worse in the short run, because the government would have to borrow additional trillions of dollars to compensate for funds diverted from the Social Security trust fund into these accounts. Many critics also emphasized the risks of the president's plan, questioning the reliability of net gains from personal account investments. In addition, they challenged the view that low-income persons would be able to risk not purchasing an annuity—and losing their ability to pass on their accounts in the process. More broadly, Bush's opponents expressed concern that privatizing a portion of Social Security would diminish the social insurance aspect of it in which the public collectively supported seniors' retirement income.

Throughout the winter and early spring of 2005, the president never said what steps he favored to put the Social Security system on a sound financial footing in order to solve the solvency problem. Instead, he maintained that it was up to Congress to offer proposals. Democrats refused to come to the bargaining table without specifics from the administration. Finally, on April 28, the president held a prime-time press conference in which he continued to press for private accounts but also added a proposal that would cut Social Security spending by reducing increases for upper- and middle-income workers.

The Pew Research Center found that the president's association with a plan to limit the growth of Social Security benefits appeared to undermine support for the concept. Pew split its large sample and, as table 5.5 shows, by a 53 percent to 36 percent margin most Americans said they would support limiting the growth of benefits for wealthy and middle-income retirees, while keeping the current system intact for lower-income people. This was a considerably higher figure than the 38 percent level of support Gallup found about two weeks earlier.[37] However, the public's support was significantly lower when Pew explicitly associated the proposal with Bush. When the phrase "George W. Bush has proposed . . ." preceded the idea, the public was divided (45 percent in favor, 43 percent opposed).

Equally striking were the responses of different partisan groups. Without any mention of Bush, the proposal was slightly more popular among Democrats than among Republicans (54 percent to 47 percent). When pollsters attributed the proposal to Bush, however, Republican support increased 15 percentage points to 62 percent while Democratic support dropped 20 points to 34 percent. Support among Independents for limiting future benefit growth for wealthy and middle-income retirees dropped 12 percentage points, from 55 percent to 43 percent, when the poll question attributed the proposal to the president.[38]

In this case, we see both the positive and negative reactions to presidential signaling. Republicans seem to have used the president's signal as a cue that the president's proposal was consistent with their policy predispositions. Democrats, on the other hand, used Bush as a cue that they

TABLE 5.5. Public Support for Social Security Indexing

Question Wording	%			
	All	Republicans	Democrats	Independents
Described without Bush's Name[1]				
Favor	53	47	54	55
Oppose	36	41	37	36
Don't know	11	12	9	9
Described as Bush's Proposal[2]				
Favor	45	62	34	43
Oppose	43	27	57	47
Don't know	12	11	9	10
Change in Support	–8	+15	–20	–12

Source: Pew Research Center for the People and the Press poll, May 11–15, 2005.

Questions:

[1] "One proposal for dealing with Social Security's financial situation is to keep the system as it is now for lower income retirees, but limit the growth of future benefits for wealthy and middle-income retirees. Would you favor or oppose this proposal?"

[2] "George W. Bush has proposed dealing with Social Security's financial situation by keeping the system as it is now for lower income retirees, but limiting the growth of future benefits for wealthy and middle-income retirees. Would you favor or oppose this proposal?"

should oppose a policy associated with him. Given increased partisan polarization, this is a topic that requires further exploration.

KISS OF DEATH?

We have hypothesized that partisan-motivated reasoning should be a two-edged sword, encouraging opposition party identifiers to maintain or increase their opposition to the president's policies. We saw in the case of support for the Affordable Care Act that Republican opposition was both stable and overwhelmingly negative. In such circumstances, it is difficult to determine the relative contributions of motivated reasoning and ideological preference. We have also seen that in the more mixed situation of Republican George W. Bush's Social Security reform proposal, association with the president served as a powerful negative signal to Democrats.[39]

There is other work that has found that association with the president can be the kiss of death. Jeffrey Mondak found that in a nonrandom set of comparisons between questions providing the cue of the president's position and those that did not, the public offered less support for the president's policies 41 percent of the time.[40] In an early experiment, Lee and Carol Sigelman asked sample groups whether they supported two proposals, a domestic policy proposal dealing with welfare and a proposal dealing with foreign aid. One of the groups was told that President Carter, who was low in the polls at the time, supported the proposals, while the president was not mentioned to the other group. The authors found that attaching the president's name to either proposal not only failed to increase support for it, but actually had a negative effect because those who disapproved of Carter reacted very strongly against proposals they thought were his.[41]

At least in some circumstances, then, presidential signals weaken support for their policies. In both the examples cited in the previous paragraph and the examples that follow, we typically lack the data to determine exactly who is reacting negatively to White House signaling. Nevertheless, it is reasonable to conclude that it is opposition party identifiers who are moving in the negative direction.

Ronald Reagan and the MX Missile

In October 1981, Ronald Reagan unveiled his plan for a major national defense strategic modernization program, including adding the 10-warhead MX missile to the U.S. arsenal. The MX missile was politically controversial because many considered it a destabilizing first-strike weapon. The White House scrapped the original plan to shuttle MX missiles on an extensive rail network in the western United States in response to strong bipartisan opposition, and in November 1982, the Reagan administration proposed deployment of 100 MX missiles in fixed silos. However, Reagan's revised MX deployment plan was unpopular in Congress, so the president responded by appointing a commission on U.S. strategic nuclear forces, led by Lt. Gen. Brent Scowcroft. In April 1983, the commission endorsed MX deployment.

The president needed congressional backing for the new weapons system, and he needed public support to obtain it. However, for most of his second and third years in office (1982–1983), Ronald Reagan did not enjoy high public approval ratings. Table 5.6 shows public support for the MX missile during November 1982 through September 1983. Reagan's approval during this period ranged from 37 percent to 47 percent. The questions used to supply data for table 5.6 are organized as three sets, and

TABLE 5.6. Public Support for MX Missile, 1982–1983

Poll Date	% Favor	% Oppose	% Don't Know
November 23–28, 1982[1]	**35**	**58**	**7**
January 18–22, 1983[2]	38	51	10
June 1–5, 1983[3]	**41**	**53**	**6**
June 15–19, 1983[2]	46	44	10
September 9–14, 1983[3]	**50**	**45**	**5**
September 22–26, 1983[2]	51	39	10

Rows in **bold** indicate questions specifically referencing Reagan.

Sources and Questions:

[1]Harris: "President Reagan has now proposed going ahead with building the MX missile system, which would be designed to allow the U.S. to retaliate with atomic weapons against an enemy who attacked the U.S. with atomic weapons. The Reagan administration says the MX system is necessary to make our atomic weapons capability equal to that of the Russians. Opponents of the MX missile system argue that it will cost much more than the administration says, and probably won't even work effectively. All in all, do you favor or oppose going ahead with the building of the MX missile system proposed by the Reagan administration?"

[2] ABC/*Washington Post*: "Do you think the U.S. should build the MX missile or not?" [Asked of those who had heard or read of the MX missile proposal. 88% in January 1983; 85% in June 1983; and 83% in September 1983.]

[3]Harris: "President Reagan has proposed going ahead with building the MX missile system, which would be designed to allow the U.S. to retaliate with land-based nuclear weapons against an enemy who attacked the U.S. with nuclear weapons. The Reagan administration claims that the MX system is necessary to make our nuclear weapons equal to that of the Russians and that by having the MX, the U.S. can better negotiate a nuclear weapons agreement with the Russians. Opponents of the MX missile system argue that it will cost much more than the administration says and won't even work effectively. All in all, do you favor or oppose going ahead with the building of the MX missile system proposed by the Reagan administration?"

the results for the first question in each set appear in bold. Those questions contain Reagan's name and thus can serve as a cue to respondents.

Comparing the responses within each set of questions, we find that in each case the public provided somewhat *lower* support for the missile when Reagan was present as cue giver. Identification with the president may not have been the kiss of death, but it did not help him expand public support for his proposal.

Ronald Reagan and Aid
to the Contras

Perhaps Reagan would serve as a more effective cue for the public when he was ranked higher in its esteem. In the spring of 1986, the president enjoyed high approval ratings of 63 percent in March and 62 percent in April. The Iran-Contra scandal would not break until after the November midterm elections. Thus, conditions should have favored the impact of Reagan as a cue giver.

One of Reagan's highest priorities was stopping the spread of communism in Central America. At the core of his policy response to this threat was an effort to undermine the Sandinista government of Nicaragua through support of the opposition Contras. Reagan required congressional support to obtain aid for the Contras, and he made substantial efforts to mobilize the public behind his program of support for the Contras. Yet he consistently failed.[42]

As he lamented in his memoirs,

> Time and again, I would speak on television, to a joint session of Congress, or to other audiences about the problems in Central America, and I would hope that the outcome would be an outpouring of support from Americans who would apply the same kind of heat on Congress that helped pass the economic recovery package.
>
> But the polls usually found that large numbers of Americans cared little or not at all about what happened in Central America—in fact, a surprisingly large proportion didn't even know where Nicaragua and El Salvador were located—and, among those who did care, too few cared enough about a Communist penetration of the Americas to apply the kind of pressure I needed on Congress.[43]

The problem Reagan is referring to is reflected in table 5.7, which shows public support for aid to the Contras over a one-month period in March and April 1986. We must be cautious in our analysis because of the small size of some of the polls (making comparisons of subgroups unreliable). Nevertheless, the data do not indicate much impact from the Reagan cue. There is a modest difference in the two polls on March 25, but similar questions invoking Reagan's name on March 6 and March 16 elicited levels of support *lower* than for the March 25 question that did not include the Reagan cue. Similarly, the two questions asking respondents about their support for "$100 million" in aid (March 20–24 and April 5–8) have a difference of only 2 percentage points in support and opposition despite the Reagan cue in the first question.

TABLE 5.7. Public Support for Aid to the Contras, 1985–1986

Poll Date	Poll N	% Support Aid	% Oppose Aid	% Don't Know
March 6, 1986[1]	**543**	**34**	**59**	**8**
March 16, 1986[1]	**511**	**30**	**54**	**16**
March 20–24, 1986[2]	**1,148**	**35**	**60**	**4**
March 25, 1986[3]	**530**	**42**	**53**	**5**
March 25, 1986[4]	606	37	44	19
April 5–8, 1986[5]	1,254	33	62	5
April 5–8, 1986[6]	1,254	39	54	7

Rows in **bold** indicate questions specifically referencing Reagan.

Sources and Questions:

[1] ABC News: "President Reagan is asking Congress for new military aid for the Nicaraguan rebels known as the 'Contras'. Do you agree or disagree with Reagan that Congress should approve that money?"

[2] ABC News: "The House of Representatives has refused Reagan's request for $100 million in military and other aid to the Contra rebels in Nicaragua. Do you approve or disapprove of that action by the House?" [Because the question asks respondents whether they approve of the House's negative action, a response of "approve" means opposing aid to the Contras. Thus, we have reversed the results to make them consistent with the portrayal of the results from the other questions.]

[3] ABC News: "As you may know, President Reagan has asked Congress for new military aid for the Nicaraguan rebels known as the 'Contras'. Do you agree or disagree with Reagan that Congress should approve that money?"

[4] *USA Today*: "Do you favor or oppose military aid to the Contras fighting the Sandinista government in Nicaragua?"

[5] Harris: "Do you favor or oppose the U.S. sending $100 million in military and non-military aid to the Contra rebels in Nicaragua?"

[6] Harris: "Do you favor or oppose the U.S. sending just $30 million in non-military aid to the Contra rebels in Nicaragua?"

Barack Obama and Health Care Reform

Much closer to the present, in September 2013 CNBC asked half the respondents to a national poll if they supported "Obamacare" and the other half if they supported the "Affordable Care Act." Those asked about Obamacare were more likely to express opinions, both positive and negative, than those asked about the ACA (table 5.8).[44] The president's name provided a heuristic that helped those on both sides reach an opinion.

Opinions among demographic groups within these small samples are difficult to measure accurately, but the differences are revealing. Sixteen

TABLE 5.8. Obama Effect on Support for Affordable Care Act

Question Wording	% Positive	% Neutral	% Negative	% Don't Know
Obamacare[1]	29	13	46	12
Affordable Care Act[2]	22	11	37	30

Source: CNBC poll, September 16–19, 2013, conducted by Hart Research/Public Opinion Strategies.

Questions:
[1] "What are your feelings toward Obamacare? Do you feel very positive, somewhat positive, neutral, somewhat negative, very negative, or do you not know enough to say?" [asked of one-half the sample]
[2] What are your feelings toward the Affordable Care Act? Do you feel very positive, somewhat positive, neutral, somewhat negative, very negative, or do you not know enough to say?" [asked of one-half the sample]

percent of Republican and Republican leaners moved from negative to either support or neutrality when the president's name was not in the question, while an equal percentage of Democrats and Democratic leaners moved away from support without the signal from the president. As we would expect, those with high disapproval rates of the president were more negative on Obamacare than the ACA. On the other hand, those more likely to support the president were also more positive about Obamacare. Tellingly, in the absence of the signal about the president's position, many more people expressed no opinion. More important from the standpoint of the president, the impact of signaling with his name proved to be a wash. Admirers moved toward support and opponents moved toward opposition.

Unfortunately, the CNBC poll had a modest sample, with just over 400 respondents in each half. Gallup remedied this problem two months later when it conducted a large survey experiment to test the impact of mentioning Obama's name in a question on the ACA. Gallup read the same basic question to four randomly selected groups of the Gallup Daily tracking sample each night in the November 4–17, 2013 period, but with four different descriptions of the law. A total of 1,725 to 1,885 respondents received each version of the question.

The results of this experimental test show that the health care law descriptions made a difference in the responses (table 5.9). Only mentioning the Affordable Care Act yielded the highest support (45 percent), while only mentioning Obamacare resulted in the lowest support (38 percent). Support for the law when using the other labels, including the president's

TABLE 5.9. Impact of Obama on Support for Affordable Care Act

Question Wording	% Approve	% Disapprove	% No Opinion
ACA, no mention of Obama[1]	45	49	6
Mention Obama and ACA[2]	41	54	5
No Mention of Obama or ACA[3]	41	52	7
Obamacare, no mention of ACA[4]	38	54	7

Source: Gallup Daily Tracking polls, November 4–17, 2013.

Questions: "Next, we'd like to ask you about the Affordable Care Act, the 2010 law that restructured the U.S. health care system. Do you generally approve or disapprove of . . ."
[1] "the Affordable Care Act?"
[2] "the Affordable Care Act, signed into law by President Obama that restructured the U.S. health care system?"
[3] "the health care law?"
[4] "Obamacare?"

name, fell in between, at 41 percent. Again, the signal of the president's name was not useful in increasing support for his most significant policy.

Barack Obama and Immigration Reform

The debate over immigration reform during the second Obama term is also instructive regarding signaling. Republican antipathy for Obama was so great that he had to avoid proposing his own immigration bill, because doing so made it more difficult for Republican members of Congress to support it. Because Republicans in Congress come from solidly Republican states or districts, it is easier for them to support an immigration bill that has broad-based support in the business and farming communities (and that also happens to be supported by Obama and the Democratic leadership) than to back a bill so popularly identified with the other side.

After outlining in a general fashion what he wanted in an immigration bill, the president adopted a hands-off approach to designing the legislation, deferring to negotiations among a bipartisan group of senators known as the Gang of Eight. He adopted this strategy soon after his inauguration, as he was preparing to introduce his own bill during a January 29 visit to Las Vegas. Several Democratic senators among the Gang of Eight members told the White House the group was close to reaching consensus on a bill and asked Obama to hold off on announcing his own plan in order to avoid disrupting the talks. Obama agreed.[45]

The imperative of avoiding a Republican backlash only increased when the House took up the issue. Thus, in July the White House released reports and videos that argued the economic benefits of an immigration overhaul but that used neither the president's image nor his voice.[46]

Senate Democrats feared that an Obama bill would scare off Republicans like Senator Marco Rubio of Florida, who had presidential ambitions. Indeed, Rubio's office once issued a statement to deny that he was discussing immigration policy "with anyone in the White House," even as it criticized the president for not consulting Republicans. Indeed, Republican antipathy put the president in a catch-22 bind. If he stayed aloof from legislative action, Republicans and others accused him of a lack of leadership. If he got involved, they complained that they could not support any bill so closely identified with him without risking the contempt of conservative voters.[47]

Obama recognized the problem he faced.

> I cannot force Republicans to embrace those common-sense solutions. . . . Ultimately, they, themselves, are going to have to say, we want to do the right thing. . . . And I think there are members certainly in the Senate right now, and I suspect members in the House as well, who understand that deep down. But they're worried about their politics. It's tough. Their base thinks that compromise with me is somehow a betrayal.[48]

Similarly, Senator Patty Murray had to keep the White House at arm's length as she negotiated a budget deal with House Republican Paul Ryan. As she put it, the president's voice in the room would have made it more difficult to reach agreement.[49]

CONCLUSION

Typically, a significant percentage of the public (although often not a majority) supports the president's policies. We should not conclude that such responses are the result of presidential persuasion, however. Presidents find it difficult or impossible to *change* opinion. Nevertheless, the White House may benefit from a built-in set of supporters who are predisposed to support them—their fellow partisans. Ignoring predispositions is a fatal logical flaw in analyzing presidential leadership and obscures the actual dynamics of leadership.

Because the core of presidential leadership is facilitating coalitions of the willing, it is important to understand how the White House can maintain or increase support for its initiatives by sending signals to its potential supporters. Determining the impact of signaling is difficult because of the confounding effects of other influences on public opinion, including the fact that many partisan supporters simply support the substance of the policies the president advocates. Nevertheless, it is important that we investigate signaling as rigorously as possible.

Motivated reasoning encourages co-partisans to follow the president's lead. At least in some instances, the president's association with a policy is an especially powerful signal to those predisposed to support his initiatives. Moreover, by reinforcing his partisans' predispositions, a president can counter opposition party attacks and discourage his supporters from abandoning him. In addition, co-partisans appear to be resilient in returning to support after periods of bad news.

It is important not to exaggerate the significance of signaling. Many of the president's co-partisans may still oppose his initiatives, as we saw in Democrat opposition to the Affordable Care Act and Republican opposition to George W. Bush's Social Security reform proposals. As with other tools of presidential leadership, signaling is at the margins of coalition-building.

In addition, reinforcement is a two-edged sword. There is a substantial percentage of the public predisposed to oppose the president. Motivated reasoning encourages such people to oppose his policies, and we have seen evidence that association with the president can lower support for his initiatives, at least among those inclined to oppose him.

CHAPTER 6

Exploiting Existing Opinion

PRESIDENTS ARE FACILITATORS; they exploit opportunities but rarely create them. They are unlikely to *change* public opinion to obtain more support for their policies. It is possible, however, for the White House to exploit *existing* public opinion to achieve the president's policy goals. At the core of this strategy is choosing the issues to emphasize and presenting policy initiatives most effectively.

Reinforcement involves influencing specific attitudes by providing cues to those predisposed to support the president. In effect, the president is asking his co-partisans to infer from the general to the particular. Sometimes, however, the president finds that many in the public already hold views compatible with his policy initiatives, although these views may not be clear or prominent in political discourse. In such cases, the president's goal is to show the public how its specific views are compatible with his policies or to increase the salience of White House initiatives that are popular with the public and thus intensify pressure on Congress.

Although previous commitments, current crises, and unresolved problems left by their predecessors impose much of their agenda upon them, presidents still have substantial discretion to choose their own initiatives and the manner in which they present them to the public. From the perspective of the White House, "the key to successful advocacy is controlling the public agenda."[1] As a result, the White House invests a substantial amount of staff, time, and energy into focusing the public's attention on the issues it wishes to promote and encouraging the public to see its proposals for dealing with those issues in a positive light.[2]

A special form of existing public opinion occurs when the public holds *no* opinion. On new issues, there are no existing views to exploit. However, motivated reasoning should still provide the president with an advantage among his co-partisans, and he may benefit from the absence of an organized opposition.

ARTICULATING OPINION

In reinforcement, the president signals his views to those generally predisposed to support him and relies on motivated reasoning to convince co-partisans to support specific policies. There are times when the currents of opinion have already shifted in the president's direction, driven by conditions largely beyond the White House's control. Nevertheless, public opinion about matters of politics and policy is often amorphous. It lacks articulation and structure. To exploit the congruence of the public's views with those of the White House, the president needs to articulate opinion in a way that clarifies its policy implications and shows the public that its wishes are consistent with his policies.

Woodrow Wilson urged leaders to interpret public opinion and identify issues that "reflected majority will even if the majority was not yet fully aware of it. The leader's rhetoric could translate the people's felt desires into public policy." As Jeffrey Tulis points out, success at interpretation requires understanding majority sentiment underlying the contradictions of factions and discordant views, and explaining people's true desires to them in an easily comprehended and convincing fashion.[3]

In his study of agenda-setting in the national government, John Kingdon found that people in and around government believed strongly that there was such a thing as a "national mood," that they could measure it, and that it had consequences for policy.[4] Frank Baumgartner and Bryan Jones cite Brutus' advice to Cassius:

> There is a tide in the affairs of men
> Which, taken at the flood, leads on to fortune;
> Omitted, all the voyage of their life
> Is bound in shallow and in miseries,
> On such a full sea are we now afloat,
> And we must take the current when it serves
> Or lose our ventures.
>
> —(William Shakespeare, *Julius Caesar*, IV, iii)

They argue that it is important for leaders to discern whether the flow of events favors their proposals and skillfully exploit the opportunity when it does.[5]

Once public opinion aligns with the president's views, he will desire to exploit the opportunity. To make the most of latent opinion, the president must not only recognize it but also articulate that opinion in a clear and compelling manner and relate it to specific policy initiatives. Michael Nelson concludes that, above all, successful presidents require not only a strategic sense of the grain of history but also an ability to sense, define, and articulate the public mood to fulfill the historical possibilities of the time.[6] Doing so may require waiting for opinion to mature to the point that it supports White House initiatives. The most effective means of articulating newly clarified opinion may be in the form of policy proposals that encapsulate the public's views.

Reviewing the presidency of Abraham Lincoln illustrates how critical a role articulating developing opinion can play. No president has exceeded Lincoln's eloquence in public discourse, and only George Washington can make a similar claim on the hearts of the American people. Lincoln was a brilliant politician who rose to power by expressing ideas on the great questions of his time. Many writers have commented on his talent for establishing a rapport with the public, and there is no doubt that he was skilled at speaking candidly without giving offense.[7] Once in office, did he position himself ahead of public opinion and employ his rhetorical skills to sway the public on the two great issues of his time—support of the Civil War and, later, the emancipation of the slaves?

Certainly, many authors have claimed that Lincoln shaped public opinion.[8] The *Wall Street Journal* asked a prominent expert in public relations to name the five best books in his field. His list included a work on Lincoln, and he argued, "Abraham Lincoln's words moved public opinion as no other U.S. politicians have before or since." For example, "However great the public dismay over the Civil War's length and costs, Lincoln succeeded in uniting the country behind him—in large part . . . because of the moral clarity and the eloquence of his appeal." [9] Yet there is nothing in that—or any other book—that shows the impact of Lincoln's eloquence.

Rather than swaying opinion with the intellectual and aesthetic force of his rhetoric, Lincoln acted in a strategic manner that would be familiar to politicians in the twenty-first century. He invested heavily in reading public opinion, relying on election returns, politicians, newspapers, mail, and visitors (including many ordinary citizens). One of his primary goals in this effort was to avoid moving too far ahead of the public. He well understood that any individual politician would fail if he tried to swim against or resist the larger tide.[10] As one contemporary supporter put it, "Lincoln . . . always moves in conjunction with propitious circumstances, not waiting to be dragged by the force of events or wasting strength in premature struggles with them."[11]

Lincoln's task was to identify and promote the means by which he could help advance the larger forces at work.[12] To do so, he tapped into the Union's deep well of religious-patriotic sentiment and effectively guided the forces of mainstream Protestant orthodoxy, the most potent agents of American nationalism. Lincoln's deep familiarity with Americans and his political and social context gave him an extraordinary sensitivity to the direction of events. Although not religious in the sense of formal membership in a church, Lincoln was "alert to the power of religious opinion and fused appeals to Protestant millennialism and Enlightenment rationalism." According to biographer Richard Carwardine, it is "no overstatement" that "the combined religious engines of the Union—and the motor of evangelical Protestantism in particular—did more than any other single force to mobilize support for the war."[13]

Similarly, Lincoln's election in 1860 "depended far less on his individual appeal than on the skill with which Republican organizers projected him as the embodiment of the party's philosophy and platform." Moreover, the demonstrations of fidelity to the Union following the hostilities at Fort Sumter and his call to arms did not require inspiration from the White House.[14]

The president was also a master of timing. "Lincoln's great—possibly greatest—achievement was to take a stethoscope to Union opinion and read it with such skill that he timed to perfection his redefinition of the national purpose." "Lincoln openly acknowledged that the steps by which he redefined the war for the Union as a war against slavery were guided by his reading of public opinion and that he feared too early an embrace of emancipation would shatter the Union consensus." This redefinition was successful because he took the initiative and persisted in his goals, but also because he was acutely sensitive to public opinion and had a gift for knowing when the public would support his policies. He articulated the rationale for the war and its sacrifices in terms that he knew from his reading of public opinion would resonate with mainstream Unionists and cement the war coalition. When he was confident that the public mood had shifted and border state opposition to military emancipation could be contained, he prepared to act.[15] Thus, he waited for the Union "victory" at Antietam before issuing the preliminary Emancipation Proclamation.[16]

Lincoln knew full well that he could not direct events, and he was not inclined to doing so. David Herbert Donald remarks in the preface to his biography of the sixteenth president that his volume "highlights a basic trait of character evident throughout Lincoln's life: the essential passivity of his nature."[17] In 1864, he famously confessed to Albert G. Hodges, the editor of the Frankfort, Kentucky, *Commonwealth*, "I claim not to have controlled events, but confess plainly that events have controlled me. Now, at the end of three years of struggle the nation's condition is not what either party, or any man devised, or expected. God alone can claim it."[18] His equally famous declaration that his policy was "to have no policy"[19] allowed him to bend to the demands of the situation.

Naturally, Lincoln was constantly trying to obtain public support, albeit it less directly than contemporary presidents.[20] After his nomination for president on the Republican ticket in 1860, he never again took the stump, never held a formal press conference, and granted only one major interview.[21] Although he spoke to the public nearly one hundred times as president, most of these instances involved modest, unscripted remarks—comments to troops passing through Washington, impromptu responses to visiting well-wishers, and statements to visiting delegations of clergymen, free blacks, state representatives, and others. His two inaugural addresses and his speech at Gettysburg were rare exceptions.

To disseminate his views, Lincoln wrote carefully crafted public letters on issues crucial to the conduct and outcome of the war to individuals or mass meetings. He designed them to rally opinion and prepare the way for changes in policy. Many of these appeared in newspapers and pamphlets. A core of Republican Party loyalists proved invaluable as interpreters of the administration's purpose to the people, and Republican editors trumpeted the cause of the Union. The administration also imaginatively exploited a formidable network of governmental, religious, and philanthropic organizations, including the Union army, to spread the word, and Lincoln's image was visible in mass-produced woodcuts, lithographs, photographs.[22]

Nevertheless, Lincoln did not make a case to either the public or Congress for transforming change until the country was ready to embrace it. His power came not from challenging or subverting the routine political system or the state itself but from defending the status quo, as Unionists defined it—a widely shared goal. It was the secessionists who were attempting to transform the system. In contrast, he emphasized and represented continuity, not radical disjunction.[23] Thus, Lincoln was a highly skilled facilitator. By brilliantly playing the hand history had dealt him, Lincoln's facilitative leadership transformed the nation forever.

Despite his caution in not getting too far ahead of public opinion, his mastery of timing, and his administration's extensive efforts to influence the public, Lincoln experienced many setbacks. On the core issue of emancipation, "[d]espite his skillful avoidance of partisanship, moral reproach or an argumentative tone, and his emphasis on opportunity for securing change that would come 'gently as the dews of heaven, nor rending or wrecking anything,' his appeal went unanswered." Poor white laborers and border state slave owners were unresponsive (encouraging the Republicans to soft-pedal the emancipation theme in the 1864 elections). On the other hand, the president could not convince black leaders of the advantages of freed slaves colonizing another country.[24] In addition, the Republicans suffered substantial losses in the 1862 midterm elections, and Congress did not heed Lincoln's plea for "malice toward none, with charity for all" when it established its Reconstruction policy.

It does not detract from Lincoln's uplifting and highly principled eloquence to conclude that his words were something less than "swords." Although he did have deep popular support, which his personal qualities encouraged and sustained, there is no evidence that he swayed many Americans with his rhetoric. Instead, he was a brilliant politician who mobilized his supporters and carefully read public opinion so as not to be too far ahead of it. His understanding of the public also helped him seize opportunities to move when opinion was disposed to support his changes in policy.

It is interesting to note that, four generations later, Franklin D. Roosevelt faced another existential threat to the nation. He was well aware that Americans were ambivalent about involvement in World War II. As a result, he carefully gauged public opinion and typically relied on events to change opinion about issues such as the nature of the threat posed by the Nazis and the Japanese and the appropriate national response to it. When opinion moved in the direction he wished to go, like Lincoln, he quickly clarified and solidified this change by announcing policies consistent with it, such as aiding the Allies in June 1940 by asking Congress for the Lend-Lease bill.[25] As distinguished historian Richard Hofstadter said of Franklin D. Roosevelt, he was not able to move the public, but "he was able to give it that necessary additional impetus of leadership which can translate desires into policies."[26]

Framing Issues

The president is interested in not only what conclusions the public reaches about a policy but also *how* they are thinking about it. As a result, the White House attempts to influence the public's understanding of what issues are about and the questions it asks about them as it evaluates the president's positions. At its core, this effort focuses on associating the president's policies with views and values the public already holds. Structuring the choices about policy issues in ways that favor the president's programs may set the terms of the debate on his proposals and thus the premises on which the public evaluates them. As one leading adviser to Reagan put it, "I've always believed that 80 percent of any legislative or political matter is how you frame the debate."[27]

Framing and Priming

Policy issues are usually complex and subject to alternative interpretations. Both issues within the direct experience of citizens, such as poverty, health care, and racial inequality, as well as issues more remote from everyday life, such as arms control and international trade, are susceptible to widely different understandings. The crux of the decision regarding which side to support in the debate over abortion is the relative weight given to the two well-known values: the life of the unborn and the right of the mother to choose to have the child. Similarly, the parties contending over the minimum wage often seem to be talking past each other. Advocates of increasing the minimum wage focus on *equity*: it is important to pay those making the lowest wages at least enough to support a minimally acceptable lifestyle. Opponents of increasing the minimum wage, on the other hand, focus on *efficiency*: raising the cost of labor puts businesses that employ low-wage earners at a disadvantage in the marketplace and may cause some employers to terminate workers in order to reduce their costs. Each side emphasizes different values in the debate in an attempt to frame the issue to its advantage.

The sheer complexity of most issues combined with the competing values that are relevant to evaluating them create substantial cognitive burdens for people. They cope by acting as cognitive misers and employing shortcuts to simplify the decisional process.[28] When people evaluate an issue or a public official, they do not search their memories for all the considerations that might be relevant; they do not incorporate all the dimensions of a policy proposal into the formulation of their preferences. The intellectual burdens would be too great and their interest in politics too limited for such an arduous task. Instead of undertaking an exhaustive search, citizens minimize their cognitive burdens by selecting the dimensions they deem to be most important for their evaluations. In this decisional process, people are likely to weigh most heavily the information and values that are most easily accessible. Recent activation is one factor that determines their accessibility.[29]

The cognitive challenges of citizens are both an opportunity and a challenge for the White House. Because individuals typically have at least two, and often more, relevant values for evaluating issue positions, and because they are unlikely to canvass all their values in their evaluations, the president cannot leave to chance the identification of which values are most relevant to the issues he raises. Instead, the president seeks to influence the values citizens employ in their evaluations.

In most instances, the president does not have much impact on the values that people hold. Citizens develop these values over many years, starting in early childhood. By the time people focus on the president, their values are for the most part well established. So the president is not in a position to, say, convince people that they ought to be more generous to the poor or more concerned with the distribution of wealth in the country.

However, as we have seen, people use cues from elites as to the ideological or partisan implications of messages (the source of a message is itself an important cue). By articulating widely held values and pointing out their applicability to policy issues, events, or his own performance, the president may increase the salience (and thus the accessibility) of those values to the public's evaluations of them. In the process, the president attempts to show the public that his position is consistent with their values. For example, if the president's argument on behalf of expanding Medicaid focuses on compassion for the poor, then those who hold such a value may be more likely to see compassion as relevant to evaluating health policy and thus be more likely to support the president's position. Many people also value frugality and personal responsibility, and such people are more likely to resist the president's appeals for support if these values are dominant in their evaluation of Medicaid.

Through framing, the president attempts to define what a public policy issue is about. A *frame* is a central organizing idea for making sense of an issue or conflict and suggests what the controversy is about and what is at stake.[30] Thus, a leader might frame welfare as an appropriate program necessary to compensate for the difficult circumstances in which the less fortunate find themselves, or as a giveaway to undeserving slackers committed to living on the dole.

By defining and simplifying a complex issue through framing, the president hopes to influence which attitudes and information people incorporate into their judgments of his policies and performance.[31] It is not clear whether an issue frame interacts with an individual's memory so as to *prime* certain considerations, making some more accessible than others and therefore more likely to be used in formulating a political preference, or whether framing works by encouraging individuals to deliberately think about the importance of considerations suggested by a frame.[32] In either case, the frame raises the priority and weight that individuals assign to particular attitudes already stored in their memories.[33]

The president may also attempt to prime perceptions of objective circumstances such as the level of economic prosperity. The White House would prefer to have citizens look on the bright side of their environments so that positive elements will play a more prominent role in their evaluations of the president and his administration. Similarly, presidents try to prime people to view them in terms of positive characteristics such as strength, competence, and empathy.[34]

Framing and priming have a number of advantages for the president, not the least of which is that they demand less of the public than directly persuading citizens on the merits of a policy proposal. The president does not have to persuade people to change their basic values and preferences. The underlying mechanism in framing is cognitive accessibility, not persuasion. The president also does not have to convince citizens to develop expertise and acquire and process extensive information about the details of a policy proposal. In addition, framing and priming— because they are relatively simple—are less susceptible to distortion by journalists and opponents than direct persuasion on the merits of a policy proposal.[35]

Presidential Framing

Instead of trying to persuade the public directly on the merits of a proposal, then, the White House often uses public statements and the press coverage they generate to articulate relatively simple themes. Public opinion research may have identified these themes as favoring the president's positions.[36] For example, on the eve of the vote in the House on the climate change bill, President Obama shifted his argument for the bill to emphasize its potential economic benefits. "Make no mistake," he declared, "this is a jobs bill."[37] Climate change is a controversial topic, but everyone is for jobs, especially in a period of high unemployment.

Attempts to frame issues are as old as the Republic.[38] Each side of a political contest usually attempts to frame the debate to its own advantage. Byron Shafer and William Claggett argue that public opinion is organized around two clusters of issues, both of which are favored by a majority of voters: social welfare, social insurance, and civil rights (associated with Democrats) and cultural values, civil liberties, and foreign relations (associated with Republicans). Each party's best strategy is to frame the choice for voters by focusing attention on the party's most successful cluster of issues.[39] John Petrocik has found that candidates tend to campaign on issues that favor them in order to prime the salience of these issues in voters' decision making.[40] Similarly, an important aspect of campaigning is activating the latent predispositions of partisans by priming party identification as a crucial consideration in deciding for whom to vote.[41]

Portraying policies in terms of criteria on which there is a consensus and playing down divisive issues is often at the core of efforts to structure choices for both the public and Congress. The Reagan administration framed the 1986 Tax Reform Act as revenue-neutral, presenting the choice on the policy as one of serving special interests or helping average taxpayers. Few people would choose the former option. Federal aid to education had been a divisive issue for years before President Johnson proposed the Elementary and Secondary Education Act in 1965. To blunt opposition, he successfully changed the focus of debate from teachers' salaries and classroom shortages to fighting poverty and from the separation of church and state to aiding children. This changed the premises of congressional decision making and eased the path for the bill.[42]

Similarly, Richard Nixon articulated general revenue sharing as a program that made government more efficient and distributed benefits widely. He deemphasized the distributional aspect of the policy, which redistributed federal funds from traditional Democratic constituencies to projects favored by Republicans' middle-class constituents.[43] Dwight Eisenhower employed the uncontroversial symbol of national defense during the Cold War, even when it came to naming legislation, to obtain support for aiding education (the National Defense Education Act) and building highways (the Interstate and Defense Highway Act).

At other times, the president must try to frame choices in an atmosphere inflamed by partisanship. Independent Counsel Kenneth Starr accused President Clinton of 11 counts of impeachable offenses, perjury, obstruction of justice, witness tampering, and abuse of power. The White House fought back, accusing Starr of engaging in an *intrusive* investigation motivated by a *political vendetta* against the president. The basic White House defense was that the president made a mistake (*personal failing*) in his *private* behavior, apologized for it, and was ready to move on to continue to do the people's business of governing the nation. Impeachment, the president's defenders said, was grossly *disproportionate* to the president's offense. The public found the White House argument compelling and strongly opposed the president's impeachment.

Ronald Reagan understood instinctually that his popular support was linked to his ability to embody the values of an idealized America. He continually invoked symbols of his vision of America and its past—an optimistic view that did not closely correspond to reality but did sustain public support. He projected a simple, coherent vision for his presidency that served him well in attracting adherents and countering criticism when the inevitable contradictions in policy arose. For example, he maintained his identification with balanced budgets even though he never submitted a budget that was even close to balanced and his administration was responsible for more deficit spending than all previous administrations combined. More broadly, Reagan employed the symbols of an idealized polity to frame his policies as consistent with core American values.[44]

According to Pat Buchanan, who served Reagan as the White House director of communications: "For Ronald Reagan the world of legend and myth is a real world. He visits it regularly and he's a happy man there."[45] In his 1965 autobiography, Reagan described his feelings about leaving the military at the end of World War II: "All I wanted to do . . . was to rest up awhile, make love to my wife, and come up refreshed to a better job in an ideal world."[46] The reader would never realize from this that Reagan never left Hollywood while serving in the military during the war! However, in politics, perceptions are as important as reality; consequently, many people responded positively to the president's vision of history and his place therein.

Presidents may manipulate symbols in attempts not only to lead public opinion, but also to deliberately mislead it. Perhaps the most important and effective televised address President Reagan made to the nation in

1981 was his July 27 speech seeking the public's support for his tax-cut bill. In it he went to great lengths to present his plan as "bipartisan." It was crucial that he convince the public that this controversial legislation was supported by members of both parties and therefore was, by implication, fair. Despite the fact that two days later House Democrats voted overwhelmingly against the president's proposal, Reagan described it as "bipartisan" 11 times in the span of a few minutes! No one could miss the point.

Frustrations in Framing

Despite presidential efforts at framing, setting the terms of debate is not a silver bullet. Presidents usually fail to move the public. Bill Clinton's first major proposal as president in 1993 was a plan to stimulate the economy. The Clinton White House wanted the public to view its plan as an effort to get the economy moving again, but congressional Republicans opposed him, defining the president's economic program in terms of wasteful pork barrel expenditures. Similarly, Republicans focused public debate on the president's budget on tax increases rather than economic growth or deficit reduction.[47]

Clinton tried to present the issue of taxes as one of fairness, but there is little evidence that many shared this perception. "The Clinton administration has lost control of its agenda," complained White House pollster Stan Greenberg.[48] The budget also injected tax increases into the debate over the fiscal stimulus bill, and Senate Republicans pointed to tax increases repeatedly in their successful effort to defeat it.[49] In the end, the president could not obtain the public's support: four months after the White House introduced the fiscal stimulus bill, a plurality of the public opposed it, and the bill never came to a vote in the Senate.[50]

The president was well aware of his inability to set the terms of the debate over his proposals. When asked why he was having such a difficult time obtaining the support of the "new" Southern Democrats, Clinton responded, "In their own districts and states, they've let the Republicans dominate the perception of what we're trying to do. . . . the Republicans won the rhetorical debate."[51] He could not reach the American people— and it frustrated him. Six months after taking office, when he appeared on *Larry King Live*, the president reflected on the unexpected dimensions of his job: "The thing that has surprised me most is how difficult it is . . . to really keep communicating what you're about to the American people."

Most presidents seek a strong, clear narrative to help them connect with the public and explain the essence of their administrations. Franklin D. Roosevelt's "New Deal" is perhaps the best known modern example. Barack Obama has an eclectic ideology. This complexity, along with his preference for complex explanations,[52] complicated the president's ability to articulate a clear, simple narrative to frame his presidency in his own terms. In his first Inaugural Address, Obama introduced the phrase "new foundation" to encapsulate his ambitious program and then repeated it in a wide range of venues over the next few months.[53] The phrase did not catch on in either the press or the public. Thus, in early 2010, the White House decided it needed to reinvigorate Obama's most successful message of the 2008 campaign: that he was an agent of change.[54]

The lack of a positive narrative, of course, invites opponents to craft a less flattering portrayal. In a question and answer session with the House Republicans in Baltimore on January 29, 2010, the president expressed his frustrations at the framing wars.

> That's why I say if we're going to frame these debates in ways that allow us to solve them, then we can't start off by figuring out A, who's to blame; B, how can we make the American people afraid of the other side? And unfortunately, that's how our politics works right now. And that's how a lot of our discussion works. That's how we start off—every time somebody speaks in Congress, the first thing they do, they stand up and all the talking points—I see Frank Luntz sitting in the front. He's already polled it, and he said . . . I've done a focus group and the way we're going to really box in Obama on this one or make Pelosi look bad on that one. . . . It's all tactics. It's not solving problems.
>
> So the question is, at what point can we have a serious conversation about Medicare and its long-term liability, or a serious . . . conversation about Social Security, or a serious conversation about budget and debt in which we're not simply trying to position ourselves politically? That's what I'm committed to doing. We won't agree all the time in getting it done, but I'm committed to doing it.[55]

In its first major proposal, the White House did not want to impose a bill on Republicans or to let them pick apart its own proposal. So it chose to let the House and Senate work their wills on the stimulus bill. One consequence of this strategy was a bill that Republicans and even some Democrats criticized for focusing too heavily on spending that would not provide an economic stimulus. Because the package was sold mostly as a short-term employment boost, the huge sums for long-term investments in health care, energy, education, and infrastructure were vulnerable to the charge that they did not immediately create many jobs.

Working with Congress behind closed doors to deal with the rising opposition, the president left a vacuum on 24-hour cable news that conservative critics eagerly exploited.[56] "We are definitely losing the framing of what this thing is," fretted one veteran Democratic operative.[57] Nothing sells news like confrontation with the president.

During the first two weeks of the Obama presidency, the media's use of the unflattering term "pork" in association with the stimulus bill increased about 400 percent.[58] The White House was losing control of the debate as the Republicans framed discourse on the bill in terms of wasteful spending. Indeed, by the end of the first week of February, 49 percent of the public reported that what it had been hearing about the stimulus plan was "mostly negative," while only 29 percent replied that what they were hearing was "mostly positive."[59]

The administration's second major proposal was health care reform. In a presentation to House Republicans on May 6, 2009, consultant Frank Luntz, an expert on the language of politics, advised framing the Democratic plan as a big government takeover that would deny care, interfere with the "doctor-patient relationship," cost too much, and restrict patients' choices. The next week, senior White House adviser David Axelrod and deputy White House chief of staff Jim Messina visited Senate Democrats and presented polling data on what Americans wanted from a health care plan. The White House aides suggested framing the Democrats' health care overhaul as one that would reduce costs, increase access to health care coverage, and allow people to keep their plan if they wished.[60]

Obama's team won early, high marks for diverging from the Clinton approach by emphasizing the need to control costs and improve choices and coverage for those who were already insured instead of making the moral-duty argument about the need to cover the uninsured. He more often cited as potential beneficiaries the working and middle classes rather than the uninsured poor. When the president spoke of covering the uninsured, he argued that doing so would also help the insured because hospitals, doctors, and insurers would no longer have to pass on unpaid expenses in higher premiums and prices to paying patients. Mindful that supporters would not agree on all details, Obama distilled his position to a frame involving three principles: reduce cost, ensure quality, and provide choice, including a public insurance option.[61]

Yet for all the president's efforts, the bill's sticker shock drew taxpayers' attention to the main expense, which was covering the uninsured. The White House's stress on abstract cost controls in order to address the cost of retooling the system also made it difficult to rally support. In addition, Republicans ridiculed his plan, offering competing frames of it as a government takeover that could limit Americans' ability to choose their doctors and course of treatment while also bankrupting the country.

In response, the White House recalibrated its message. Obama began framing the issue more as health *insurance* reform instead of health care reform, a change calculated to appeal to the satisfied majority. Guided by polls,[62] the administration framed the health care debate as a campaign against insurance companies—prohibiting practices that made buying coverage impossible or excessively expensive for many who are sick, older, or had a prior illness and bringing a degree of security and stability that they lacked. The White House website listed eight "Health Insurance Consumer Protections" that would "bring you and your family peace of mind." Democrats also zeroed in on the health insurance industry's hefty profits.

Nevertheless, the White House lost the battle of competing frames. The president could not even achieve a plurality of support for his reform effort, and this lack of enthusiasm persisted for years after the Affordable Care Act passed.[63]

In September 2013, the White House focused on the rollout of the ACA and began a six-month campaign to persuade millions of uninsured Americans to sign up for health coverage as part of insurance marketplaces that would open for business on October 1. The rollout provided another opportunity for the administration to frame discourse about the Affordable Care Act. In response to the highly publicized malfunctioning of HealthCare.gov, the White House argued that the problems were simply technical glitches that would soon be fixed and were partially the result of overwhelming public demand for access to the online exchanges.

In an eloquent reflection of polarized politics, Republicans worked to discourage people from enrolling. They feared that once people begin receiving health care benefits they would be loath to give them up. Thus, they tried to deepen the nation's anger about the health insurance program. The rollout provided them an opportunity to offer their own frame: that the website's problems reflected the fatally flawed nature of the policy and the high level of mismanagement in the executive branch, similar to the George W. Bush administration's response to Hurricane Katrina.

Jennifer Hopper analyzed media coverage of a range of nightly news broadcasts, major newspapers, cable news programming, and online news sources for the first week of October and then the period of November 11–25. She found that although the White House's framing dominated media coverage in the first days of the rollout, the administration soon lost this advantage and the media resorted to the comparison with Katrina frame. The stakes were high in this case, because the real issue was the competence of the administration to govern. Moreover, the rollout was on the heels of the government shutdown, which had given the Democrats an advantage in the polls. In the end, the White House lost this advantage and raised serious questions about its competence that lingered through the midterm elections the following year.[64]

In July 2013, reprising a phrase Obama employed during his reelection campaign, the White House settled on "from the middle out rather than the top down" to signal both a diagnosis of the problems that ailed the economy and the policies that might act as an antidote. The president

TABLE 6.1. Obama Focus on the Economy and the Middle Class, Summer 2013

Date	Location	Subject
July 13	White House Radio Address	Strengthening our economy by passing bipartisan immigration reform
July 16	White House	Interviews with four local anchors from America's biggest Spanish-language television networks
July 18	White House	Affordable Care Act
July 24	Galesburg, IL	Economy
July 25	Warrensburg, MO	Economy
	Jacksonville, FL	Economy
July 27	White House Radio Address	A better bargain for the middle class
July 30	Chattanooga, TN	Jobs for the middle class
August 6	Phoenix, AZ	Responsible homeownership
	Burbank, CA	*Tonight Show with Jay Leno*
August 9	White House	Student loans bill signing
	White House	Press conference (Introductory Remarks)
August 17	White House Radio Address	Working to implement the Affordable Care Act
August 22	Buffalo, NY	College affordability
	Syracuse, NY	College affordability
August 23	Binghamton, NY	Remarks in Town Hall meeting
	Scranton, PA	College affordability

Source: Whitehouse.gov.

elaborated on the middle-out theory in a series of speeches (table 6.1) intended to focus the nation's political discourse on his agenda for reinvigorating the nation's economy.[65] He also appeared on the *Tonight Show with Jay Leno*, spending 42 minutes reflecting on global and domestic issues and even cracking jokes about his odd-couple alliance with Senator John McCain. There is no evidence that the president's attempts to frame his economic policy were successful with the public.

Limits on Framing

We know very little about the terms in which the public thinks about issues. Studies that have shown powerful framing effects typically have carefully sequestered citizens and restricted them to hearing only one frame, usually in the context of a controlled experiment.[66] These frames tend to be confined to brief fragments of arguments, pale imitations of frames that often occur in the real world.

Although frames may evolve over decades,[67] presidents do not have the luxury of such a leisurely perspective. Chief executives need public support during their tenures, usually in their first terms when they are more likely to have majorities in Congress. Research has found that when people are offered competing frames, as they actually are on a daily basis, they adopt positions consistent with their preexisting values and discount those from the opposition party.[68]

Similarly, when people can choose their sources of information, as almost everyone can, they are unresponsive to opinion leadership.[69] Studies have found that conversations that include conflicting perspectives,[70] credible advice from other sources,[71] predispositions,[72] levels of education,[73] and relevant expertise[74] condition the impact of framing efforts. Even what appears to be successful framing may not be.[75]

Using an impressive data set and advanced methods for studying language, Daniel Hopkins carefully measured the frames used by political elites and the mass public to describe their views on the Affordable Care Act over the 2009–2012 period. He found that elites offered a variety of frames, but the public did not mirror those frames. Instead, their language changed little from the period before health care reform became highly salient.[76]

Frank Baumgartner and his colleagues carefully examined elite frames on a wide range of issues and found little impact on the frames used by others. They also found that it is difficult to coordinate the use of frames among allies, who are reluctant to adopt new frames when they are invested in existing frames.[77]

Thus, the challenges that Bill Clinton and Barack Obama faced are commonplace for presidents, who often fail in their efforts to frame issues for the public. Aside from the difficulties of systematically employing a frame, several other factors limit the success of presidential framing.

MEDIA RESISTANCE

The media is unlikely to adopt uniformly or reliably the White House's framing of issues. Most news outlets devote little attention to a typical issue, making it difficult for the president to educate the public. The press, especially the electronic media, is reluctant to devote repeated attention to an issue, even though this might be necessary to explain it adequately to the public. As a deputy press secretary in the Carter administration said: "We have to keep sending out our message if we expect people to understand. The Washington press corps will explain a policy once and then it will feature the politics of the issue."[78]

An important limitation on presidential framing is the increasing reluctance of journalists to let the president speak for himself. Instead, reporters increasingly feel the need to set the story in a meaningful context. The construction of such a context may entail reporting what was *not* said as well as what was said; what had occurred before; and what political implications may be involved in a statement, policy, or event. More than in the past, reporters today actively and aggressively interpret stories for viewers and readers. They no longer depend on those whom they interview to set the tone of their stories, and they now regularly pass sweeping (and frequently negative) judgments about what politicians are saying and doing.[79]

Even when the president speaks directly to the people, the media presents an obstacle to his framing issues in ways that favor his positions. Commentary following presidential speeches and press conferences may influence what viewers remember and may affect their opinions.[80] Although the impact of commentary on presidential addresses and press conferences is unclear, it is probably safe to argue that it is a constraint on the president's ability to lead public opinion.[81]

PUBLIC AWARENESS AND KNOWLEDGE

On January 17, 2014, President Obama delivered a speech at the Department of Justice outlining changes to the National Security Agency's collection of telephone and Internet data. The issue was important and salient to the public. Nevertheless, his remarks did not register widely with the public. Half said they had heard nothing at all about the president's proposed changes to the NSA's surveillance policy, and another 41 percent said they had heard only a little bit. Even among those few who heard a lot about the president's speech, only 21 percent thought it would improve privacy protections.[82]

It is not surprising, then, that the address had no impact on overall approval of the program or on opinions about whether adequate safeguards were in place. Pew found no difference in three nights of interviewing conducted after the speech (January 17–19, 2014) as compared with the two nights of interviewing conducted prior to the address (January 15–16).[83]

Thus, a fundamental limitation on presidential priming is the public's lack of attention to politics, which restricts its susceptibility to taking cues from political elites. Russell Neuman estimates that in the United States less than 5 percent of the public constitute a politically sophisticated elite. Another 75 percent are marginally attentive and 20 percent are apolitical. Even the marginally attentive lack the background information and rich vocabulary for quick and convenient processing of large amounts of political information. The apolitical 20 percent do not respond to political stimuli in political terms. Even in the middle, he argues, people frequently interpret political stimuli in nonpolitical terms.[84] If attempts to set the terms of debate fall on deaf ears, they are unlikely to be successful.

Among Americans, there are widely varying levels of interest in and information about politics and public policy.[85] From one perspective, those citizens with less interest and knowledge present the most potential for presidential persuasion. Such people cannot resist arguments if they do not possess information about the implications of those arguments for their values, interests, and other predispositions. However, these people are also less likely to be aware of the president's messages, limiting the president's influence. Even substantial public discourse does not reliably compensate for lack of information.[86] To the extent that they do receive the messages, they will also hear from the opposition how the president's views are inconsistent with their predispositions.

Even if their predispositions make them sympathetic to the president's arguments, less interested and informed citizens may lack the understanding to make the connection between the president's arguments and their own underlying values. Moreover, the more abstract the link between message and value, the fewer people who will make the connection.[87]

In addition, people are frequently *misinformed* (as opposed to uninformed) about policy, and the less they know, the more confidence they have in their beliefs. Thus, they resist correct factual information. Even when presented with factual information, they resist changing their opinions, including those that were the objects of elite framing.[88] Those who pay close attention to politics and policy are likely to have well-developed views and thus be less susceptible to persuasion. Better-informed citizens possess the information necessary to identify and thus reject communications inconsistent with their values. They are also more sensitive to the implications of messages. In the typical situation of competing frames offered by elites, reinforcement and polarization of views are more likely than conversion among attentive citizens.[89]

John Zaller argues that those in the public most susceptible to presidential influence are those attentive to public affairs (and thus who receive messages) but who lack strong views (and thus who are less likely to resist messages).[90] At best, such persons make up a small portion of the population. In addition, these persons will receive competing messages. There is no basis for inferring that they will be most likely to find the president's messages persuasive. Such a conclusion is especially suspect when we recognize that most attentive people have explicit or latent partisan preferences. The president is leader of one of the parties, and those affiliated with the opposition party must overcome an inherent skepticism about him before they can be converted to support his position.

PUBLIC PERCEPTIONS

For framing to work, people must first perceive accurately the frame offered by the president. We know very little about how people perceive messages from the president or other elites. Nor do we know much about how citizens come to understand public issues or develop their values and other predispositions that the president seeks to prime. (We also do not know whether the potential impact of frames is restricted to priming existing values or whether they may also affect understanding, which may in turn alter opinion.) There is reason to believe, however, that different people perceive the same message differently.[91] With all his personal, ideological, and partisan baggage, no president can assume that all citizens hear the same thing when he speaks. Partisanship is especially likely to bias processing perceptions, interpretations, and responses to the political world.[92]

A related matter of perception is the credibility of the source. Experimental evidence supports the view that perceived source credibility is a prerequisite for successful framing.[93] The president is likely to be more credible to some people (those predisposed to support him) than to others. Many people are unlikely to find him a credible source on most issues, especially those on which opinion is divided and on which he is the leader of one side of the debate.

NATURE OF ISSUES

The president faces yet other challenges in setting the terms of debate. Although there are occasions on which a president can exploit an external event such as arms control negotiations to structure choices on a single issue, he cannot rely on his environment to be so accommodating. In addition, the White House must advocate the passage of many proposals at roughly the same time, further complicating its efforts to structure choice on any single issue.

INEPTNESS

Attempts to structure decisions may actually hurt the president's cause if they are too heavy-handed and thus create a backlash. In 1986, Ronald Reagan was engaged in his perennial fight to provide aid to the Contras in Nicaragua. The president equated opposition to his aid program with support for the Sandinistas. More graphically, the White House communications director, Patrick J. Buchanan, wrote an editorial in the *Washington Post* that characterized the issue in stark terms: "With the contra vote, the Democratic Party will reveal whether it stands with Ronald Reagan and the resistance or [Nicaraguan President] Daniel Ortega and the communists." These overt efforts to set the terms of debate were not successful.

Instead, they irritated members of Congress and provoked charges that the White House was engaged in red baiting.[94]

OVERUSE

The White House can go to the well only so often. Later in this chapter I discuss Ronald Reagan's effort in 1985 to frame the issue of approval of the MX missile as supporting his credibility in arms control negotiations. The next year, he faced opposition from Congress and the public over the sale of arms to Saudi Arabia. The president argued that a defeat on this highly visible foreign policy issue would undermine his international credibility and destroy his role as a mediator in the Middle East. Despite all his efforts, the president was able to garner only 34 votes in the Senate, then controlled by Republicans.[95]

INCREASING THE SALIENCE OF POPULAR ISSUES

Even if the president cannot change the public's views on issues, he may be able to influence *what* it is thinking about. Instead of seeking to change public opinion regarding an issue, presidents may make appeals on policies that already have public support in an attempt to make them more salient to the public and thus encourage members of Congress to support White House initiatives to please the public.[96]

Brandice Canes-Wrone found that presidents are "more likely to publicize a domestic initiative the more popular it is and almost never appeal to the public about an initiative likely to mobilize popular opposition." "Only on popular domestic proposals can presidents increase their prospects for legislative success by going public." Presidents are also more likely to publicize foreign policy initiatives if a majority of the public favors them and will generally avoid going public on initiatives that face mass opposition.[97]

In 2001, George W. Bush made large tax cuts a top priority of his presidency. Although most people were not clamoring for tax cuts, the president's Republican base was enthusiastic, there was little organized opposition to the principle of the policy, many people found the prospect of lower taxes attractive, and the budget surplus in 2000 made tax cuts plausible. Bush traveled extensively to speak on behalf of his tax-cut initiative, and his travels seemed motivated more by demonstrating his support in states where he ran well in the election than by convincing more skeptical voters of the soundness of his proposals. He did not travel to California until May 29 and visited New York even later. Instead, the White House gave priority to states that Bush had won and that were represented by Democratic senators, including Georgia, Louisiana, Arkansas, Missouri,

North and South Dakota, Montana, and North Carolina. The goal of these trips seemed to be to demonstrate preexisting public support in the constituencies of members of Congress who were potential swing votes. In 2003, the president seemed to be following the same strategy as he campaigned for another tax-cut proposal. His travel seemed designed to work at the margins to convince moderate senators of both parties that his tax-cut proposal enjoyed public support in their states.

Exploiting existing support for an issue by making the issue more salient to the public requires that (1) the president's initiative be popular, (2) the president has the ability to increase the salience of issues among the public, and (3) the president has the time and energy to take his case to the public. Some presidential initiatives do have public support, but many do not. Ronald Reagan's efforts to decrease government spending on domestic policy, increase it on defense policy, win support for the Contras, and reduce regulation all typically lacked majority support. Bill Clinton's proposals for stimulating the economy, reforming health care reform, intervening in Haiti, and enacting NAFTA (North American Free Trade Agreement) faced at least plurality opposition once their opponents responded to them. George W. Bush's most ambitious proposals in his second term, reforming Social Security and immigration policy and maintaining troops in Iraq, confronted a similar lack of popular support. Barack Obama's signature policy, health care reform, was never popular with the public. Presidents are most likely to be advantaged when seeking to make modest alterations to existing policies.

We know little about the president's success in increasing the salience of issues, but there is reason to be cautious about attributing influence to the White House. Bill Clinton sought to start national discussions on affirmative action and Social Security, trying to develop a consensus on how to reform them. He even participated in roundtables with citizens to discuss the policies. The president's goal was laudable, but there is no evidence that he succeeded in stimulating national discussions, much less forging agreement on solutions.

Christopher Olds found that the president does not have the capacity to directly guide public attention, nor does the president have the capacity to indirectly guide public attention through the media.[98] Jeffrey Cohen found that presidents can influence the public's agenda through symbolic speech in State of the Union messages, at least in the short run. He also found, however, that presidents are only able to affect the public's agenda over time on foreign policy and that substantive policy rhetoric has no impact on the public's policy agenda. In general, Cohen found the president to have only a very modest impact on public opinion.[99]

Yet this influence may be even less than Cohen suggests, because presidential issue priorities in the State of the Union message may actually be a response to rather than a cause of public issue concerns. Kim Hill replicated Cohen's work to consider the possibility of reverse causality and found it operating for public concern with the economy and foreign policy, although not for civil rights.[100] B. Dan Wood found that the intensity of presidential rhetoric on the economy responds to public concerns about economy.[101] In other words, presidential issue priorities are often a response to the public rather than a cause of the public's agenda.

Tying Initiatives to Popular Policies

Nevertheless, there are steps a president can take to increase the odds of exploiting existing support for policies. On January 27, 1998, Bill Clinton delivered one of the most anticipated State of the Union messages in modern history. News about his relationship with a White House intern, Monica Lewinsky, had broken, instantly becoming the biggest story of the day and focusing attention on how the president would handle the strain of public discussion of his personal life. Clinton showed no effects of the scandal, and never mentioned it, but he did use the occasion to promote his agenda.

The president wanted to use the new budget surplus to pay down the national debt rather than to cut taxes, as Republicans favored. He articulated the rationale for this stance in the most memorable line of his speech, which was an appeal to "save Social Security first." As one of his speechwriters put it, "The presidential pulpit had never been put to more effective use." Social Security was not a matter of great public concern at that time, but Republicans had to applaud this widely supported policy, and that gave the president the upper hand in the battle over using the budget surplus.[102]

Clinton's deft use of rhetoric is an example of a president increasing the saliency of a widely supported policy when doing so helped advance his own agenda. Stopping Republican proposals for tax cuts was not at the core of Social Security policy, but the president was able to frame the issue of using the budget surplus to pay down the national debt as being for or against the popular policy of Social Security. By showing how Social Security was relevant to paying down the national debt, the president increased the salience of the latter by making it relevant to more people, people who did not previously see debt payment as pertinent to their interests.

This strategy is the classic case of expanding the scope of conflict by making issues salient to a wider segment of the public and thus adding to a supportive coalition.[103] The primary means of making an issue relevant to more people is the inclusion of new attributes to the policy.[104] In other words, the president attempts to show that a policy that people have evaluated principally in some terms should also be evaluated in other terms. If a new group cares about the second set of attributes, it may add a crucial component to the president's coalition.

Another example of adding a popular dimension to a policy initiative occurred in 1985, when Ronald Reagan asked Congress to appropriate funds for 21 additional MX missiles. He had been unable to win the money he had sought in 1984, when the debate focused on the utility of the missiles as strategic weapons. He succeeded the next year, however, after the terms of the debate changed to focus on the impact the building of missiles would have on the arms control negotiations with the Soviet Union that had recently begun in Geneva. Senators and representatives who lacked confidence in the contribution of the MX to national security were nevertheless reluctant to go to the public and explain why they were denying American negotiators the bargaining chips they said they required. According to a senior official at the Pentagon, "By the end, we gave up on technical briefings on the missile. . . . It was all based on the unspoken bargaining chip. Without Geneva, we would have died right there."[105]

The program that the president proposed had not changed. The MX was the same missile with essentially the same capabilities in 1985 as in 1984. There is scant evidence that anyone changed his or her mind about these capabilities. Conversion was not the key to success. What had changed were the premises on which discourse on the issue occurred. The burden of proof had shifted from the administration ("MX is a useful weapon") to its opponents ("canceling the MX will not hurt the arms control negotiations") because the president had added a new and widely supported dimension to evaluation of the MX.

Despite the success of Clinton and Reagan in these examples, it is usually difficult to frame a policy as central to the success of another, popular policy. Presidents are rarely in a position to make such claims. Indeed, as we have seen, it is generally difficult to frame issues in ways that favor the president.

INFLUENCING FLUID OPINION

Sometimes new policies arise on which there is little or no existing opinion. When opinion is not crystallized and thus fluid, there is an increased utility to external cues. At first glance, it would seem that such situations offer opportunities for the president to develop support, especially among his co-partisans, before an organized opposition develops.

On rare occasions, a crisis may befall the United States, creating new issues overnight. The onset of the Great Depression in 1929, the Japanese attack on Pearl Harbor in 1941, the captivity of U.S. hostages in Iran in 1975, and the terrorist attacks of September 11, 2001, are examples. In such cases, partisan-motivated reasoning may play less of a role in the formation of public opinion because of the nationalization of policy concerns and the consensus on goals.[106] The public may look to the White House to respond to the new problem rapidly. This potential for deference provides the president an opportunity to build support for his policies by demonstrating competence and resolution. Franklin D. Roosevelt exploited the crisis atmosphere to obtain passage of his New Deal legislation. George W. Bush won most of what he sought for fighting the war on terrorism abroad, investigating and prosecuting terrorism at home, and reorganizing the government to enhance domestic security.

Lee Sigelman ascertained public opinion on six potential responses to the 1979–1980 hostage crisis in Iran. He then asked those who opposed each option whether they would change their view "if President Carter considered this action necessary." In each case a substantial percentage of respondents changed their opinions in deference to the supposed opinion of the president.[107] Such results no doubt reflect the highly consensual policy goal of obtaining the return of American hostages. In addition, foreign policy issues are often complex and relatively far removed from most peoples' experiences. They should provide the best opportunities for the president to receive the benefit of the doubt from those predisposed to trust him.

At other times, the president may choose to advocate a policy to which the public has not been attentive. This inattention could be the result of the freshness of an issue or a general lack of concern for a matter. In either case, the public is not clamoring for action and contending sides have not mobilized for action. Public indifference may signal a tolerance for a presidential initiative, providing an opportunity for the White House.

Immediately after taking office in 1963, Lyndon Johnson began his War on Poverty. Poverty was not a pressing issue in the United States at the time,[108] but such an effort animated liberals, and giving people a hand up is consistent with broad currents of American ideology. Thus, the White House launched what Jeffrey Tulis has termed a "massive rhetorical campaign" to develop a sense of urgency about poverty, and the president made it the most visible theme of his first State of the Union message.[109] In such a case, partisan opinion may be responsive because of the ideological compatibility of the president's policy thrust, and opinion among opposition party identifiers may be temporarily subdued because of the lack of cues from party leaders.[110]

The president's cues can provide helpful shortcuts for fellow party identifiers to reach conclusions about what they should think about an issue. If the president is able to activate latent policy views by linking his initiatives to existing views, such as concern for the underprivileged or support for a strong national defense, he may be able to obtain rapidly a sizable core of supporters for his program. For example, in an experiment conducted during the Reagan presidency, Dan Thomas and Lee Sigelman posed policy proposals to sample subjects. When informed that the president was the source of the proposals, enthusiastic supporters of Reagan evaluated them in favorable terms, but when interviewers withheld the source, Reagan supporters evaluated these same proposals unfavorably.[111]

Opinion may be fluid even on elements of highly salient ongoing policies. In September 2007, the Gallup poll asked whether respondents favored the plan of General David Petraeus and President Bush to withdraw about 40,000 troops from Iraq by the summer of 2008, but not to make a commitment to further withdrawals until that time. Gallup also asked whether respondents supported a plan introduced by Democratic senators that called for the withdrawal of most U.S. troops within nine months. The muddled results revealed that similar and large percentages of Americans favored each plan—and 45 percent of the public favored both plans.[112] Although the president was not able to obtain the public's support solely for his preferred option, he was able to buy himself time to pursue his policy.

However, not all new issues provide an opportunity for presidential leadership. Some new issues, such as the 1970 U.S. invasion of Cambodia, are so closely related to issues about which public opinion is well developed that the public's responses are strongly influenced toward the overall policy. In addition, new issues often surge into the public arena and receive a flood of attention, especially in the age of 24 / 7 news programs. This cascade of publicity may provide enough information for people to become sufficiently informed that they do not need to defer to presidential cues. Finally, some issues readily elicit an instinctual response and do not require knowledge or deliberation to arrive at a conclusion.[113] In such cases, there is little need for the cognitive efficiency provided by White House cues.

Ronald Reagan's Strategic Defense Initiative

One of Ronald Reagan's most notable proposals in national security policy was the Strategic Defense Initiative (SDI). Critics often referred to it as "Star Wars." Reagan first broached SDI in a national address on national security in March 1983, when he was near the nadir of his approval ratings. The goal of the initiative was to protect the United States against nuclear attack, an aspiration shared by virtually everyone.

Opinion about SDI was slow to crystallize. Through the end of 1987, less than half the public felt they knew enough to have an opinion about SDI.[114] (When asked to offer an opinion, however, most complied.) The absence of prior opinion about a policy with a consensual goal provides a best-test case for White House opinion leadership.

TABLE 6.2. Public Support for the Strategic Defense Initiative, 1984–1988

Poll Date	% Favor			
	All	Republicans	Democrats	Independents
October 22–24, 1984	40	57	26	42
August 27–28, 1985	45	56	36	45
January 29–30, 1986[1]	47	66	32	50
December 4–5, 1986	52	64	42	50
April 25–May 10, 1987	44	61	34	41
June 24–26, 1988[2]	38			

Source: Gallup Poll.

[1] N = 533

[2] Registered voters

Question: "Some people feel the U.S. should try to develop a space-based 'Star Wars' system to protect the U.S. from nuclear attack. Others oppose such an effort because they say it would be too costly and further escalate the arms race. Which view comes closer to your own?"

Question August 1985: "Some people feel the United States should try to develop a space-based Star Wars system to guard against a nuclear attack. Others oppose such an effort because they say it would be too costly and escalate the arms race. Which view comes closer to your own?"

Nevertheless, Gallup found that public support for SDI increased 12 percentage points over a two-year period from 1984 to 1986 but then fell notably in Regan's last two years in office (table 6.2). Reagan's own pollster, Richard Wirthlin, also found that support for SDI fell during the president's second term.[115]

Perhaps because opinion was not crystallized on such a new and technical issue, support for the SDI was volatile, especially among Democrats and Independents. In the last half of 1985, for example, overall approval increased by 34 percent (table 6.3). (This change occurred before President Reagan's summit meeting with Mikhail Gorbachev in Geneva on November 19–20, 1985.)

Reagan's experience on SDI also shows that opinion changes may well be temporary. Even under unusual circumstances when people have participated in intense deliberations with fellow citizens and listened to the testimony of politicians and policy experts, research finds changes of opinion to be largely temporary.[116] Members of the public who are the easiest to sway in the short run are those without well-formulated opinions. However, as issues fade into the background, as the realities of daily life confront positions, and as the implications of supporting the president become more clear, opinions that were altered in response to presidential

TABLE 6.3. Public Support for Strategic Defense Initiative, 1985

| | % Approve/Favor | | | |
Poll Date	All	Republicans	Democrats	Independents
July 25–29, 1985	41	59	26	44
October 24–28, 1985	48	65	33	48
November 10–13, 1985	55	67	43	58

Source: ABC News/*Washington Post* Poll.

Questions:
July: "Supporters say such weapons (Star Wars or the Strategic Defense Initiative) could guarantee protection of the United States from nuclear attack and are worth whatever they cost. Opponents say such weapons will not work, will increase the arms race, and that the research will cost many billions of dollars. How about you: Would you say you approve or disapprove of plans to develop such space-based weapons?"
October and November: "Supporters say such (space-based) weapons ('Star Wars,' or Strategic Defense Initiative) could guarantee protection of the United States from nuclear attack and are worth whatever they cost. Opponents say such weapons will increase the arms race, and cost many billions of dollars. How about you: Would you say you favor or oppose plans to develop such space-based weapons?"

leadership may quickly be forgotten. This slippage is especially likely to occur in foreign policy, the area where the president's influence on public opinion may be greatest.

George W. Bush's Stem Cell Research Decision

Stem cell research was not on the minds of most voters in the early summer of 2001. At that time, President George W. Bush was weighing advice about whether the federal government should fund medical research using cells obtained from human embryos in the first few days after fertilization. Gallup reported that most Americans were not following the issue closely and did not know enough about the facts involved to render an opinion. The issue was (and is) controversial because scientists destroy embryos during their research. As a presidential candidate, Bush committed to eliminating this funding, but pressure on him to reverse his stance developed, especially from reactions to a report issued by the National Institutes of Health arguing that adult stem cells were not as useful as embryonic stem cells in stem cell research and that a large number of embryonic stem cells could be generated in the laboratory.

In July 2001, only 38 percent of Americans reported they were following the stem cell research issue very or somewhat closely. A clear majority of Americans, 57 percent, said they did not know enough to venture an opinion on whether the federal government should fund the particular kind of stem cell research using human embryos created in laboratories. Of the remainder, 30 percent said the government should fund it, while 13 percent disagreed. Responses to more specific questions varied greatly with the question wording.[117] By August, however, the issue heated up, and 57 percent of the public were following the debate over stem cell research at least "somewhat closely," while 78 percent felt the issue was at least "somewhat important."[118]

The precipitating factor in the change in opinion was discussion over George W. Bush's deliberations on the issue. He announced his decision in a nationally televised address on August 9, 2001, declaring that he would allow the federal government to fund research using stem cells that had been created in the past in a process that destroyed human embryos, but he would not allow funding for stem cell research that would destroy additional embryos in the future.

A few days before Bush's speech, 55 percent of the public supported federal funding for stem cell research *and* for using embryos discarded from fertility clinics. Forty-six percent even supported using embryos created in laboratories specifically for the purpose of research.[119]

Initially the president's decision *not* to fund stem cell research that would destroy additional embryos in the future seemed to change the public's views. Sixty percent of the public approved his decision, and most of those disapproving felt he was not strict enough. There was a partisan split, however. Republicans approved of Bush's decision by a 79 percent to 16 percent margin. Democrats, on the other hand, disagreed. Only 42 percent approved while 52 percent disapproved. Independents were in the middle, with 58 percent approving and 36 percent disapproving.[120]

Whatever advantage the president enjoyed from the novelty of the issue of stem cell research soon faded. Indeed, the opinion finding the use of human embryonic stem cells in research morally acceptable *increased* by 8 percentage points following Bush's speech. By the following May, a small majority of the public felt medical research using stem cells obtained from human embryos was morally acceptable (table 6.4). Five years later, in 2007, by which time the issue was no longer novel, the percentage of the public that found stem cell research morally acceptable increased to 64 percent.

The source of that change was partisan. Although there was little difference between party identifiers in 2001–2003, a partisan gap soon appeared (table 6.5). Republicans' opinions did not change at all from 2002. On the other hand, Democrats increased their agreement with the moral acceptability of stem cell research by nearly 88 percent—to 77 percent—a 36-percentage-point increase. Independents also increased their support, up to 63 percent. It appears that in the end Bush's opinion leadership was more reinforcement than persuasion.

TABLE 6.4. Moral Acceptability of Research Using Human Embryonic Stem Cells

Poll Date	% Morally Acceptable	% Not Morally Acceptable
July 10–11, 2001[1]	39	54
August 10–12, 2001[1]	47	49
May 6–9, 2002	52	39
May 5–7, 2003	54	38
May 2–4, 2004	54	37
May 2–5, 2005	60	33
May 8–11, 2006	61	30
May 10–13, 2007	64	30

Source: Gallup Poll and Gallup/CNN, USA Today Poll.

Question: "Regardless of whether or not you think it should be legal, for each one, please tell me whether you personally believe that in general it is morally acceptable or morally wrong. How about . . . medical research using stem cells obtained from human embryos?"
[1] "Which comes closest to your view of this kind of stem cell research—it is morally wrong and is unnecessary, it is morally wrong, but may be necessary, it is not morally wrong and may be necessary, or it is not morally wrong but is unnecessary?" (Categories for morally acceptable and categories for morally wrong combined.)

TABLE 6.5. Partisan Opinion on Moral Acceptability of Research Using Human Embryonic Stem Cells

	% Morally Acceptable			
Poll Date	All	Republicans	Democrats	Independents
July 10–11, 2001[1]	39	37	41	38
August 10–12, 2001[1]	47	43	46	52
May 6–9, 2002	52	50	52	55
May 5–7, 2003	54	53	55	55
May 2–4, 2004	54	50	57	55
May 2–5, 2005	60	47	72	61
May 8–11, 2006	61	51	68	62
May 10–13, 2007	64	50	77	63

Source: Gallup Poll and Gallup/CNN, USA Today Poll.

Question: "Regardless of whether or not you think it should be legal, for each one, please tell me whether you personally believe that in general it is morally acceptable or morally wrong. How about . . . medical research using stem cells obtained from human embryos?"
[1] "Which comes closest to your view of this kind of stem cell research—it is morally wrong and is unnecessary, it is morally wrong, but may be necessary, it is not morally wrong and may be necessary, or it is not morally wrong but is unnecessary?" (Categories for morally acceptable and categories for morally wrong combined.)

TABLE 6.6. Partisan Opinion on Government Funding of Stem Cell Research

| | % No Restrictions or Ease Restrictions | | | |
Poll Date	All	Republicans	Democrats	Independents
August 3–5, 2001[1]	46	37	53	49
October 9–10, 2004	55	37	76	54
May 20–22, 2005	53	36	60	60
August 5–7, 2005[2]	56	42	67	61
April 13–15, 2007	60	45	72	61

Source: Gallup Poll, Gallup/USA Today Poll, and Gallup/CNN/USA Today Poll.

Question: "Which would you prefer the government do—[ROTATED: place no restrictions on government funding of stem cell research, ease the current restrictions to allow more stem cell research, keep the current restrictions in place, (or should the government) not fund stem cell research at all]?"
[1]"Some stem cells are developed from embryos that are created in laboratories specifically for the purpose of conducting this research and not to help women have a child. Do you think the federal government should or should not fund research on stem cells from this kind of embryo?"
[2] "Do you think the federal government should—or should not—fund research that would use newly created stem cells obtained from human embryos?"

By 2005, 56 percent of the public felt the federal government should fund research that would use newly created stem cells obtained from human embryos (table 6.6). Fifty-eight percent of the public disapproved of Bush's veto of a bill in 2006 that would have expanded federal funding for embryonic stem cell research.[121] By April 2007, 60 percent of the public, including 72 percent of Democrats and 61 percent of Independents, wanted fewer or no restrictions on federal funding for stem cell research.[122] Even Republicans were not immune from national trends, increasing their support to 45 percent.

CONCLUSION

Although presidents are unlikely to change public opinion, there are times when the White House may exploit existing public opinion in its efforts to change public policy. The president may clarify the public's wishes and show how they are consistent with his policies, frame proposals to emphasize their consistency with the public's existing views, increase the salience of White House initiatives that are popular with the public, and exploit opinion fluidity or public indifference regarding an issue. The basic strategy for the White House is to position the president in front of a parade and then lead it in a direction and with a tempo that will serve his programmatic needs.

Such strategies often fail, however. Articulating public opinion in a way that clarifies its policy implications and shows the public that its wishes are consistent with his policies can be essential for achieving major changes in policy, but it takes a finely tuned ear and a deft hand. Not all presidents will possess these attributes. Similarly, the president cannot depend on successfully framing how the public views his policies and his performance. One can sympathize with Bill Clinton when he declared, "Americans don't want me to help them understand. They just want me to do something about it."[123]

In addition, it is difficult for the president to focus the public's attention and make his popular initiatives more salient, especially for extended periods. Despite the fact that rhetoric cascades from the White House, chief executives disperse their public remarks over a broad range of policies, and wide audiences hear only a small portion of them. The president faces strong competition for the public's attention from previous commitments of government, congressional initiatives, opposing elites, and the mass media. Equally important, presidents often compete with themselves as they address other issues. Reaching the public is a continual and sizeable challenge for the president.

Not all presidential policies deal with well-established issues. Occasionally there is a White House initiative on which the public has not developed attitudes. Although such situations may seem to offer the president especially favorable conditions for obtaining support, there is little evidence that the president can overcome either partisan predispositions, which soon develop, or the broad trends in public attitudes.

CHAPTER 7

Cross-Pressuring Opinion

THE PRESIDENT'S SIGNALS are not always consistent with the preferences of his fellow party identifiers. Sometimes the president's stances conflict with the views of his co-partisans, who are thus cross-pressured between their policy predispositions and the policies of their party's leader. Although many people may be primed to follow the lead of "their" president, they may also offer more resistance to that leadership. Thus, cross-pressured citizens provide an excellent test of the impact of opinion leadership.

Cross-pressuring is not limited to the president's co-partisans. There are two conditions under which the president takes stands consistent with those of opposition party identifiers and thus exposes them to cross-pressuring. First, specific White House policies may appeal to members of the opposition. Examples of such cross-pressuring are an aggressive foreign policy stance by a Democratic president that Republicans find compatible with their orientation toward national security or a "liberal" policy on a social welfare issue by a Republican president that appeals to Democratic identifiers.

There are times, however, when presidents emphasize broader themes designed to expand their coalitions in the long run by attracting support from the opposition party. If the White House succeeds in such efforts, the consequences for American politics can be profound.

CROSS-PRESSURING

The president's co-partisans, especially attentive partisans, have broad views about the appropriate level of government intervention in the economy, the obligations of society to help the less fortunate, the fairness of approaches to policy, the threats of policies to civil liberties, and other matters. If signals from the White House run counter to these views, identifiers with the president's party will find themselves cross-pressured. Even if co-partisans support a policy stance that seems to be inconsistent with the general tenor of the party's stances in the short run, the fact that they are cross-pressured may weaken their support over time. There is some evidence that cross-pressured partisans abandon partisan motivated reasoning,[1] perhaps because they are encouraged to give deeper thought to their views.[2] Thus, Republican presidents taking leftward stances and Democrats taking conservative positions should not expect their parties to simply snap into step.

If the president's stands are consistent with the views of members of the opposition party, it is possible that he may obtain some additional support from that quarter. Opposition party identifiers will not defer to the president or be persuaded by him. Instead, they may support the president's policies because they already agree with them. However, partisan polarization may negate the attractiveness of the White House's policies to the opposition. If an opposition party president is for something, it might be not such a good idea after all.

There is more potential for public support, however, under conditions of low partisan polarization. In such an environment, the president may appeal to opposition party identifiers, even attracting them to change their party allegiance to more closely align their partisan identification with their ideologies.

Thus, the tension between existing opinion and presidential signals provides the best test of the power of signaling. It is here that we are most likely to find an actual change of views among the president's co-partisans. Four issues that arose during Barack Obama's second term illustrate cross-pressuring. The first is the anti-terrorism policy of surveillance of the nation's email and phone calls. The president's aggressive policy in this area cross-pressured Democrats, who are typically sensitive to potential violations of civil liberties. The second policy is military action on behalf of rebels in Syria. Again, the president's drawing a line in the sand and calling for military action created tension among Democrats, who on average wished to avoid the use of force and further involvement in armed conflict in the Middle East. Next was the president's decision to delay enforcing the mandate for businesses with more than 50 employees to provide health care insurance for their employees. This decision cross-pressured Democrats, who supported the mandate, and Republicans, who opposed it. Finally, the president ordered military action against the brutal Islamic fundamentalist group, ISIS. Once again, many Democrats were cross-pressured by their desires to avoid military action and to support their party leader. Most, but not all, Republicans, on the other hand, were eager to strike against ISIS but virtually all of them also had disdain for President Obama.

NSA Surveillance

In 2013, Edward Snowden, a former contract employee of the National Security Agency, released thousands of classified documents revealing the existence of numerous global surveillance programs, many run by the NSA and nations closely allied with the United States. The programs received prominent coverage in the news and elicited a steady stream of commentary by public officials and private citizens alike. In 2014, the *Washington Post* received a Pulitzer Prize for its coverage of Snowden and the government surveillance issue.

Table 7.1 shows that, when questioned under a Republican president, George W. Bush, in 2006, Republican support was high for secretly listening in on telephone calls and reading emails of some people in the United States and other countries without prior court approval. That support declined 23 percentage points when respondents were queried about track-

TABLE 7.1. Partisan Views of NSA Surveillance Programs

Party Group	January 2006		June 2013		Change
	% Acceptable	% Unacceptable	% Acceptable	% Unacceptable	% Unacceptable
All	51	47	56	41	+5
Republican	75	23	52	47	−23
Democrat	37	61	64	34	+27
Independent	44	55	53	44	+9

Source: Pew Research Center polls, January 4–8, 2006 and *Washington Post*/Pew Research Center poll, June 6–9, 2013.

Questions:
January 2006: "The National Security Agency (NSA) has been investigating people suspected of involvement with terrorism by secretly listening in on phone calls and reading emails between some people in the United States and other countries, without first getting court approval to do so. Would you consider this wiretapping of telephone calls and emails without court approval as an acceptable or unacceptable way for the federal government to investigate terrorism?"
June 2013: "It has been reported that the National Security Agency has been getting secret court orders to track telephone call records of millions of Americans to investigate terrorism. Would you consider this access to telephone records an acceptable or unacceptable way for the federal government to investigate terrorism?"
"Don't know/Refused" responses not shown.

ing telephone calls under Democrat Barack Obama seven years later. Similarly, only 37 percent of Democrats found the NSA surveillance acceptable under Bush, but their support increased 27 percentage points to 64 percent acceptable under Obama. There is no question that underlying ideologies affected the partisans' responses, but the change in partisan opinion in response to the president's party is striking.

It is always important to note the exact wording of poll questions. The 2006 question includes secretly listening to phone calls and reading emails without a court order, a clear invasion of privacy. However, the question also confines itself to inquiring about government surveillance of persons suspected of terrorism. On the other hand, the second question covers a broader group of Americans ("millions"), but it also specifies court orders and only refers to tracking call records. One can easily view the latter question as referring to a less aggressive invasion of privacy than actually listening to calls and reading emails, albeit one that happens to more people.

Regardless of the impact the question wording had on the respondents, that impact should affect the absolute levels of acceptability of the surveillance programs. However, our focus is on the differences among the party groups and especially the changes in the views of those groups.

A week after the 2013 poll shown in table 7.1, 58 percent of Democrats approved the government's collection of phone and Internet data as part of its anti-terrorism efforts, while only 45 percent of Republicans offered the same response. Only 29 percent of those who agreed with the Tea Party, Obama's staunchest foes, approved of these policies.[3] Gallup found considerably lower levels of approval, but the same patterns of partisan differences (table 7.2).

TABLE 7.2. Partisan Approval of NSA Surveillance Programs

Pary Group	% Approve	% Disapprove	% No Opinion
All	37	53	10
Republicans	32	63	5
Independents	34	56	10
Democrats	49	40	11

Source: Gallup poll, June 10–11, 2013.

Question: "As you may know, as part of its efforts to investigate terrorism, a federal agency obtained records from larger U.S. telephone and Internet companies in order to compile telephone call logs and Internet communications. Based on what you have heard or read about the program, would you say you approve or disapprove of this government program?"

TABLE 7.3. Partisan Concerns about Anti-terrorism Programs

Party Group	October 2010		July 2013		Change
	Too Far in Restricting Civil Liberties	Not Far Enough to Protect Country	Too Far in Restricting Civil Liberties	Not Far Enough to Protect Country	Concern about Civil Liberties
Total	32	47	47	35	+15
Republican	25	58	43	38	+18
Democrat	33	49	42	38	+9
Independent	35	44	52	33	+17

Source: Pew Research Center polls, October 13–18, 2010 and July 17–21, 2014.

Question: "What concerns you more about the government's anti-terrorism policies?" [options] "Have gone too far in restricting civil liberties"; "Have not gone far enough to protect country."

Similarly, there was a large partisan shift in those who would feel their personal privacy had been violated if they knew the government had collected data on them. In 2006, Gallup found that 77 percent of Democrats said they would feel their privacy had been violated, compared with just 28 percent of Republicans.[4] Pew found that in 2013, only about half of Democrats (53 percent) said they would feel their privacy had been violated if they knew the government had collected their personal data. By contrast, the percentage of Republicans who would feel their privacy had been violated more than doubled to 68 percent.[5]

We can also see the impact of signaling on the public's trade-offs between security and civil liberties. The data in table 7.3 show that in 2010, before the Snowden revelations, Republicans prioritized security over civil liberties, as they had for years. Democrats held the same basic views, although to a lesser extent. After Snowden released the NSA documents, the entire country became more concerned about civil liberties. However, Republicans moved 18 percentage points in switching their priorities to civil liberties. Independents moved 17 percentage points in the same direction. Democrats, however, only moved 9 percentage points toward a prioritization of civil liberties. Republicans and Republican leaners supporting the Tea Party made the greatest changes of all, moving 35 percentage points toward a greater concern for civil liberties.

Similarly, when asked about their support for the news media reporting on the government's secret anti-terrorism programs in 2006, only 26 percent of Republicans agreed that the media should do so (table 7.4). Conversely, a clear majority (59 percent) of Democrats supported such actions. By mid-2013, the national totals had not changed at all. This seeming

TABLE 7.4. Partisan Opinion of Media Reporting on Secret Anti-terrorist Programs

Party Group	% Agreeing News Media Should Report on Secret Anti-terrorism Programs		
	May 2006	July 2013	Change
All	47	47	0
Republican	26	43	+17
Democrat	59	45	−14
Independent	53	51	−2

Source: Gallup/USA Today poll, May 12–13, 2006, and Pew Research Center poll, July 17–21, 2013.

Question:
May 2006: "Should the news media report information it obtains about the secret methods the government is using to fight terrorism?"
July 2013: "Please tell me whether you agree or disagree with the following statement: The news media reports too much information that can harm the effectiveness of the government's anti-terrorism programs."

stability in opinion masked a partisan dynamic, however. Republicans increased their support for the news media reporting on government secrets by 17 percentage points, while Democrats decreased their support by 14 percentage points.

Syria

Wishing to avoid dragging the country into another Middle Eastern quagmire but distressed by the deaths of 100,000 people in the civil war in Syria, President Obama struggled to determine the appropriate U.S. response. Until June 2013, the administration opposed providing military aid to the Syrian rebels. On June 13, however, the White House announced that the president had ordered direct military aid to anti-government groups. The core of the rationale for the shift in policy was the conclusion reached by U.S. intelligence agencies that the Syrian government had used chemical weapons against the rebels.

A poll conducted shortly after the president's announcement found that only 37 percent approved of the president's action while 54 percent disapproved (table 7.5). Even the provision of military aid to the rebels—as opposed to direct U.S. military intervention—provoked a partisan response. Following the president's lead, a slight majority of Democrats overcame their normal reluctance regarding foreign interventions and approved of providing military aid to anti-government forces, while about

TABLE 7.5. Partisan Support for Military Aid to Syrian Rebels

Party Group	% Approve	% Disapprove	% Don't Know
All	37	54	9
Republicans	29	63	9
Independents	33	60	7
Democrats	51	42	7

Source: Gallup poll, June 15–16, 2013.
Question: "Do you approve or disapprove of the Obama administration's decision to supply direct military aid to Syrian rebels fighting against the government in Syria?"

TABLE 7.6. Support for Military Aid to Syrian Rebels

Poll Date	% Favor	% Oppose	% Unsure/ Refused
March 30–April 3, 2011	25	66	11
March 7–11, 2012	29	63	9
December 5–9, 2012	24	65	11
March 4–18, 2013	25	64	11
June 12–16, 2013	20	70	9

Source: Pew Research Center Poll.

Question: "Would you favor or oppose the U.S. and its allies sending arms and military supplies to anti-government groups in Syria?"

six in ten Independents and Republicans disapproved. Even the support of some Republican leaders, most notably Senator John McCain, was not enough for Republicans to overcome their antipathy for any Obama initiative and voice their typical support for a more aggressive foreign policy. More broadly, opposition to military aid *increased* after the president supported it (table 7.6). In general, the public always overwhelmingly opposed military aid to the Syrian rebels.

On August 20, 2013, the president set a "red line" against the use of chemical weapons—without defining what crossing the line would entail. Although he was determined to keep the American military out of Syria, "a red line for us is we start seeing a whole bunch of chemical weapons moving around or being utilized," he said at an impromptu news conference. "That would change my calculus. That would change my equation."[6]

Shortly afterward, U.S. intelligence agencies reported that the government of Bashar al-Assad had launched a poisonous sarin gas attack in the

TABLE 7.7. Partisan Support for U.S. Military Action against Syria

Party Group	% Favor	% Oppose	% Unsure
All	36	51	13
Republicans	31	58	11
Independents	34	53	13
Democrats	45	43	12

Source: Gallup poll, September 3–4, 2013.

Question: "Would you favor or oppose the U.S. taking military action against Syria in order to reduce that country's ability to use chemical weapons?"

outskirts of Damascus on August 21, 2013, killing more than 1,400 civilians. Within hours, administration officials began signaling that they were preparing for an immediate military strike to punish the Syrian government—an idea the officials had dismissed repeatedly in the past.

Such a move was likely to be a hard sell with some allies, a war-weary public, and Congress. When the British declined to participate in the operation, Obama, over the objections of his staff and without consulting his secretary of state, John Kerry, or his secretary of defense, Chuck Hagel, suddenly decided on August 31 that he would seek congressional authorization for the strike.

To win that support, the White House mounted a massive public relations campaign—testifying in Congress, organizing private briefings and dinners with lawmakers, holding conference calls, and blanketing the news media. On September 9, CNN, PBS, Fox News, ABC, CBS, and NBC aired interviews with the president in which he argued that it was critical for the United States to hold Assad accountable and send a global message that the use of poison gas as a weapon was unacceptable. This effort culminated on September 10 in a national prime-time television address from the White House.

In general, the president faced majority opposition to his call for military strikes against the Syrian government's forces.[7] Americans believed that Bashar al-Assad had used chemical weapons against his citizens, but they did not see it in the national interest for the United States to be involved in military actions in Syria.[8]

Despite the public's overall opposition to military strikes, there was a differential response among the party groups. When asked about "military action"—a vague term to be sure—Democrats were much more supportive than Republicans (table 7.7). When asked more specifically about "military airstrikes," Democrats were once again by far the most supportive of the partisan groups (table 7.8).

TABLE 7.8. Partisan Support for U.S. Military Strikes against Syria

Party Group	% Favor	% Oppose	% Unsure
All	30	61	9
Republicans	28	65	7
Independents	23	67	10
Democrats	41	50	9

Source: CBS News/New York Times poll, September 6–8, 2013.

Question: "In response to the Syrian government's use of chemical weapons, do you favor or oppose the United States launching military airstrikes against Syrian military targets?"

The Pew Research Center asked the same question about support for military strikes twice during the period of the White House's intense public relations effort to obtain the backing of voters. The results in table 7.9 show that initially Republicans provided more support for the strikes than did Democrats or Independents. However, Republican support declined by 40 percent in a few days as the initiative became more clearly identified with the president, while GOP opposition climbed 30 percentage points, from 40 percent to 70 percent. The rule of thumb seemed to be, when in doubt, oppose Obama.

Conversely, Democrats increased their support for military strikes by six percentage points, no doubt for the same reason as the Republicans withdrew theirs. By September 8, before the complicating factor of the president's acceptance of Russia's plan for securing Syria's chemical weapons, Democrats were 40 percent more likely to support military strikes than were Republicans and 25 percent more likely to support the strikes than were Independents. Each side appears to have taken its cues from party leaders.

In his September 10 address to the nation, the president made a surprise move and asked Congress to postpone a vote authorizing the use of force against Syria to allow time for the Russian initiative to work. In a poll conducted shortly afterward, the Pew Research Center found somewhat more support for military airstrikes among all three party groups if Syria did not give up control of chemical weapons than there had been a week earlier, when the prospect of a failed diplomatic solution was not raised in the question it posed to respondents. Support for airstrikes increased by 9 percentage points overall and 13 points among Republicans, 9 points among Independents, and 8 points among Democrats (table 7.10). Nevertheless, majorities of both Republicans and Independents opposed airstrikes, while Democrats were tied at 43 percent in favor and 43 percent opposed.

TABLE 7.9. Partisan Response to White House in Support for U.S. Military Strikes against Syria

Party Group	% Favor	% Oppose	% Don't Know
All	29	48	23
Republicans	35	40	24
Independents	29	50	20
Democrats	29	48	23

Source: Pew Research Center poll, August 29–September 1, 2013.

Party Group	% Favor	% Oppose	% Don't Know
All	28	63	9
Republicans	21	70	9
Independents	28	66	6
Democrats	35	53	12

Source: Pew Research Center/USA Today poll, September 4–8, 2013.

Question: "Would you favor or oppose the U.S. conducting military airstrikes against Syria in response to reports that the Syrian government used chemical weapons?"

TABLE 7.10. Partisan Support for Military Strikes against Syria Following Obama's Speech

Party Group	% Favor	% Oppose	% Don't Know
All	37	49	14
Republicans	34	51	15
Independents	37	51	11
Democrats	43	43	14

Source: Pew Research Center, September 12–15, 2013.

Question: "If Syria does not give up control of its chemical weapons, would you favor or oppose the U.S. conducting military airstrikes against Syria in response to reports that the Syrian government used chemical weapons?"

In general, public opinion was remarkably stable regarding U.S. intervention in Syria, despite the president's public relations efforts. As an overview, we can see this stability in table 7.11, where Pew asked about U.S. responsibility for intervening in the civil war. The public clearly did not think the United States should become involved. Moreover, after the

TABLE 7.11. Responsibility of United States to Intervene in Syria

Poll Date	% Has Responsibility	% Does Not Have Responsibility	% Unsure/No Answer
December 12–16, 2012	27	62	11
March 20–24, 2013	20	69	11
April 24–28, 2013	24	62	14
May 31–June 4, 2013	28	61	10
September 6–8, 2013	28	65	7
September 19–23, 2013	26	68	5

Source: CBS News/New York Times poll.

Question: "Do you think the United States has a responsibility to do something about the fighting in Syria between government forces and anti-government groups, or doesn't the United Sates have this responsibility?"

Syrian government crossed the "red line," the percentage of the public finding no responsibility actually increased.

ACA Employer Mandate

The Obama administration faced a number of challenges in the early implementation of the Affordable Care Act. One of these challenges was the mandate for businesses with more than 50 employees to provide health care insurance for their employees. In mid-2014, the president announced a delay in enforcing the mandate. This decision cross-pressured those identifying with the two parties because Democrats supported the mandate while Republicans opposed it. In two polls in July 2014, the *Economist*/YouGov Poll asked the public about their support for delaying the business health insurance mandate. As table 7.12 shows, the answers depended heavily on whether the question mentioned the president.

In the first poll, the question referred to a decision by "the president." The responses were highly partisan, with Americans taking their cues, positive and negative, from the person associated with the action. In fact, the cues were so strong that they overcame the policy preferences of the two groups of partisans. Democrats, who supported the mandate, also supported President Obama's delaying it. Conversely, Republicans, who opposed the mandate, also opposed delaying it when the action was associated with the president.

In the second poll, taken just one week later, the question only mentioned "the government delaying" the mandate. Without the partisan cues, the responses of those identifying with the two parties were remark-

TABLE 7.12. Obama Effect on Support for Delaying Employer Mandate

Question Wording	Democrats		Republicans	
	% Support	% Oppose	% Support	% Oppose
President's Decision[1]	67	23	31	47
Government[2]	41	38	37	38

Source: Economist/YouGov polls, July 12–14, 2014 and July 19–21, 2014.

Questions:
[1] July 12–14, 2014: "Do you support or oppose the president's decision to delay enforcing the law requiring businesses with more than 50 employees to provide a health insurance option for their employees?"
[2] July 19–21, 2014: "Do you support the government delaying the mandate requiring businesses with more than 50 employees to provide a health insurance option for their employees?"

ably similar. Moreover, Democratic support for the delay dropped 26 percentage points and opposition increased by 15 percentage points. Republican support and opposition changed by more modest amounts, but, like the Democrats, Republicans changed their responses in the direction of their basic policy views.

ISIS

Beginning as an al Qaeda splinter group, ISIS (the Islamic State in Iraq)—also known as Islamic State in Iraq and the Levant (ISIL) and the Islamic State (IS)—thrived and mutated during the civil war in Syria and in the security vacuum that followed the departure of American forces from Iraq. In June 2014, ISIS came to the attention of Americans when it captured several Iraqi cities, including Mosul, the second largest city in the country. ISIS proclaimed the creation of a caliphate that erased all state borders and claimed authority over all the world's Muslims. In July, several Syrian cities fell to ISIS, as did the country's major oil field. By September, ISIS controlled hundreds of square miles in Iraq and Syria where state authority had evaporated.

Pictures of thousands of refugees fleeing the fighting and stories of the potential of genocide raised public alarm, as did words of warning from military leaders and intelligence officials. Graphic videos of the beheading of two American journalists, James Foley and Steven Sotloff, angered and scared the public, who were horrified by the brutality of ISIS rule.

In the first days of September 2014, 59 percent of the public felt that ISIS posed a "very serious threat" to the United States, and another 41 percent viewed the threat as "somewhat serious." There was diversity within this seeming consensus, however. Republicans were much more likely than Democrats or Independents to view the threat from ISIS as "very serious."[9] Similarly, Republicans were much more concerned about Islamic extremism than Democrats or Independents.[10] Nevertheless, large majorities of each party group were apprehensive about ISIS.

The predispositions of the partisan groups were somewhat complicated. The 2014 Chicago Council on Global Affairs survey found that both Republicans and Independents, along with Democrats, had become disillusioned with the wars in both Afghanistan and Iraq. Democrats were somewhat more likely than Republicans to support an active international role for the United States, a first in the 40-year history of the Council's polling. Independents, as in the past, were the most likely to want the United States to stay out of world affairs. Nevertheless, Republicans were generally more willing than other partisans to use force.[11]

The first three polls listed in table 7.13 reveal that public support for military action against ISIS in Iraq grew substantially and uniformly from June to the first week of September. In June, only Republicans displayed support for military action, while Independents and Democrats were reluctant to do so. At least for Democrats, this reluctance reflected their core orientation toward military action. By early September, no doubt in response to the graphic violence in the news, Republicans had increased their support for air strikes by 25 percentage points, Independents by 26 percentage points, and Democrats by 23. Support for air strikes against ISIS in Syria in the September 4–7 poll was also high for all partisan groups. Americans appeared to be responding to what they saw on television and YouTube.

Obama responded to the concerns of both the public and elites in a nationally televised address on September 10, 2014. He announced his intention to use U.S. military force to "degrade and destroy" ISIS, ordering airstrikes against its forces in Iraq and Syria. The president argued that the powers vested in him as commander in chief, coupled with the Authorization for the Use of Military Force Against Iraq that Congress passed in 2002, provided the authority for his actions. He also asked Congress to authorize the arming and training of Syrian rebel forces.

How did the public react to the president? First, overall opinion about the seriousness of the threat ISIS posed to the United States did not change at all in the period following the president's speech. Indeed, the stability of opinion is striking. There was no net movement from the "fairly serious" to the "very serious" category (table 7.14).

There were differences among partisan groups in views of the appropriate response to the ISIS threat, however. Table 7.15 shows the results of a poll taken in the days immediately after the president's national address.

TABLE 7.13. Support for Military Action against ISIS

Poll Date	All	Republicans	Independents	Democrats
		% Support		
Airstrikes in Iraq				
June 18–22, 2014[1]	45	58	41	44
August 13–17, 2014[1]	54	61	49	54
September 4–7, 2014[1]	71	83	67	67
September 11–14, 2014	*53*	*64*	*47*	*60*
September 12–15, 2014[2]	71	83	64	72
October 3–6, 2014[2]	73	71	70	71
Airstrikes in Syria				
September 4–7, 2014[3]	65	74	64	60
September 11–14, 2014	*53*	*64*	*47*	*60*
September 12–15, 2014[4]	69	84	63	68
October 3–6, 2014[4]	72	70	70	69

Sources and Questions

Pew Research Center Poll: "As you may know, Barack Obama has announced a plan for a military campaign against Islamic militants in Iraq and Syria, involving U.S. airstrikes and U.S. military training for opposition groups. Overall, do you approve or disapprove of this plan?"
[1] *Washington Post*-ABC News Poll: "Overall, do you support or oppose U.S. airstrikes against the Sunni insurgents in Iraq?"
[2] CBS News/*New York Times* Poll: "Do you favor or oppose U.S. airstrikes against ISIS militants in Iraq?"
[3] *Washington Post*-ABC News Poll: "Do you support or oppose expanding U.S. air strikes against the Sunni insurgents into Syria?"
[4] CBS News/*New York Times* Poll: "Do you favor or oppose U.S. airstrikes against ISIS militants in Syria?"

TABLE 7.14. Seriousness of the ISIS Threat

Poll Date	% Very Serious	% Fairly Serious	% Somewhat Serious	% Not So Serious
September 5–7, 2014	45	22	23	10
September 25–28, 2014	45	23	23	8

Source: CNN/ORC Poll.

Question: "How serious a threat do you think ISIS poses to the United States—very serious, fairly serious, just somewhat serious, or not so serious?"

TABLE 7.15. Concerns about Military Action against ISIS

Party Group	% Go Too Far	% Not Go Far Enough
Republicans	21	71
Independents	42	40
Democrats	54	27

Source: Pew Research Center poll, September 11–14, 2014.

Question: "What concerns you more about U.S. military action? That the U.S. will go too far in getting involved in the situation. [or] That the U.S. will not go far enough in stopping Islamic militants."

We can see that Republicans were worried that his proposal did not go far enough and thus would not effectively counter ISIS. Conversely, Democrats worried that the president's actions would go too far and thus involve the United States more deeply in combat. Independents were split between these fears.[12]

Response to the president's proposals was not what the White House hoped. The results of the Pew Research Center September 11–14, 2014, poll reported in table 7.13, which are displayed in italics in both halves of the table, show public support for Obama's proposed course of action, including airstrikes in Iraq and Syria and military training for opposition groups. Unlike the other poll questions covered in the table, this one mentions the president by name.

Republicans had a strong aversion to Obama, as we have seen, and gave him only 8 percent approval in the week of September 1–7. Independents accorded him only 34 percent approval during the same period. Both figures were near the all-time lows for the groups.[13] Similarly, Americans' trust in the federal government to handle international problems fell to a record low of 43 percent in Gallup's September 4–7, 2014, poll. Republicans were at 27 percent and Independents were at 39 percent. Democrats' trust in the federal government had been far less shaken than that of Republicans and Independents over the previous two years and stood at 70 percent.

It is perhaps unsurprising that when asked specifically about Obama's plan, the support of both Republicans and Independents for the president's plan *decreased* dramatically from their support for airstrikes in Iraq just a week earlier. Republican approval dropped by 19 percentage points while Independents' support dropped by 20 percentage points. Similarly, Republican support for airstrikes in Syria dropped 10 percentage points from its levels regarding airstrikes against Syria, while that of Independents declined by 17 percentage points.

In the face of the substantial decline in approval of the president's plan among other party groups, Democratic support held steady in relation to the week-earlier poll on air strikes in Syria and declined by only 7 percentage points from its previous reading on air strikes in Iraq. It is possible that motivated reasoning played a role for at least some Democrats, who were reassured by their party's leader. Nevertheless, it seems clear that the president's association with the policy of military action against ISIS was not a net advantage. Indeed, it appears to have lowered support for military action.

Of equal importance, however, was the public's support for the core of the president's policy, air strikes against Iraq and Syria, in the absence of reference to the president. In this case, support was remarkably stable, as we can see in the poll taken on September 12–15, 2014. Republican support for airstrikes in Iraq did not change at all from where it stood before the president's speech, and Independent support declined just 3 percentage points. Democratic support increased 5 percentage points. It is possible that Democrats were responding to the president, but the basic ratios of support among the party groups remained similar to what they were in August. Overall, cross-pressuring seems to have had a modest impact at best.

The results for Independents and Democrats for airstrikes in Syria were more encouraging for the White House. Although Independents decreased their support by 1 percentage point, Democratic support increased by 8 percentage points and, in the absence of direct reference to the president, Republicans increased their support for the airstrikes by 10 percentage points, bringing it to a similar level as their support for airstrikes against Iraq.

The next step was congressional authorization for the arming and training Syrian rebel forces. Speaker John Boehner—who took the unusual step of voting for the Syria proposal—and his leadership team worked closely with White House officials and congressional Democrats to whip nervous lawmakers and drive the vote count as high as possible. On September 17, in a rare bipartisan show of support, the House approved the president's plan to arm and train rebels in Syria by a vote of 273-156. The majority included 159 Republicans and 114 Democrats. The Senate voted to authorize the president to arm and train Syrian rebels to fight against ISIS the next day by a vote of 78-22. Forty-five Democrats and 33 Republicans supported the bill.

Despite the pleas of party leaders and personal lobbying by Obama and other senior White House officials, an unusual coalition of antiwar Democrats, isolationist-leaning Republicans, libertarians, and hawks with grave doubts that the training mission would work opposed the bill. Many thought the administration's proposal was a step toward sending American combat troops back into Iraq or dragging the United States into Syria's bloody civil war. Thus, 85 Democrats (43 percent) and 71 Republicans (30 percent) opposed the measure in the House. In the Senate, 10 Democrats and 12 Republicans opposed the bill. These dissenters reflected the division of opinion within the parties in the electorate, as we have seen in table 7.15.

When the dust settled in early October, an unusual convergence of opinion occurred among the partisan groups and across airstrikes in both Iraq and Syria. Support for airstrikes in Iraq and in Syria was within 1 percentage point for each group (table 7.13). Moreover, there was virtually no difference among the groups in their support for airstrikes in each country. Either presidential leadership was so dominant that every group deferred to the White House uniformly, which seems highly unlikely, or broader forces were at work influencing public opinion.

If we examine changes in the public's support over the previous month, starting from before the president addressed the nation, we see how this consensus developed. Support for air strikes in Iraq decreased by 12 percentage points for Republicans, increased by 3 points for Independents, and by 4 percentage points for Democrats. There are somewhat similar results for air strikes in Syria. Republican support was down 4 percentage points, Independent support increased by 6 points, and Democratic support was up 9 points.

In sum, the highly visible threat posed by ISIS seems to have impelled the bulk of public opinion. The response of the greatly conflicted and entanglement-averse Independents indicates that the issue itself rather than presidential persuasion was driving opinion. Nevertheless, some Democrats may have been reassured by their party's leader and overcome their concerns of greater involvement in foreign conflicts. Even if we attribute all the net increase in support for air strikes in Iraq over the period of early September to early October to the president's leadership, the net gain was very modest—2 percentage points. It was slightly greater—7 percentage points—for air strikes in Syria.

Lessons

What do these cases tell us about the impact of presidential cross-pressuring? On the issue of NSA surveillance programs, the president did not engage in a fruitless attempt to persuade Democrats to change either their basic values or their orientations toward policy. Obama defended the surveillance programs, of course, offering reassurance about the protection of civil liberties. However, he did not engage in the kind of campaigning he employed, for example, on behalf of health care reform or fiscal cliff–related tax increases. Unsurprisingly, some, although certainly not

TABLE 7.16. Partisan Approval of NSA Surveillance Programs

Party Group	June 2013		January 2014		Change
	% Approve	% Disapprove	% Approve	% Disapprove	% Approve
All	48	47	40	53	–8
Republican	45	51	37	56	–8
Democrat	58	38	46	48	–12
Independent	42	53	38	57	–4

Source: Pew Research Center poll (June 6–9, 2013) and Pew Research Center and USA Today poll (January 15–19, 2014).

Question: "Overall, do you approve or disapprove of the government's collection of telephone and Internet data as part of anti-terrorism efforts?"

all, Democrats in the public were reassured. There is no evidence that Democrats changed their concerns for either privacy or security. They simply were more likely to trust the government to make the appropriate trade-off with one of their own in the White House.

Because cross-pressuring asks people to move against their policy proclivities, it may have only short-term effects, if it has any at all. Despite the pull of partisanship, it is difficult to turn people against their core instincts. The support of Democrats for the NSA surveillance programs was short-lived. By January 2014, approval had declined among all partisan groups, especially among Democrats (table 7.16). Although they remained more supportive of the surveillance program than Republicans, they now disapproved by a 48 percent to 46 percent margin.

Rather than attracting support from the opposition party, cross-pressuring may antagonize it. Those predisposed to oppose the president may increase their opposition to his policy—even if they otherwise might support it. Despite the fact that most Republican leaders *supported* the NSA's surveillance programs, grassroots Republican opinion changed toward *opposition* to those programs. This change reflected the response of Republicans to a Democrat in the White House and reflected their broad, implacable opposition to the president.

Regarding military action on behalf of the Syrian rebels, the president did not ask Democrats to change their general opposition to a more aggressive foreign policy or the use of force. Instead, he asked them to trust him to limit U.S. involvement and defend consensual humanitarian interests. Democrats' initial responses to aid to the Syrian rebels were to the party leader rather than the policy. Nevertheless, the president's attempts to gain public support for military intervention in Syria were even less successful than his efforts to obtain support for NSA surveillance of the American people.

The public simply would not support military aid or military strikes. Democrats were more responsive to the White House than were Republicans. Even so, they *increased* their opposition at the very time the president was intensifying his persuasive efforts. Even a nationally televised address could not garner a Democratic plurality. Similarly, some Republican leaders supported U.S. military interventions in Syria but the Republican grassroots responded negatively to both aid and airstrikes. Moreover, Republican support for airstrikes, already low, plummeted as the president increased his efforts to obtain public support.

The president also did not ask Democrats to weaken their support for health care reform. He only asked them to trust him that a delay in the employer mandate was necessary for the long-term health of the policy. In this case, his co-partisans responded to him rather than to their policy preferences, while Republicans moved in the other direction. Perhaps because the policy was only a "delay" made it easier for Democrats to accept.

When faced with the advance of ISIS, the president emphasized the consensual value of protecting the country against terrorism. He also asked Democrats to trust him to limit U.S. involvement. There is some evidence that a small percentage of Democrats overcame their initial reluctance to support military action against ISIS in response to the president, but events on the ground and news coverage of them seemed to be more important than the White House in driving public opinion.

Indeed, in this case Republicans were not put off by the president's leadership and favored an aggressive use of American force, including sending troops. By February 2015, 86 percent of Republicans saw ISIS as a threat to the security of the United States, and 72 percent favored sending ground troops to fight ISIS militants.[14]

In the end, the absence of persuasion, the potential of only short-term effects, and the negative impact of on opposition party identifiers limited the utility of cross-pressuring for building supportive coalitions for the White House.

CHANNELING THE PUBLIC

Cross-pressuring the public on specific issues is a short-term strategy. Channeling opposition party identifiers to support a broader party program is a longer process but one that may have significant consequences for politics and public policy. Channeling involves parties and leaders signaling to opposition party identifiers a commonality of interests and increasing the salience of these shared interests in voting decisions.

There is a substantial literature on party coalitions. We know who is in them and how their allegiances have changed over time. However, we have just scratched the surface of understanding the role that presidents and their top supporters play in exploiting the potential of channeling the public and thus facilitating change. In an era in which the parties are less polarized than they are in the twenty-first century, such as in the decades before the election of Ronald Reagan in 1980, the leaders of one party may find large numbers of identifiers with the other party agree with them on key issues. Under such conditions, the president may appeal to opposition party identifiers, even attracting them to change their party allegiance to more closely align their partisan identification with their ideology.

The rise of new issues has the potential to destabilize or even destroy party coalitions, and effective leaders will recognize and channel this potential to help build a new governing coalition. The most dramatic example of such leadership in the past half century occurred after pressure from the civil rights movement, along with Lyndon Johnson's unwavering commitment and legislative acumen, resulted in the passage of the 1964 Civil Rights Act.

Republican Barry Goldwater's victory in five southern states in the presidential election that fall marked a critical stage in the transformation in the political allegiance and voting behavior of citizens in the South. Republicans, led by Richard Nixon, saw that the alienation of many southerners from their former home in the Democratic Party provided them the opportunity to engage in a "southern strategy" to win converts among conservative white southerners—and they did.

Edward Carmines and James Stimson have shown how the emergence of race as a new issue cleavage in the 1960s caused many Americans to change their party allegiances.[15] Although race was the issue that pushed many conservative Democrats toward the Republican Party, Republican leaders also attracted support by stressing patriotism, religious values, and traditional (and thus conservative) positions on social issues to attract voters alienated by the Democrats' antiwar stances and apparent sympathy for views ranging from support for greater protections for alleged criminals to a wide separation between church and state. Republicans also began stressing economic issues,[16] which the emerging white middle class in the South found especially attractive.[17] When the Supreme Court made abortion a constitutional right in *Roe v. Wade* in 1973, opposition to abortion fit seamlessly with the Republicans' emphasis and further defined the parties, attracting additional adherents and mobilizing new legions of activists.

The result of the party realignment was Republican domination of presidential elections for two generations after 1964. Only two Democrats won in the four decades following that election, and only one, Jimmy Carter in 1976, running on the heels of Watergate, received a majority of the vote. The changes in party identification that aided Republican candidates did not occur overnight, nor even within the period of one presidency. Nevertheless, by recognizing and exploiting the opportunity to build a new governing coalition, Republican leaders profoundly influenced the direction of public policy.

The political landscape did not change because leaders persuaded people to alter their views about race, abortion, or other issues. (It is noteworthy that grassroots organizations and local protests of ordinary people had more impact in shaping public opinion on civil rights than did elites.[18]) As Gary Jacobson put it, "as strategic vote-seekers, candidates and parties anticipate voters' potential responses to their political initiatives and so are constrained by them. . . . In adopting positions, politicians are guided by the opportunities and constraints presented by existing configurations of public opinion on political issues."[19]

Instead of changing the public's opinions, leaders acted consistent with Morris Fiorina's view that leaders can take positions that split the public in a new way without the public changing its opinions.[20] Republican leaders attracted new voters to their party by reacting to events that were not of their making, such as the war in Vietnam, urban riots, and Supreme Court decisions. They responded by articulating views with which the voters agreed and making these views more salient in voting decisions.

CONCLUSION

There are times when the president's stances are contrary to the views of his co-partisans. Such positions cross-pressure co-partisans between their policy predispositions and the policies of their party's leader. We have found that some partisans follow the president's signals, even when his views are contrary to their own policy preferences. Such changes in opinion may be short-lived, however, providing the president a fragile base for coalition-building.

When the president is cross-pressuring his co-partisans, he may very well be doing the same with opposition party identifiers. In this case, however, he is taking stands consistent with their policy preferences. Yet the president cannot depend on successfully reaching out to the opposition. Indeed, in an era of partisan polarization he is more likely to antagonize it and thus increase disapproval of his policy.

In some eras, presidents emphasize broad themes designed to expand their coalitions in the long run by attracting adherents from the opposition party. It is possible for the White House to succeed in such efforts, changing the face of American politics without changing the policy preferences of individual Americans.

CHAPTER 8

Reaching the Base

THE PREVIOUS THREE chapters have explored the utility of the president leading without persuading by exploiting the views of those who agree with him on specific policies or who are generally predisposed to follow his lead. Chapter 6 also examined the president's ability to influence fluid opinion. In each case, the simplifying assumption has been that the president signaled his views directly to the public. This assumption, of course, is not strictly correct.

Despite all their efforts to lead public opinion, presidents do not directly reach the American people on a day-to-day basis. For more than two centuries the primary intermediary between the president and the public was the press, first newspapers and then radio and television. It was the traditional news media that provided people with most of what they knew about chief executives, their policies, and their policies' consequences. The press, in turn, found coverage of the president indispensable in satisfying its audience and reporting on the most significant political events through a story line that personalized government and policymaking.

The White House communications environment has undergone a sea change, however. The president cannot depend on broadly focused newspapers, network television, and radio to reach the public. In response, the White House has embraced the latest technology to take its case to the people. At its core, the new modes of communication offer an opportunity to bypass the press and communicate directly with the public.

These changes raise a host of important questions about how the current technology impacts the president's relations with the traditional media and the nature of the media's coverage of the president. For our purposes, however, the key question is whether advances in technology make it easier for the president to lead without persuading. In this chapter I explore the challenges the new communications environment presents for the White House and the potential for the president to exploit the new media to signal likely supporters and reinforce their predispositions to back his initiatives.

THE FRAGMENTED AUDIENCE

One of the most salient characteristics of the modern media environment is its fragmentation. Reflecting on the presidency as recently as the tenure of Ronald Reagan, Barack Obama's press secretary, Jay Carney, observed, "You would reach almost every voter in the country. And that's not even remotely the case now. The only way you get that many eyeballs at one time is to have an enormous event, something like killing bin Laden."[1]

"Like any period of tumultuous change, it's not a happy one," adds Obama's former communications director Anita Dunn. "This idea that somehow there's a bully pulpit that can be used effectively," Dunn says, "to communicate with everybody in this country at the same time and get them all wrapped around one issue—it's very much an idea whose time has passed."[2] "That's why we do all the unorthodox stuff, putting him [the president] in unusual places," Carney said—like Obama's appearance on the Web series *Between Two Ferns*—"just to try to reach people where they are. Because where they're not is watching the news or reading the newspapers."[3]

Wide viewership was common during the early decades of television. Presidential speeches routinely attracted more than 80 percent of those watching television.[4] Things have changed. Audiences for presidential speeches and press conferences have declined steadily since the Nixon administration in the early 1970s.[5] Only 40 million viewers saw at least part of George W. Bush's first nationally televised address on February 27, 2001, compared with 67 million viewers for Bill Clinton's first nationally televised address in 1993.[6]

Barack Obama attracted more than 52 million viewers to his nationally televised first address in February 2009, which occurred during a severe economic crisis. The size of his audience dropped off substantially, however. When he spoke on behalf of his health care reform proposal the following September, for example, he drew only 32 million viewers, a typical audience for his national addresses (table 8.1).

The root cause of this drop in viewership is access to alternatives to watching the president provided by cable, the Internet, and television.[7] Almost all households receive cable service and also own a DVD player (providing still more opportunities to avoid watching the president).[8] Doz-

TABLE 8.1. Audiences for Obama Nationally Televised Speeches and Press Conferences

Date	Venue	Topic	Audience Size
February 9, 2009	White House	Press conference	49.5 million
February 24, 2009	Joint Session of Congress	Overview of administration	52.4 million
March 24, 2009	White House	Press conference	40.4 million
April 29, 2009	White House	Press conference	28.8 million
July 22, 2009	White House	Press conference	24.7 million
September 9, 2009	Joint Session of Congress	Health care reform	32.1 million
December 1, 2009	USMA, West Point	Afghanistan	40.8 million
January 27, 2010	Joint Session of Congress	State of the Union message	48.0 million
June 15, 2010	Oval Office	Gulf of Mexico oil spill	32.1 million
August 31, 2010	Oval Office	End of Iraq War	29.2 million
January 12, 2011	Tucson, Arizona	Memorial for shooting victims	30.8 million
January 25, 2011	Joint Session of Congress	State of the Union message	42.8 million
March 28, 2011	National Defense University	Libya	25.6 million
May 1, 2011	White House	Death of Osama bin Laden	56.7 million
June 22, 2011*	White House	Troops cuts in Afghanistan	25.4 million
July 25, 2011	White House	Debt limit	30.3 million

September 8, 2011	Joint Session of Congress	Jobs proposals	31.4 million
January 24, 2012	Joint Session of Congress	State of the Union message	37.8 million
May 1, 2012†	Afghanistan	War in Afghanistan	NA
September 6, 2012	Charlotte, North Carolina	Acceptance of Democratic nomination	35.7 million
January 21, 2013⁺	Capitol	Inaugural Address	20.6 million
February 12, 2013	Joint Session of Congress	State of the Union message	33.5 million
September 10, 2013	White House	Syria	32.3 million
September 27, 2013†	White House	Budget	NA
September 30, 2013†	White House	Budget	NA
October 16, 2013	White House	Budget/government shutdown	NA
November 23, 2013†	White House	Iran nuclear capability	NA
January 28, 2014	Joint Session of Congress	State of the Union message	33.3 million
September 10, 2014	White House	Islamic State of Iraq and the Levant	34.2 million
November 20, 2014‡	White House	Immigration	13.8 million
January 20, 2015	Joint Session of Congress	State of the Union message	31.7 million

Source: Nielsen Company.

* Univision did not carry the speech.

† Not delivered in prime time; no audience ratings.

⁺ Not delivered in prime time.

‡ ABC, CBS, and NBC did not broadcast the speech.

ens of new networks have no news departments and thus run entertainment programming during important speeches, creating yet another distraction from tuning in to the president.

Television is a medium in which visual interest, action, and conflict are most effective. Unfortunately, presidential speeches are unlikely to contain these characteristics. Only a few addresses to the nation—such as President George W. Bush's address to a joint session of Congress on September 20, 2001—occur at moments of high drama.

The public's general lack of interest in politics constrains the president's leadership of public opinion in the long run, as well as on any given day. Although they have unparalleled access to the American people, presidents cannot make much use of it. If they do, their speeches will become commonplace and lose their drama and interest. That is one reason why presidents do not make formal speeches to the public on television very often—only four or five times a year, on average.[9] Recent presidents, beginning with Richard Nixon, have turned to radio and midday addresses to supplement their prime-time televised addresses,[10] although media coverage of these addresses has diminished over the years.[11]

In addition to the challenge of attracting an audience for the president's television appearances, the White House faces the obstacle of obtaining television coverage in the first place. Traditionally, presidents could rely on full network coverage of any statement they wished to make directly to the American people or any press conference they wished to be televised. The networks began to rebel against providing airtime in the 1970s and 1980s when one or more of them occasionally refused to carry an address or a prime-time press conference held by Presidents Ford, Carter, Reagan, or Bush. Bill Clinton encountered so much resistance from the networks to covering his speeches and press conferences that he held only four evening press conferences in his eight years in office (only one of which all the networks covered live) and made only six addresses on domestic policy, all of them in his first term.

In the two months following the terrorist attacks on the United States on September 11, 2001, George W. Bush received plenty of prime-time coverage for his speeches and a press conference. By November 8, however, most networks viewed the president's speech on the U.S. response to terrorism as an event rather than news and did not carry it. Nearly a year later, on October 7, 2002, Bush made his most comprehensive address regarding the likely need to use force against Saddam Hussein's regime in Iraq. Nevertheless, the TV networks ABC, CBS, NBC, and PBS chose not to carry the president's speech, arguing that it contained little that was new.

The president has a problem sending his signals more indirectly, as well as through prime-time presentations. The audience for the network evening news broadcasts stood at 23.7 million people in 2014, a 55 percent decline in viewership since 1980. The audience for prime-time cable news dropped to about 2.8 million in November 2014.[12] Between 1980 and 2014, daily newspaper circulation dropped nearly 21.8 million to 40.4 million—a decline of 35 percent; Sunday circulation dropped 11.9 million to 42.8 million—a decline of 22 percent.[13] Thus, the Obama White House had to innovate to reach the public and survive in this new communications environment.

REACHING THE AUDIENCE

Although technological change and corporate resistance have made it more difficult for the president to attract an audience on television, other changes may have increased the White House's prospects of reaching the public. Teddy Roosevelt gave prominence to the bully pulpit by exploiting the hunger of modern newspapers for national news. Franklin D. Roosevelt broadened the reach and immediacy of presidential communications with his use of radio. More recently, John F. Kennedy and Ronald Reagan mastered the use of television to speak directly to the American people. Now Barack Obama has positioned himself as the first Internet president.

It is a good thing he has. The Pew Research Center reports:

> The vast majority of Americans now get news in some digital format. In 2013, 82 percent of Americans said they got news on a desktop or laptop and 54 percent said they got news on a mobile device. Beyond that, 35 percent reported that they get news in this way "frequently" on their desktop or laptop, and 21 percent on a mobile device (cellphone or tablet).[14]

The Internet, which emerged in 2008 as a leading source for campaign news, has now surpassed all other media except television as a main source for national and international news. More people say they rely mostly on the Internet for news than say they rely mostly on newspapers (although people often turn to the websites of traditional news sources for their news).[15] Young people are even more likely to report that they rely on the Internet as a main source of national and international news.[16]

The 2008 Campaign

Realizing that they could no longer depend on reaching the public through the traditional media, Obama's 2008 election campaign team made great efforts to put the candidate's messages directly in voters' inboxes, social-media feeds, and television sets.[17] Significant strategy announcements were often made in the form of videos, with campaign manager David Plouffe speaking directly at the camera, rather than through news releases or strategic interviews.[18]

Obama distributed his 2007 announcement of his candidacy for the presidency via Web video, revealed his vice presidential selection via text message, recruited about 13 million online supporters during the campaign, and used the electronic medium to sidestep mainstream media and speak directly with voters throughout the primaries and general-election campaign. This practice forged a firsthand connection and may have encouraged some supporters to feel they had a greater stake in the campaign's success. Some Obama videos became YouTube phenomena: millions of people viewed his speech on the Rev. Jeremiah A. Wright, Jr., and race in America and his victory speech in Grant Park on November 4, 2008.

The new administration was oriented to exploiting advances in technology to communicate more effectively than ever with the public. Bush State Department spokesman Sean McCormack started filing posts from far-flung regions during trips with his boss, Secretary of State Condoleezza Rice. On October 31, 2008, McCormack unveiled "Briefing 2.0" in the press briefing room of the State Department in which he took questions from the public rather than the press and then put the session on YouTube.[19]

The Obama White House wanted to do more. "It's really about reaching an extra person or a larger audience of people who wouldn't normally pay attention to policy," said Jen Psaki, a spokeswoman for Obama's transition team. "We have to think creatively about how we would do that in the White House, because promoting a speech in front of 100,000 people is certainly different than promoting energy legislation."[20]

Videos

On November 18, 2008, about 10 million of Barack Obama's supporters received an email message from the president-elect's campaign manager, David Plouffe. Labeled "Where we go from here," Plouffe asked backers to "help shape the future of this movement" by answering an online survey, which in turn asked them to rank four priorities in order of importance. First on the list was "Helping Barack's administration pass legislation through grassroots efforts."[21]

Plouffe's email message revealed much about Obama's initial approach to governing. Even before taking office, the president-elect began making Saturday radio addresses—but with a twist. In addition to beaming his addresses to radio stations nationwide, he recorded them for digital video and audio downloads from YouTube, iTunes, Myspace, and the like. As a result, people could access them whenever and wherever they wanted. "Turning the weekly radio address from audio to video and making it on-demand has turned the radio address from a blip on the radar to something that can be a major news-making event any Saturday we choose," declared Dan Pfeiffer, the incoming White House deputy communications director. Videos are also easy to produce: a videographer can record Obama delivering the address in fewer than 15 minutes.[22] After his inauguration, the White House put the president's Saturday videos on both the White House website and a White House channel on YouTube.

The Obama White House produces and distributes much more video than any past administration. To do so, it maintains a staff devoted to producing online videos for whitehouse.gov, Obama's YouTube channel, and other video depots such as Vine. A search for "Barack Obama" is stacked with videos approved and uploaded by the administration (which viewers may not realize). When filming a presidential speech, the production team tailors the video to the site, with titles, omissions, crowd cutaways, highlight footage, and a dozen other manipulations of sound and image that affect the impression they make, including applause that is difficult to edit out.[23] The president's YouTube channel had more than 650 video uploads in its first year alone.[24]

The administration provides an extensive blog (The White House Blog) offering short stories accompanied by photos and videos. In addition, the White House streams live events and provides podcasts of speeches, remarks, events, and briefings. The administration also introduced *West Wing Week*, a video blog consisting of six- to seven-minute compilations that appear each week on the White House's website and on such video-sharing sites as YouTube. The items offer what a narrator on each segment calls "your guide to everything that's happening at 1600 Pennsylvania Avenue."The White House has adopted other strategies such as hosting an animated page, making a video on BuzzFeed, having Obama appear on the Internet show *Between Two Ferns* and on the comedy website *Funny or Die*, and agreeing to interviews with the president on *The Daily Show* and *The Colbert Report*. (Obama's aides took unusual steps to cultivate *The Daily Show* host Jon Stewart, including arranging two visits to see the president.[25]) White House assistants even encourage the president and others to pose for "selfies" and other funny pictures. In hopes of it going viral, staff members promote such content to popular sites such as Upworthy, which is known for its eye-catching headlines. Within a week, the BuzzFeed video, which was designed to encourage young people to sign up for Obamacare, had nearly 1.75 million viewers on BuzzFeed and within two weeks had more than 50 million more on Facebook.

Messaging

"What's the first page on Google and Bing look like?" asked Dan Pfeiffer, the president's senior adviser and longtime communications strategist. "Let's take Benghazi," referring to the partisan battle over the administration's response to the attacks on U.S. facilities in Libya in 2012. "Is it five things from *Free Beacon* and *Breitbart*? Or is it something from the *New York Times* or is it from the *New Republic*?" If the administration's perspective is not well represented in the Google search results, "we have to ask: Does it mean we need to do a better job of getting our message out?"[26]

Pfeiffer maintained that the White House is not bypassing traditional media such as news conferences and other events. But he said it is more important than ever to do late-night comedy and daytime talk shows, ESPN, and MTV. "It used to be that Ronald Reagan or, to a lesser extent, Bill Clinton could give a national address," he said. "We don't have that option. We have to go where the public is."[27]

To more fully exploit developments in communications technology, the Obama White House established an Office of New Media, which would later become the Office of Digital Strategy. It has flooded niche media markets via blogs, Twitter feeds, Facebook posts, and Flickr photo streams in addition to videos on YouTube, Vine, Upworthy, and other outlets. For example, in the months following the 2014 midterm elections, the president announced his plans for immigration, net neutrality, and increasing the affordability of college on social media platforms—rather than issuing press releases for the traditional press.[28]

The White House regularly alerts its more than 5 million Twitter followers of the president's policy stances. When he nominated Sonia Sotomayor to the U.S. Supreme Court, Obama sent a video appealing for support for his candidate to the huge email list of supporters accumulated during his campaign and the Democratic Party's own lists. The email message included a directive from the president to share his views via Facebook, Twitter, and other Web connections.[29]

Even more impressive, Obama's official Twitter feed, with 62 million followers in 2015, reaches more people than all of the nightly news broadcasts combined and more than the total circulation of all daily newspapers. On May 18, 2015, President Obama started his own Twitter account. By July 21, he had 67 million followers. Equally imposing is the president's Facebook page, which has 45 million likes.

In addition, the White House tracks journalists' tweets for comments it might view as inaccurate, incomplete, or unfair, as well as for clues about what the press is reporting and how it might portray the president or the administration. An aide then flags the tweets in mass emails to more than

80 Obama aides, who then respond, sometimes with "obscenity-laced yelps of outrage."[30]

The Obama administration has shown some deftness at catering to a nonstop, Internet- and cable-television-driven news cycle. For example, the White House went to great lengths to project an image of competence in U.S. relief efforts in Haiti, in implicit contrast to the way the Bush administration handled Hurricane Katrina and its aftermath. The administration and the military set up a busy communications operation with 25 people at the American Embassy and in a cinder-block warehouse at the airport in Port-au-Prince, Haiti's capital. The public relations team released a torrent of news releases, briefings, fact sheets, and statements, including a "ticktock" (a newspaper term of art for a minute-by-minute reconstruction of how momentous events unfolded), a link to a Flickr photo of a meeting on Haiti in the Situation Room, presided over by the president, a video of American search teams rescuing a Haitian woman from a collapsed building, and a list of foreign leaders he had telephoned.[31]

Politico.com is a prominent face of the new media at the White House. It is a bulletin board of the stories on which the media is focused and what is happening in Washington on a given day. The White House starts communicating with Politico early in the day to try to influence what others will view as important. It also uses Politico as a forum to rebut directly its adversaries in front of the rest of the news media.[32]

Internet Interviews

Obama made the case for his economic agenda in a variety of forums, including *The Tonight Show*, *60 Minutes*, and a prime-time news conference. On March 26, 2009, he added a new arrow to his quiver. The president held an "Open for Questions" town hall meeting in the East Room of the White House. Bill Clinton and George W. Bush answered questions over the Internet, but Obama was the first to do so in a live video format, streamed directly onto the White House website.

For more than an hour, the president answered questions culled from 104,000 sent via the Internet. Online voters cast more than 3.5 million votes for their favorite questions, some of which an economic adviser who served as a moderator then posed to the president. The president took other queries from a live audience of about 100 nurses, teachers, businesspeople, and others assembled at the White House.

The questions covered topics such as health care, education, the economy, the auto industry, and housing. In most cases, Obama used his answers to advocate his policies. Although the questions from the audience in the East Room were mostly from campaign backers, the White House was not in complete control of the session. One of the questions that drew the most votes online was whether legalizing marijuana might stimulate the economy by allowing the government to regulate and tax the drug. (The White House listed the question on its website under the topics "green jobs and energy" and "budget." White House officials later indicated that interest groups drove up those numbers.[33])

On February 1, 2010, the president sat for a first-of-its-kind group interview with YouTube viewers, who submitted thousands of questions and heard the president answer some in a live Webcast. YouTube viewers voted for their favorite questions, and Steve Grove, the head of news and politics at YouTube, selected the ones to ask in the half-hour session.

On April 21, 2011, Obama sat down with Facebook founder Mark Zuckerberg and answered questions from Zuckerberg and Facebook users. The president next turned to Twitter. On July 6, 2011, he held the first Twitter town hall meeting, live from the East Room of the White House. The hour-long session involved the president answering questions submitted by Twitter users and selected in part by ten Twitter users around the country chosen by Twitter. Twitter's chief executive, Jack Dorsey, moderated the session. The president also answered questions in a town hall meeting on LinkedIn on September 26, 2011.

In January 2015, the president met with three YouTube stars—GloZell Green (aka "The Queen of YouTube"), Bethany Mota, and Hank Green—to discuss his upcoming State of the Union address. The next month Obama granted a pair of fast-growing digital media companies, Vox and BuzzFeed, their first interviews with the president.

Specialized News

The fragmentation of the media has provided the White House opportunities to tap into the market for specialized news. For example, the Obama administration holds regular question-and-answer Webcasts, "Open for Questions," with policy officials on White House.gov. In addition, the president has granted interviews to websites that are largely ignored in Washington but have large online audiences, such as Zillow for housing or WebMD for health care news.

In early May 2014, Obama and his staff spent hours giving top weather forecasters the royal treatment—a briefing in the Roosevelt Room with multiple cabinet secretaries and senior officials on a major new report on climate change, plus Rose Garden interviews with the president. The explanation for this outreach effort is that Americans have more trust in meteorologists than in political figures or the mainstream media to discuss climate change.[34]

The White House has made special efforts to speak directly to the huge and politically powerful audience of Latinos. A multimedia public relations campaign pushing for an overhaul of the nation's immigration system—delivered in Spanish and in English daily—reached millions of Hispanics across the country. The president sat for six lengthy interviews on Telemundo and Univision in January, March, and May 2013. In addition, Cecilia Muñoz, the director of the White House domestic policy council, appeared on the networks regularly, and the president's weekly Internet address was matched each Saturday by a corresponding one in Spanish by an administration official. Online, the White House office of Hispanic media posted messages on Twitter in both English and Spanish from @lacasablanca, which had more than 40,000 followers.[35]

Local News

Another way to reach the public is when they are watching local television news. Nearly three-quarters of Americans watch local television news at least once a month, more than watch the network news.[36] Once the Washington press reports an issue, it tends to drop it and move on to the next one; however, repetition is necessary to convey the president's views to the generally inattentive public. Moreover, the Washington press tends to place more emphasis on the support of, or opposition to, a program than on its substance, although the White House wants to communicate the latter. The Washington- and New York-based national media also have substantial resources to challenge White House versions of events and policies and to investigate areas of government not covered by briefings or press releases, resources the local media lacks. As a result, the White House caters to the local as well as the national media.

During the rollout for the Affordable Care Act in the autumn of 2013, Obama and members of his cabinet visited nine of the top ten cities with the highest concentration of uninsured, while senior administration officials held almost daily conference calls with reporters in nearly a dozen states to challenge Republican governors who refused to expand Medicaid and to point out the consequences of such actions for the citizens of those states. Organizing for Action took a similar approach, holding protests— some only attended by a dozen or so people—that won coverage on the local pages of the nation's small-town newspapers.[37]

The White House invites local editors, reporters, and news executives to Washington for exclusive interviews and briefings by the president and senior administration officials. Recent presidents have also arranged to be interviewed from the White House by television and radio stations through satellite hookups, and the White House provides briefings for the local press using the same technology. It also sends administration briefing teams around the country to discuss the president's policies with local media representatives and provides press releases, speeches, other documents, and audio clips for local media.

Contemporary presidents also meet frequently with journalists representing local media during their trips throughout the country. These efforts enable the White House to tailor unedited messages for specific groups and reach directly into the constituencies of members of Congress while reinforcing its policy message. Naturally, presidents hope to create goodwill and to receive a sympathetic hearing from journalists who are grateful for contact with the White House and, perhaps, susceptible to presidential charm.

There are limits to the utility of such efforts, however. Bill Clinton took office with an antagonistic attitude toward the national media, which he planned to bypass rather than use as part of his political strategy. As he told an audience of journalists shortly after taking office: "You know why I can stiff you on press conferences? Because [talk-show host] Larry King liberated me by giving me to the American people directly." After a rocky start in his press relations, Clinton's orientation changed. He found that he could not avoid the national press, which remains the primary source of news about the federal government. "I did not realize the importance of communications," he confessed, "and the overriding importance of what is on the evening television news. If I am not on there with a message, someone else is, with their message."[38]

Another problem is the diminishing number of local news outlets. The Pew Research Center reported in 2014 that one-fourth of the 952 U.S. television stations that air newscasts do not produce their news programs. Additional stations have sharing arrangements where much of their content is produced outside their own newsroom, and such arrangements are increasing.[39]

THE INSULATED AUDIENCE

Although technology provides the theoretical potential for the White House to communicate more effectively with greater numbers of people, other features of that same environment create obstacles to successfully realizing that potential. According to Obama press official Reid Cherlin, "people are increasingly getting information from an atomized, partisan, choose-your-news smorgasbord, where you're as likely to process the State of the Union through your brother-in-law's Facebook rants, the tweets of a few favorite reporters, and the top 17 GIFs of Nancy Pelosi blinking as curated by BuzzFeed."[40] Obama political strategist David Axelrod adds, "In today's media age, Teddy Roosevelt's 'bully pulpit' has been

atomized. . . . Presidents must try to steer their agenda through a tumultuous environment in which anyone with a cell phone camera has the potential to hijack the story of the day."[41]

Americans increasingly read and view material that matches their political beliefs. Newspaper editorial pages always offered different takes on
the news, but now cable news networks and an extraordinary range of
websites do so as well. Moreover, the algorithms of search engines and
social media guide people toward material that is likely to reinforce their
views. Ideological insulation poses a new challenge for White House communications, a challenge that cannot be overcome by simply communicating in different venues.

The Web was an enormous asset for reaching young people in the 2008
campaign. By his second term, Obama was faced with an ideologically
fragmented media that made it more difficult to reach the public. "In
every year, this project gets harder, the media gets more disaggregated,
people get more options to choose from, and they self-select outlets that
speak to their preconceived notions," said Pfeiffer.[42]

He was correct. On November 28, 2012, the White House created a
hashtag of "#my2k" to represent the estimated $2,000 in increased taxes
an average household was potentially facing unless Congress acted to prevent the country going over the fiscal cliff. The Pew Research Center studied a network of 688 Twitter users who tweeted a message that mentioned
"my2k" starting January 6 and ending January 8, 2013. It found two
large, dense groups of people talking about the same subject but not connecting to each other or using the same words, URLs, and other hashtags.
More generally, Twitter conversations around political issues often quickly
polarize into disconnected groups, with people citing different information sources to make their case.[43]

Thus, although the Internet offers new opportunities for the president
to reach the public, it also fragments the president's audience, making it
more difficult to reach those predisposed to oppose the president with
unfiltered messages. The obverse of this situation may seem to be that the
president can now reach those predisposed to follow his lead in a context
that facilitates reinforcement of those predispositions. Yet such a conclusion is only partially true.

Active Supporters

On the positive side are those most committed to the president's programs. When the Obama White House texts its supporters, it is preaching
to the choir. Such communications are useful because perhaps the first
rule in the politics of coalition-building is solidifying the core. Moreover,
committed congregants can be very helpful evangelists. The explosion of

social media, the fragmentation of news, and the erosion of the institutional press not only provide ample opportunity for the expression of partisan views, they also actively encourage it. Backing your friends and belittling your enemies is a healthy business model, one rewarded by a torrent of clicks, re-tweets, "likes," and links.

In early May 2014, Republicans used a newly released email to once again attack the president on the administration's handling of the assault on the U.S. diplomatic mission in Benghazi, Libya. However, the White House had plenty of help in answering critics. The *New Republic*'s Brian Beutler dismissed Benghazi as "nonsense." *Slate*'s David Weigel, along with the *Washington Post*'s *Plum Line* blog, debunked any claim that the new email was a "smoking gun." *Media Matters for America* labeled Benghazi a "hoax." *Salon* wrote that the GOP had a "demented Benghazi disease." *Daily Kos* featured the headline: "Here's Why the GOP Is Fired Up about Benghazi—and Here's Why They're Wrong." The *Huffington Post* offered "Three Reasons Why Reviving Benghazi Is Stupid—for the GOP."[44]

On issues ranging from health care reform to Syria, such aid has become typical. When critics attack the president, progressive bloggers jump to his defense. Moreover, they employ sharper arguments than the White House. Although presidential administrations have relied on friendly opinion-shapers since 1789, no White House has ever enjoyed the luxury of having its arguments and talking points advanced on a day-by-day, minute-by-minute basis. No longer must it await the evening news or the morning op-ed page to make its case and answer its critics.

Naturally, the White House is attentive to its blogging supporters. It should not be surprising that the administration holds off-the-record briefings, sometimes with Obama in the room, for select progressive bloggers from outlets such as *TPM* and *ThinkProgress*. Moreover, the press pool that takes turns covering the president up close now includes Web-only publications like *Talking Points Memo*, the *Huffington Post*, BuzzFeed, and the *Daily Caller*.

Resistance

Widespread home broadband and mobile access to the Internet has created the potential for people to communicate easily with each other as well as to receive communications from leaders. Conservatives have exploited this technology to reinforce their and Republicans' opposition to the Obama administration. Indeed, nothing has served conservative organizers better than Barack Obama, whom they have vilified as the devil incarnate. The fragmented news audience has allowed Fox News and conservative radio hosts to dominate the cable and radio airwaves. The ideological segmentation of the audience has allowed conservative discourse to go largely unanswered in many venues, which will not feature the president's responses. Moreover, conservatives employ the same range of videos, emails, tweets, and blogs as the White House and its supporters. All of these developments make leading the public more difficult for the president.

Also important has been the potential for *liberals* to use the new technologies to oppose the president's pragmatism and tendencies toward moderation. Americans glory in the freedom to dissent that is at the heart of blogging. Even during the transition, there were hints of conflict within the base. Candidate Obama allowed his supporters to wage an online revolt—on his own MyBarackObama.com website—over his vote in favor of legislation granting legal immunity to telecommunications firms that participated in the Bush administration's domestic wiretapping program. President-elect Obama, however, did not provide a forum for comments on his YouTube radio address, prompting grumbling among some that YouTube without comments was no different from radio.[45]

Internet users are creative, however. The day after Obama announced that the Rev. Rick Warren would deliver the opening prayer at his inauguration, a discussion forum focused on community service instead filled with pages of comments from people opposing the choice. In early January, visitors to Change.gov, the transition website, voted a question about whether Obama would appoint a special prosecutor to investigate possible Bush administration war crimes to the top of the questions submitted to the new administration. Progressive websites blasted the new administration's efforts to dodge the issue. Within a day, MSNBC's Keith Olbermann picked up the story. A day later, Obama was compelled to answer the question in an interview with ABC's George Stephanopoulos, who quoted it and pressed Obama with two follow-ups. Obama's answer, which prioritized moving "forward" but did not rule out a special prosecutor, made the front page of the January 12 issue of the *New York Times*.

Dissent among liberals did not end with the transition. For example, MoveOn.org, one of Obama's staunchest supporters during the 2008 campaign, called on its members in April 2010 to telephone the White House and demand that Obama reinstate the ban on offshore oil drilling that he had ended.[46] It has not been supportive of the president's more aggressive foreign policy actions, and criticized him on everything from immigration to net neutrality.

Missing the Congregation

The Democratic choir is composed of true believers. They do not represent most of the Democratic congregation, and, as we have seen, sometimes the flock contains skeptics. Most of those predisposed to support the president rarely, if ever, view a White House video or watch a presidential interview on the Internet. A perusal of the official White House Channel on YouTube tells the story. Most videos have no more than a few thousand viewers, and this in a nation of 320 million people. A study found that between May 2009 and November 2010, no video of the president's radio addresses had more than 100,000 views and most had close to 20,000.[47]

Many more people receive White House emails and tweets, of course, but we know little about the effects of these messages. There is reason to be skeptical about their impact, however. We do know, for instance, that despite the massive following of @BarackObama, recipients re-tweet its tweets on average only 1,442 times.[48] This is an impressive number for most tweets, but a minuscule fraction of the president's 67 million Twitter followers.

MOBILIZING SUPPORTERS

Reaching people is useful for political leaders, but mobilizing them is better. David Plouffe's emphasis on helping the Obama administration pass legislation through grassroots efforts indicates a desire to use public backing to move Congress to support the president's program. According to Andrew Rasiej, co-founder of the Personal Democracy Forum, a nonpartisan website focused on the intersection of politics and technology, Obama "created his own special interest group because the same people that made phone calls on behalf of him [in the campaign] are now going to be calling or e-mailing their congressman."[49] A Pew study during the transition found that among those who voted for Obama, 62 percent expected to ask others to support at least some of the new administration's policies.[50]

Plouffe did not take a formal role in the White House until 2011. He did, however, remain as an adviser and began overseeing the president's sprawling grassroots political operation, which at the time boasted 13 million email addresses, 4 million cell phone contacts, and 2 million active volunteers.[51] More than 500,000 people completed surveys following the election to express their vision for the administration, and more than 4,200 hosted house parties in their communities. On January 17, 2009, Obama sent a YouTube video to supporters to announce plans to establish Organizing for America (OFA), which was to enlist community organizers around the country to support local candidates, lobby for the president's agenda, and remain connected with his supporters from the campaign. There was speculation that the organization could have an annual budget of $75 million in privately raised funds and deploy hundreds of paid staff members. It was to operate from the Democratic National Committee headquarters but with an independent structure, budget, and priorities.[52] (By 2010, OFA had virtually supplanted the party structure. It sent about 300 paid organizers to the states, several times the number the national party hired for the 2006 midterms.)[53]

During the transition, the Obama team drew on high-tech organizational tools to lay the groundwork for an attempt to restructure the U.S. health care system. On December 3, 2008, former Democratic Senate majority leader Thomas Daschle, Obama's designee as secretary of Health and Human Resources and point person on health care, launched an effort to create political momentum when he held a conference call with one thousand invited supporters who had expressed interest in health issues, promising it would be the first of many opportunities for Americans to weigh in. In addition, there were online videos, blogs, and email alerts as well as traditional public forums. Thousands of people posted comments on health on Change.gov, the Obama transition website, which encouraged bloggers to share their concerns and offer their solutions regarding health care policy.[54]

According to Rasiej, "It will be a lot easier to get the American public to adopt any new health care system if they were a part of the process of crafting it." Simon Rosenberg, president of the center-left think tank NDN, was more expansive: "This is the beginning of the reinvention of what the presidency in the 21st century could be. This will reinvent the relationship of the president to the American people in a way we probably haven't seen since FDR's use of radio in the 1930s."[55]

Democratic political consultant Joe Trippi took the argument a step further, observing, "Obama will be more directly connected to millions of Americans than any president who has come before him, and he will be able to communicate directly to people using the social networking and Web-based tools such as YouTube that his campaign mastered." "Obama's could become the most powerful presidency that we have ever seen," he declared.[56] Republican strategist and the head of White House political operations under Ronald Reagan, Ed Rollins, agreed. "No one's ever had these kinds of resources. This would be the greatest political organization ever put together, *if it works*."[57]

Organizing for America

Whether it would work was indeed the question. The Organizing for America team held several dry runs to test the efficacy of their volunteer apparatus, including a call for supporters to hold "economic recovery house meetings" in February to highlight challenges presented by the recession. The house parties were designed to coincide with the congressional debate over Obama's stimulus package and had mixed results. Although OFA touted the 30,000 responses the email drew from the volunteer community and the more than 3,000 house parties thrown in support of the stimulus package, a report in McClatchy Newspapers indicated that many events were sparsely attended.[58]

The first major engagement of OFA in the legislative process began on March 16, 2009. An mail message was sent to volunteers, asking them to go door to door on March 21 to urge their neighbors to sign a pledge in support of Obama's budget plan. A follow-up message to the mailing list a few days later asked volunteers to call the Hill. A new online tool on the DNC/OFA website aided constituents in finding their congressional representatives' contact information so they could call the lawmakers' offices to voice approval of the proposal.

The OFA reported that its door-to-door canvass netted about 100,000 pledge signatures, while another 114,000 signatures came in through its email network. Republicans scoffed at the effort, arguing that this proved that even the most die-hard Obama supporters were uncertain about the wisdom of the president's budget plan. Several GOP aides noted that the number of pledges gathered online amounted to less than 1 percent of the names on Obama's vaunted email list. The *Washington Post* reported that interviews with congressional aides from both parties found the signatures swayed few, if any, members of Congress.[59]

By June, OFA was the Democratic National Committee's largest department, with paid staff members in 31 states and control of the heavily trafficked campaign website. Public discourse on health care reform was focusing on the high costs and uncertain results of various proposals. Remembering the "Harry and Louise" television ads that served as the public face of the successful challenge to Bill Clinton's health reform efforts, the White House knew it had to regain momentum. Thus, the president emailed millions of campaign supporters, asking for donations to help in the White House's largest-ever issues campaign and for "a coast-to- coast operation ready to knock on doors, deploy volunteers, get out the facts," and show Congress people wanted change. The DNC deployed dozens of staff members and hundreds of volunteers to 31 states to gather personal stories and build support.[60]

In late June, the DNC reported roughly 750,000 people had signed a pledge in support of the president's core principles of reducing cost, ensuring quality, and providing choice, including a public insurance option; 500,000 volunteered to help; and several hundred thousand provided their own story for the campaign's use. OFA posted thousands of personal stories online to humanize the debate and overcome criticism of the president's plan. It also trained hundreds of summer volunteers and released its first Internet advertisement—a Virginia man explaining that he lost his insurance when he lost his job.[61] As the health care debate intensified in August, the president again turned to the OFA for support. Obama sent an email to OFA members: "This is the moment our movement was built for," he wrote. He also spent an hour providing bullet points for the health care debate during an Internet video. OFA asked its volunteers to visit congressional offices and flood town hall meetings in a massive show of support.[62] There is no evidence that this show of strength ever materialized.

By August, Organizing for America reported paid political directors in 44 states. Nevertheless, it had to moderate its strategy. In response to Democrat complaints to the White House about television commercials on health care, climate change, and other issues broadcast in an effort to pressure moderates to support the president's proposals, the group started running advertisements of appreciation. It also found that its events around the country were largely filled with party stalwarts rather than the army of volunteers mobilized by the 2008 campaign.[63]

Despite some success in generating letters, text messages, and phone calls on behalf of health care reform, OFA was not a prominent presence in 2009.[64] In response to the lack of action, in 2010 organizers held hundreds of sessions across the nation intended to re-engage the base from 2008.[65]

In a video to members of OFA in April 2010, Obama delivered an appeal saying that the Democratic majority in Congress—and his agenda—depended on their roles in that year's midterm elections. The recorded message was part of a new effort by the Democratic National Committee to impress upon Democrats—particularly those occasional voters who were likely to cast ballots only in presidential races—the importance of the midterm elections for the House and Senate.

At the end of 2010, OFA launched a public relations offensive to demonstrate support for repealing "don't ask, don't tell." The group ran online advertisements and staged events in the home states of moderate Republican senators inclined to support the repeal bill. OFA volunteers delivered petitions with tens of thousands of signatures to wavering senators in an effort to build momentum for repeal—and to try to show them that they were safe politically if they voted to overturn the ban.[66]

Overall, however, OFA had to be a disappointment to the White House. In the midterm elections, OFA tried to rally its network of millions of Obama supporters to help Democratic candidates across the country, but the group was not very successful. Aside from a handful of victories, such as Senate Majority Leader Harry Reid's reelection in Nevada, most OFA-backed candidates lost.[67] The president also received help from an array of interest groups, such as Health Care for America Now, a progressive coalition that deployed 120 paid organizers to 43 states, staged events, and launched ads in a number of states.[68]

Organizing for Action

In 2013, the administration tried again. It named its grassroots operation Organizing for Action (OFA) and did not turn it over to the DNC. The president's campaign manager in 2012, Jim Messina, chaired the operation, and a small group of former campaign advisers oversaw it. The aim of the group was to promote the president's policies and give Democratic activists and other allies a way to rally behind his agenda.

OFA had access to the Obama campaign's data on voters, including email addresses and social network information. In theory, OFA had a grassroots army of 2.2 million volunteers, and social media assets that included 33 million Facebook friends, 26 million Twitter followers, and 17 million email subscribers. As an outside group, OFA could raise money, broadcast television ads, and otherwise run a political campaign on issues without running afoul of government guidelines that prohibit directly advocating for legislation. The president put it to work right away, running ads in the constituencies of 13 Republican members of Congress on behalf of his proposal for background checks for gun purchasers.

On June 14, 2013, Organizing for Action mobilized more than a thousand people to attend nearly 80 public events around the country to commemorate the six-month anniversary of the December 2012 Newtown shooting incident. The group hosted scores of "action planning sessions" and celebrated events that earned local news coverage. It also hosted informational phone banks, and collected 1.4 million signatures for a pro-gun control petition with the intent of pressuring Congress.[69]

On the day after the Senate voted down all efforts to strengthen gun control laws, OFA executive director Jon Carson sent an email to the group's members vowing that "Those senators who decided that not crossing the gun lobby was more important than making our kids and communities safer—OFA supporters will call them out and hold them accountable to their constituents."[70]

OFA's pledge to punish senators presented a difficult test, given that many of the senators voting no were in deep-red states where Obama lost badly. Nevertheless, there is little evidence of any success at all. As one reporter put it, "The group did not sway a single vote for the background check proposal, and was not able to make any of those who voted against it feel any heat." Even in states Obama carried handily, such as Ohio and New Hampshire, the group could not hold big rallies, blanket the airwaves with TV ads, or motivate enough supporters to match the volume of phone calls from pro-gun advocates.[71]

More broadly, the OFA focused on promoting legislation on climate change, gun control, economic policy, and immigration in six states that

Obama won in 2012, but that were represented by at least one GOP senator: Illinois, Maine, Pennsylvania, New Hampshire, Ohio, and Nevada. It was also targeting the red states of Arizona and Georgia, whose senators could be persuaded to back parts of the president's agenda, group officials said. OFA planned to hold 500 events focused on immigration by the end of May,[72] and it also emphasized defending the Affordable Care Act and claimed to have held more than 3,000 community events in support of enrollment in the new health insurance exchanges.[73]

A study of January 30, 2009 to August 7, 2014, found that 180 times during that period of time, the OFA sent its members emails, encouraging them to contact representatives regarding presidential priorities and engage in mass persuasion campaigns in their neighborhoods.[74] There is little evidence of any notable consequences from these and other efforts (although such impact is inherently difficult to measure). Most of the activity appeared to be in Democratic areas, and the scale of nearly all the activities appeared to be small.[75] Even ardent Obama fans could not make a strong push for him on the off-time from their regular jobs, and they lacked the resources to mount the kind of field or messaging operation that made the 2012 campaign effort so successful.[76]

By mid-2014, OFA was telling its donors that it would stop requesting large contributions and began shedding much of its staff.[77] The promise of exploiting technology to mobilize supporters behind White House initiatives had yet to be realized.

CONCLUSION

Technological developments such as email, the ease of uploading videos and photos via YouTube and Flickr, and social media sites like Facebook and Twitter have fundamentally changed the relationship between the president, the media, and the public. Reporters are no longer the only—or even necessarily the main—conduit through which news flows. Now the White House has the potential to bypass the press and communicate directly and appealingly with the public.

These technological advancements offer the president opportunities to compensate for the declining audience for presidential messages over the traditional media and to be better positioned to reinforce the views of those predisposed to support him. We saw in chapter 5 that reinforcing co-partisans' views can be an advantage to the president, albeit a modest one. Given available information, it is not possible to determine the contribution, if any, of the new media to the reinforcement of supporters' views. It is likely to be small, however.[78] Most presidential communications to the public go to true believers, not to the broader pool of potential supporters. The most balanced conclusion is that the impact of the new media on the president's ability to govern is marginal.

To make matters worse for the president, audience fragmentation and ideological insulation make it more difficult to reach the bulk of the population. Moreover, the opposition is able to exploit the same tools and audience characteristics to challenge the White House and reinforce the tendencies of its adherents. And, in the unkindest cut of all, true believers among Democrats push back against the president's moderate tendencies, and there is little evidence that the president can mobilize his supporters to pressure Congress for change.

CHAPTER 9

Exploiting Partisans in Congress

BECAUSE THE U.S. system of separation of powers is really one of shared powers, presidents must obtain the consent of Congress to accomplish many of their goals. The White House especially requires congressional assent for those policies that will endure and form the core of the president's legacy. Obtaining this support is often difficult, however. Thus, one of the chief executive's most demanding and frustrating tasks, one that inevitably occupies much of the president's time and energy, is trying to move Congress to support his policies. According to Lyndon Johnson, "There is only one way for a President to deal with Congress, and that is continuously, incessantly, and without interruption."[1]

As in dealing with the public, it is natural for a new president, basking in the glow of an electoral victory, to focus on creating, rather than exploiting, opportunities for change. It may seem quite reasonable for a president who has just won the biggest prize in American politics by convincing voters and party leaders to support his candidacy to conclude that he should be able to convince members of Congress to support his policies. Moreover, the appeal of unity following an election may obscure the prospects of working with the opposition party. As with leading the public, then, presidents may not focus on evaluating existing possibilities when they think they can create their own. Yet, assuming that the White House can persuade members of Congress to change their minds and support policies they would otherwise oppose is likely to lead to self-inflicted wounds.

PARTY SUPPORT

No matter what other resources presidents may have at their disposal, they remain highly dependent on their party to move their legislative

TABLE 9.1. Presidential Support in Congress*

| | | % Support | | | | | |
| | | House | | | Senate | | |
President	Party	Rep	Dem	Difference⁺	Rep	Dem	Difference⁺
Eisenhower	Rep	63	42	21	69	36	33
Kennedy	Dem	26	73	47	33	65	32
Johnson	Dem	27	71	44	44	56	12
Nixon/Ford	Rep	64	39	25	63	33	30
Carter	Dem	31	63	32	37	63	26
Reagan	Rep	70	29	41	74	31	43
Bush	Rep	73	27	46	75	29	46
Clinton	Dem	24	75	51	22	83	61
W. Bush	Rep	83	19	64	86	18	68
Obama‡	Dem	15	85	70	19	94	75

*On roll-call votes on which the winning side was supported by fewer than 80 percent of those voting.
⁺ Percentage points
‡ 2009–2014
Dem = Democrat; Rep = Republican.

programs. Representatives and senators of the president's party usually form the nucleus of coalitions supporting presidential proposals and provide considerably more support than do members of the opposition party.

Table 9.1 shows the party support for the president on contested roll-call votes on which the White House took a stand since 1953, a period covering more than a fourth of the nation's history under the U.S. Constitution. The differences in each party's support for the president are sizeable. Moreover, the gap between the levels of support from the president's and the opposition parties has been growing since the 1970s, reaching 70 percentage points or more under Barack Obama.

Table 9.2 shows the same data organized by the party of the president. Several patterns are evident. In the 1950s, President Eisenhower received relatively modest support from his own party, only 63 percent in the House and 69 percent in the Senate. Foreign affairs was the dominant issue of the era, and there was substantial diversity of opinion among elected Republican representatives. Many were isolationist and opposed to the president's strong internationalist orientation.[2]

Kennedy and Johnson received somewhat more support from the Democrats in the House than Eisenhower received from his party, but they also

TABLE 9.2. Presidential Party Support in Congress*

| | | % Support | | | |
| | | House | | Senate | |
President	Party	Own Party	Opposition Party	Own Party	Opposition Party
Eisenhower	R	63	42	69	36
Kennedy	D	73	26	65	33
Johnson	D	71	27	56	44
Nixon/Ford	R	64	39	63	33
Carter	D	63	31	63	37
Reagan	R	70	29	74	31
Bush	R	73	27	75	29
Clinton	D	75	24	83	22
W. Bush	R	83	19	86	18
Obama†	D	85	15	94	19

* On roll-call votes on which the winning side was supported by fewer than 80 percent of those voting.
† 2009–2014

received weak support from the Republicans (26 and 27 percent, respectively), who were strongly opposed to many of the liberal initiatives of the New Frontier and the Great Society. The presidents' party support among Senate Democrats was quite modest, reflecting the heterogeneity of the Democratic Party, and the response of its conservative wing to the same programs. Democrats supported Kennedy about two-thirds of the time. Opposition to civil rights measures was especially strong among the large contingent of Southern Democrats, who supported LBJ only 36 percent of the time.[3] The combination of opposition from conservative Democrats and the support of a number of liberal Republican senators resulted in Johnson receiving 44 percent support among Senate Republicans, only slightly less than his 56 percent support among Democrats.

Since the 1970s, there has been a steady increase in the support the president received from his own party in both houses and a corresponding decrease in the support he received from the opposition party. These changes, in turn, have produced the substantial increase in the differences between the support levels of the two parties.

Significantly, presidents of both parties have experienced the increasing disparity in support. While George W. Bush received only 19 percent support from House Democrats, Barack Obama received even less support—15 percent—from House Republicans. Similarly, Bush won 18 percent support from Senate Democrats while Obama achieved 19 percent from Senate Republicans.

The realignment of the parties and the increasing party polarization we discussed in chapter 3 have been at the core of the divergence in presidential support. The consequences of these dynamics in congressional support for the White House are that the president is more dependent on his party than at any time in at least three generations. His co-partisans are likely to accord him highly reliable support for his initiatives, while the opposition's response to his proposals will be overwhelmingly negative. As we have seen, presidential leadership demarcates and deepens cleavages in Congress. The parties tend to be more cohesive on issues on which the president has taken a stand.[4]

Thus, there is little chance that the president can persuade the opposition party to support him. As we saw in chapter 4, the opposition will support the president when it is forced to accede to the president's wishes to avoid a worse outcome or in the few instances when it may agree with his policies. Even then, however, opposition backing will not result from presidential persuasion. Even a hint of cooperating with the White House can be detrimental to an opposition party member's political future.

Despite the pull of party ties, all presidents experience at least some slippage in the support of their party in Congress. When constituency opinion and the president's proposals conflict, members of Congress are more likely to vote with their constituents, whom they rely on for reelection. Moreover, if the president is not popular with their constituencies, congressional party members may avoid identifying too closely with the White House.

The primary obstacle to party unity is the lack of consensus on policies among party members. Jimmy Carter, a Democrat, remarked, "I learned the hard way that there was no party loyalty or discipline when a complicated or controversial issue was at stake—none."[5] When George W. Bush proposed reforming Social Security and immigration policy, many congressional Republicans refused to support him. Likewise, when Barack Obama negotiated deals with Republicans on taxes in 2010 and spending in 2011, many congressional Democrats voted against him.

Because the majority party has such tight control over the agenda of the House, it is possible for the White House to win House approval for its initiatives if the president's party has only a small majority, but, as we have seen, holding a narrow majority is no guarantee of success. Large majorities are not common, however. The last time a president's party held 60 percent of House seats was in 1980.

The Senate filibuster rule turns the convenience of a 60 percent into a necessity. Presidents generally need at least 60 votes to pass important legislation, and in this era almost all of these votes will come from the president's party. Aside from about six months in late 2009 and early 2010, no president has enjoyed a majority of 60 votes since 1978.

Because of the president's reliance on his own party and because he is unlikely to have large majorities in either house of Congress, he needs the support of as much of his party's cohort as possible. What can the White House do to increase the chances of obtaining party support?

PARTY LEADERSHIP

The most straightforward answer to the question of increasing party support is making appeals to co-partisans in Congress. Shared party affiliation is more than a superficial characteristic that the president and some members of Congress hold in common. In addition, most representatives and senators of the president's party share a psychological bond that generates a proclivity for supporting the White House. Members of the president's party typically have personal loyalties or emotional commitments to their party and to its leader, which shape the contours of the context in which the president attempts to lead his party.

Equally important, as we saw in chapter 3, the increasing ideological coherence of the parties has created a substantial overlap in the ideologies of the president and his party's members in Congress. Thus, representatives and senators are inclined to support White House initiatives because they agree with them and may well have advocated them in their campaigns. Moreover, the president and his congressional co-partisans were probably supported by similar electoral coalitions, reinforcing the pull of party ties.

Members of the president's party also share a desire to avoid embarrassing "their" administration and thus hurting their chances for reelection or their party's chances of maintaining or regaining a majority. Moreover, these officials have a basic distrust of the opposition party, which is quite correctly seen as eager to undermine the White House. This perception induces party members to rise to the president's defense.[6]

Thus, the president comes to his position as party leader with a clear advantage. Members of his party are open to the White House's leadership. It is not surprising, then, that earlier work found that co-partisans gave the president the benefit of the doubt, especially if they were unsure about their own opinion on an issue.[7] One presidential aide, speaking in the 1970s, described as "just amazing" how often members of the president's party voted for the administration's proposals not on substance but on loyalty and a desire to be helpful.[8] In the closely divided congresses and highly polarized politics of the twenty-first century, even though presidents receive higher average levels of support from their parties, the addition of a few votes can be critical for the White House.

The president has some assets as party leader, including congressional party leaders, services and amenities for party members, and campaign aid. Each asset is of limited utility, however. The president's relationship with party leaders in Congress is a delicate one. Although the leaders are predisposed to support presidential policies and typically work closely with the White House, they are free to oppose the president or lend only symbolic support; some party leaders may be ineffective themselves. Moreover, party leaders, especially in the Senate, are not in strong positions to reward or discipline members of Congress.

To create goodwill with congressional party members, the White House provides them with many amenities, ranging from photographs with the president to rides on *Air Force One*. Perhaps more important, districts represented by members of the president's party receive more federal outlays than those represented by opposition party members.[9] Although this largesse may earn the president the benefit of the doubt on some policy initiatives, party members consider it their right to receive such favors from the White House and as a result are unlikely to be especially responsive to the president's largesse. In addition to offering a carrot, the president can, of course, withhold favors to encourage support, but such action tends to be self-defeating. As Lyndon Johnson's chief congressional liaison aide, Lawrence O'Brien, put it, the White House sometimes offered positive inducements but "we didn't carry any big stick."[10]

If party members wish to oppose the White House, the president can do little to stop them. When Bill Clinton tried to discipline Senator Richard Shelby of Alabama, the senator switched parties to fight the president more effectively as a Republican. When George W. Bush tried to punish Jim Jeffords of Vermont, he left the Republican Party, costing the president his majority in the Senate.

The parties are highly decentralized. Neither presidents nor national party leaders control those aspects of politics that are of vital concern to members of Congress—nominations and elections. Members of Congress are largely self-recruited, gain their party's nomination by their own efforts and not the party's, and provide most of the money and organizational support needed for their elections. Party organizations do contribute millions of dollars to House and Senate candidates. However, the parties do not use these contributions as incentives to encourage party loyalty. Nor do they withhold funds to punish members who stray from the party line. Instead, the party committees act pragmatically to enhance the prospects of winning elections for all viable candidates, especially those running in competitive districts or states.[11]

PERSUADING PARTISANS

We have seen that his fellow partisans in Congress are likely to support the president's initiatives and that the bonds of party should encourage them to give him the benefit of the doubt when they are unsure of their own stands on issues. Yet no systematic study has found that presidents can reliably move members of Congress to support them. Jon Bond, Richard Fleisher, and B. Dan Wood focused on determining whether the presidents to whom we attribute the greatest skills in dealing with Congress were more successful in obtaining legislative support for their policies than were other presidents. After carefully controlling for other influences on congressional voting, they found no evidence that those presidents who supposedly were the most proficient in persuading Congress were more successful than chief executives with less aptitude at influencing legislators.[12]

In his important work on pivotal politics, Keith Krehbiel examined votes to override presidential vetoes, focusing on those members of Congress who switched their votes from their original votes on the bill. He found that presidents attracted 10 percent of those who originally supported a bill but lost 11 percent of those who originally supported him by opposing the bill. Those closest in ideology to the president were most likely to switch to his side, which may indicate they voted their true views, rather than responding to other interests, when it really counted. Even among those most likely to agree with the White House, legislators within the cluster of pivotal or near-pivotal, the net swing was only 1 in 8. The majority of switchers were from the president's party, indicating that the desire to avoid a party embarrassment rather than presidential persuasiveness may have motivated their votes.[13]

It is possible that there is selection bias in votes on veto overrides. Presidents do not veto the same number of bills, and some veto no bills at all. Moreover, presidents may often choose to veto bills on which they are likely to prevail. In addition, most override votes are not close, allowing members of Congress more flexibility in their voting. Whatever the case, Krehbiel's data do not provide a basis for inferring successful presidential persuasion.

It is not necessary to take an extreme position to obtain a better understanding of the nature of presidential leadership. There are times, of course, when presidents do persuade some members of Congress to change their votes. A famous example of apparent large-scale change occurred over the Panama Canal treaties, ratified in 1978. In the fall of 1976, shortly before Jimmy Carter became president, 48 senators introduced a resolution pledging not to approve any change in the existing treaties regarding the canal. After a full-court press, Carter obtained the two-thirds vote in the Senate to ratify the new treaties.[14]

The issue is not whether persuasion is *ever* successful in moving a member of Congress. Instead, the question is whether persuasion is typically the key to presidential success in Congress. Examples such as the Panama Canal treaties are rare. Whatever the circumstances, the impact of persuasion on the outcome is usually relatively modest. As Calvin Mouw and Michael MacKuen concluded, "presidential influence in Congress does not rely on persuasion."[15] Although potentially important, conversion is likely to be at the margins of coalition-building rather than at the core of policy change. Presidential legislative leadership is more useful in exploiting discrete opportunities than in creating broad possibilities for policy change.

LYNDON JOHNSON

Even those presidents with the strongest reputations for effectiveness in dealing with Congress were not especially persuasive. Lyndon Johnson, who presided over the greatest period of legislative productivity in the past 50 years, is a prime example.

In 1964, LBJ had the good fortune to run against an opponent, Barry Goldwater, whom many in the public viewed as an extremist outside the mainstream of American politics. The election also occurred in the shadow of the traumatic national tragedy of the assassination of John F. Kennedy. Johnson won a smashing victory, and opposition to his proposals melted. As Lawrence O'Brien, his chief congressional aide, put it, Johnson's landslide "turned the tide."[16] For the first time since the New Deal, liberals gained majorities in both houses of Congress.

Johnson did not have to convince these liberals to support policies that had been on their agenda for a generation.[17] Nor did he have to convince the public of much. His policies were popular,[18] allowing him the luxury of emphasizing in the election proposals such as Medicare that he knew the public already supported so he could claim a mandate for them after the election.[19] Both congressional leaders and White House aides felt they were working in a period of remarkable unanimity in which, as one member of LBJ's domestic staff put it, "some of the separation got collapsed. It seemed we were all working on the same thing."[20]

Was this consensus the result of Johnson's persuasion, the fabled "Johnson Treatment"? Probably not. Then Democratic House majority leader Carl Albert argued that Johnson's tenaciousness and intensity in pushing legislation were his great talents, not his persuasiveness. Although pressed for specifics on Johnson's legislative skills, Albert responded only that the president just kept pushing.[21] Congress was not rubber-stamping the president's proposals, but doing what it wanted to do. "We had the right majority," he recalled.[22]

Others close to Johnson agree. The president understood the opportunity the large, liberal majorities in the Eighty-ninth Congress presented to him, and he seized it, keeping intense pressure on Congress. After the results of the 1964 landslide were tallied, Johnson called his chief congressional liaison aide, Lawrence O'Brien, and told him, "We can wrap up the New Frontier program now, Larry."[23] In O'Brien's words, with LBJ, "Every day, every hour it was drive, drive, drive."[24]

Most would agree that John Kennedy and Lyndon Johnson had substantially different leadership styles and personal relationships with Congress. LBJ was the master legislative strategist and technician, making Congress his highest priority and leaving no stone unturned in his efforts to exercise his influence. Kennedy, on the other hand, had more non-legislative concerns and lacked Johnson's fascination with the legislative process. Kennedy, reputed to be less effective than Johnson with Congress, should have received less support in Congress, *ceteris paribus*, than Johnson.[25]

Yet leading participants in the legislative process did not view their visible differences as important for legislative success. According to Henry Hall Wilson, the White House's chief liaison aide for the House under both Kennedy and Johnson, the approach of the two presidents to the House was "practically identical."[26] Similarly, the White House liaison to the Senate for both presidents, Mike Manatos, argued that it did not make any difference on the Hill which president he represented. His members of Congress treated his appeals for support the same.[27]

Congressional leaders John McCormack, Carl Albert, Charles Halleck, and Everett Dirksen, Johnson's aides Lawrence O'Brien, Joseph Califano, and Mike Manatos, the executive branch official James Sundquist, and numerous scholars agree that had Kennedy lived and won by a large margin in 1964, he would have got much the same from Congress as Johnson did, and that the basic explanation for Johnson's phenomenal success in 1965 and 1966 was the increase in the number of liberal Democrats in Congress as a result of the elections of 1964.[28] Significantly, Kennedy and Johnson legislative liaison aides do not argue to the contrary in their published memoirs or in their oral histories in the Kennedy and Johnson presidential libraries.

Arthur Schlesinger, Jr., a historian and White House aide to President Kennedy, was also skeptical about the significance of legislative skills. Comparing President Kennedy and President Johnson, he concluded:

When Johnson lost 48 Democratic House seats in the 1966 election, he found himself, despite his alleged wizardry, in the same condition of stalemate that had thwarted Kennedy and, indeed, every Democratic President since 1938. Had the sequence been different, had Johnson been elected to the Presidency in 1960 with Kennedy as his Vice President, and had Johnson then offered the 87th Congress the same program actually offered by Kennedy, the probability is that he would have had no more success than Kennedy—perhaps even less because he appealed less effectively to public opinion. And, if Johnson had died in 1963 and Kennedy had beaten Goldwater by a large margin in 1964, then Kennedy would have had those extra votes in the House of Representatives, and the pundits of the press would have contrasted his cool management of Congress with the frenetic and bumbling efforts of his predecessor. In the end, arithmetic is decisive.[29]

We can fruitfully compare the success of Kennedy and Johnson in obtaining support in Congress. Both were Democrats and they served in the same historical era. Table 9.3 summarizes the records of Democratic support in the House and Senate for Kennedy and Johnson. Because of the ideological diversity of the Democratic Party in the 1960s, I include separate figures for Northern and Southern Democrats. The figures in the table do not support the hypothesis that Johnson was especially persuasive in influencing representatives to support his policies. The support for each partisan group for president in the House is virtually identical. In the Senate, Kennedy received more support than Johnson from Democrats of all stripes. Thus, Johnson was not able to effectively appeal to his co-partisans for support.

Even if Johnson's legislative leadership skills did not have a systematic influence on congressional support for his policies, it is possible that they had a more restricted impact, albeit still an important one. Legislative leadership may be most significant at the margins of coalition-building, that is, in gaining the last few votes needed to pass a program. Turning a sizable coalition into a victorious one after broader influences have had their impact can certainly be a critical component of leadership.

Perhaps the famous Johnson Treatment made the difference in persuading members of Congress to support the historic Great Society legislation. The evidence for the importance of legislative leadership on marginal votes is mixed. On the one hand, the White House often devotes substantial resources to obtaining votes at the margin of coalitions. Reflecting on the extraordinary economic policies Congress passed in 1981, Reagan budget director David Stockman declared, "I now understand that

TABLE 9.3. Congressional Support for Kennedy and Johnson*

	% Support			
	House		Senate	
Party Group	Kennedy	Johnson	Kennedy	Johnson
All Democrats	73	71	65	56
Northern	85	82	75	65
Southern	54	54	44	36

* On roll-call votes on which the winning side was supported by fewer than 80 percent of those voting.

you probably can't put together a majority coalition unless you are willing to deal with those marginal interests that will give you the votes needed to win. That's where it is fought—on the margins—and unless you deal with those marginal votes, you can't win."[30] Certainly, LBJ traded favors for votes when he needed them—something much less likely to occur in an era of scarce resources and polarized parties in which the opposition party refuses to negotiate.

Yet not all coalitions are of equal size. Russell Renka closely examined the House votes on major elements of Johnson's agenda. A swing of 23 votes would have been required for the White House to have lost the closest vote (a recommittal motion sponsored by Republicans on Medicare). Renka could find no indication in the White House's files that the president did anything specific to secure these 23 votes. Indeed, the White House did not even red-flag the Civil Rights Act of 1964, the Voting Rights Act of 1965, Medicare, or the Elementary and Secondary Education Act of 1965 for special presidential efforts as they came to the House floor. The president's intervention was not needed.[31]

In an earlier study, I found that in 1965, when Johnson had a large majority, and 1967, after the Democrats had suffered substantial losses in midterm elections, there were very few marginal victories in either chamber (victories of 25 votes or fewer in the House and ten votes or fewer in the Senate). In other words, there were few victories where Johnson's leadership skills could have made the difference between winning and losing. The marginal victories that did occur were generally not on major issues.[32] Similarly, Jon Bond and Richard Fleisher examined presidential success on votes decided by a margin of 10 percent or less. Controlling for the status of the president's party in each chamber, the authors found little relationship between presidential legislative leadership skills and success in winning votes.[33]

Johnson knew his own limitations. For example, when Senate Majority Leader Mike Mansfield asked LBJ to talk directly to the president's old friend, Senator Richard Russell, Johnson complained, "Well, goddamit . . . I couldn't get Dick Russell to vote with me when I was majority leader. What makes Mike think he's going to vote with me now?"[34] Similarly, after losing a skirmish with House Ways and Means Committee Chairman Wilbur Mills over taxes, Johnson grumbled, "I'm not master of nothing. . . . We cannot make this Congress do one damn thing that I know of."[35]

It is not surprising that a legislative aide to Johnson remembered, "It was a very rare thing that he called a member of the House respecting a vote."[36] The tape recordings of his White House conversations show Johnson pleading, thanking, complimenting, and consulting but rarely trying directly to persuade a legislator, and even when he did, he employed a light touch.[37]

Even if presidents are unlikely to change many congressional minds, they can still take advantage of members' ideological predispositions or their proclivities to support their party leader. The best way to do this is by working to maintain and even increase the number of co-partisans in the House and Senate.

Maintaining and Increasing Party Numbers

Because representatives and senators of the president's party give him such high levels of support, the best way to improve his chances of obtaining support in Congress as a whole is to increase the number of fellow party members in the legislature. Helping incumbents, and thus maintaining the party's cohorts of members of Congress, is also critical. There are two points at which the White House may act to influence the size of the president's party's contingent in Congress: during the presidential and midterm elections. Certainly presidents spend considerable time raising money for their parties, and the White House may also be active in encouraging attractive candidates to run for office—and occasionally discouraging less attractive ones.

The most direct potential influence of the president on the outcomes of elections, however, is through their standing with the public. According to Gary Jacobson, in the increasing nationalization of politics, "popular assessments of the president strongly affect how his party is evaluated, perceived, and adopted as an object of identification, which, in turn, helps to account for the president's influence on the electoral fates of his party's candidates."[38]

Presidential coattails occur when voters cast their ballots for congressional candidates of the president's party because those candidates support the president. We have seen that there is an increasing connection between presidential and congressional voting, with a rise in party loyalty and thus a decline in ticket-splitting. Party-line voting reached its highest level ever for House and Senate elections in 2012, with defection rates of 10 percent in House elections and 11 percent in Senate elections. Similarly, 2012 witnessed the lowest incidence ever of ticket-splitting—voting for a Democrat for president and a Republican for U.S. representative or senator, or vice versa; 11 percent for both the House and the Senate. Much of this coherence in voting is the result of views about the president.[39]

On the other hand, the president runs *behind* almost every winning congressional candidate of his party. This fact does not in itself prove he has weak coattails, but it hardly provides the basis for inferring them. The lack of competition in nearly all House seats and most Senate seats provides little potential for coattails to determine the winner.[40]

It is not surprising, then, that the change in party balance that usually emerges when the electoral dust has settled is strikingly small. In the 16 presidential elections between 1952 and 2012, the party of the winning presidential candidate averaged a net gain of 8 seats (out of 435) per election in the House and only 1 seat in the Senate, where the opposition party actually gained seats in 7 of the elections (see table 9.4). The Republicans lost seats in both houses when George W. Bush was elected in 2000. Presidents cannot rely on their coattails to carry their party's legislators into office to help pass their legislative programs.

What about the midterm elections? Recent presidents have campaigned actively for their party's candidates in these contests, and there is evidence that they reap benefits from those members who win.[41] Sometimes, however, the president is not ranked high in the polls, and his party's candidates find it better to avoid association with him. For example, in 2014, when the Democrats were in a desperate struggle to retain a Senate majority, Barack Obama campaigned in only one state—Michigan—with a competitive Senate race. Instead, he focused his efforts on Democratic states where his approval numbers remained reasonably strong.

In addition, events may constrain the president's campaign efforts. In 2014, the White House determined that the president would need to devote time to managing the new bombing campaign against the Islamic State of Iraq and the Levant. The president also wanted to avoid the optics of ordering strikes en route to political rallies.[42]

Ultimately, the president's party typically *loses* seats in midterm elections (table 9.5), sometimes with serious consequences for the president's

TABLE 9.4. Congressional Gains or Losses for the President's Party in Presidential Election Years

Year	President	House	Senate
1952	Eisenhower (R)	+22	+1
1956	Eisenhower (R)	−2	−1
1960	Kennedy (D)	−22	−2
1964	Johnson (D)	+37	+1
1968	Nixon (R)	+5	+6
1972	Nixon (R)	+12	−2
1976	Carter (D)	+1	0
1980	Reagan (R)	+34	+12
1984	Reagan (R)	+14	−2
1988	G. Bush (R)	−3	−1
1992	Clinton (D)	−10	0
1996	Clinton (D)	+9	−2
2000	G. W. Bush (R)	−2	−4
2004	G. W. Bush (R)	+3	+4
2008	Obama (D)	+21	+8
2012	Obama (D)	+8	+1
	Average	+8	+1

initiatives. For example, in 1986, the Republicans lost 8 seats in the Senate, depriving President Reagan of a majority, and in 1994, the Democrats lost 8 Senate seats and 52 House seats, in the process losing control of both houses.[43] The president's party is especially likely to lose seats in the House when the president's approval rating is low and when the party gained a large number of seats in the previous election. Thus, the Democrats suffered large losses in the 2010 midterm elections, including 6 seats in the Senate and 63 in the House. As a result, Barack Obama found it difficult to win passage of his priority programs.

Because the president cannot reliably increase his party's contingents in the House and Senate, his party often lacks a majority in one or both houses. Since 1953 there have been 30 years in which Republican presidents faced a Democratic House of Representatives and 22 years in which they faced a Democratic Senate. Democrat Bill Clinton faced both a House and a Senate with Republican majorities from 1995 through 2000. Barack Obama had to deal with a Republican majority in the House in 2011–2016, and a Republican majority in the Senate in 2015–2016.

TABLE 9.5. Congressional Gains or Losses for the President's Party in Midterm Election Years

Year	President	House	Senate
1954	Eisenhower (R)	− 18	− 1
1958	Eisenhower (R)	− 47	− 13
1962	Kennedy (D)	− 4	+ 3
1966	Johnson (D)	− 47	− 4
1970	Nixon (R)	− 12	+ 2
1974	Ford (R)	− 47	− 5
1978	Carter (D)	− 15	− 3
1982	Reagan (R)	− 26	0
1986	Reagan (R)	− 5	− 8
1990	G. Bush (R)	− 9	− 1
1994	Clinton (D)	− 52	− 8
1998	Clinton (D)	+ 5	0
2002	G. W. Bush (R)	+ 6	+ 2
2006	G. W. Bush (R)	− 30	− 6
2010	Obama (D)	− 63	− 6
2014	Obama (D)	− 13	− 9
	Average	− 24	− 3

Although there are times when a popular president may influence the size of his party cohort in Congress, doing so is not a reliable leadership resource. Therefore, the president has to rely primarily on those fellow partisans who are already in Congress.

EXPLOITING PARTISANS

Because presidents are not likely either to increase the number of their fellow partisans in Congress or to change the minds of representatives and senators once they are there, the White House needs to understand and then exploit the opportunities that its party cohorts offer.

Lyndon Johnson

No one understood Congress better than Lyndon Johnson, and he knew that his personal leadership could not sustain congressional support for his policies. The civil rights movement was peaking as Johnson assumed the presidency, providing crucial public backing for legislation to increase equality in many areas of American life.[44] In addition, LBJ recognized that the assassination of President Kennedy and the election of 1964 had provided him a rare window of opportunity in Congress and that he had to move rapidly to exploit it.[45] Thus, in February 1965, after his landslide victory, Johnson assembled the congressional liaison officials from the various departments and told them that his victory at the polls "might be more of a loophole than a mandate," and that because his popularity could decrease rapidly they would have to use it to their advantage while it lasted.[46] Moreover, LBJ knew he would probably lose his liberal Democratic margin in the 1966 midterm elections.[47]

Johnson followed his own advice. First, he was ready to send legislation to Capitol Hill immediately after Congress convened. As he explained to one aide, "You've got to give it all you can, that first year . . . You've got just one year when they treat you right and before they start worrying about themselves."[48]

To keep Congress focused on his proposals, he was ready to replace enacted legislation with new requests.[49] He told his aide Jack Valenti early in his presidency, "I keep hitting hard because I know this honeymoon won't last. Every day I lose a little more political capital. That's why we have to keep at it, never letting up. One day soon . . . the critics and the snipers will move in and we will be at stalemate. We have to get all we can now, before the roof comes down."[50]

To exploit fully the favorable political environment, he pushed as much legislation as possible through Congress, keeping it in session until October 22, just two weeks before the 1966 midterm elections.[51] In those elections, the Democrats lost 47 seats in the House and 4 in the Senate. Legislating became much more difficult as a result. Sixteen months later, in March 1968, the president declared that he would not seek reelection. Johnson had lost neither his leadership skills nor his passion for change. Instead, he had lost the opportunity to exploit a favorable environment.[52] As one biographer put it, by 1968 "Congress, the hothouse that had nurtured Johnson . . . was his enemy."[53] Another historian added, "In the Ninetieth Congress [1967–1968], he could control very little, and he could dominate nothing."[54]

Ronald Reagan

It was the Republicans' turn in 1981. Although Ronald Reagan won only 51 percent of the vote in the 1980 presidential election, he beat incumbent Jimmy Carter by 10 percentage points, and the Republicans won a majority in the Senate for the first time since the 1952 election. The unexpectedly large size of Reagan's victory and the equally surprising outcomes in the Senate elections created the perception of an electoral mandate.

Unlike the other two modern mandates, 1932 and 1964, Reagan's victory placed a stigma on big government and exalted the unregulated marketplace and large defense budgets. More specifically, the terms of the debate over policy changed from which federal programs to expand to which ones to cut; from which civil rights rules to extend to which ones to limit; from how much to regulate to how little; from which natural resources to protect to which to develop; from how little to increase defense spending to how much; and from how little to cut taxes to how much. Reagan had won on much of his agenda before Congress took a single vote.

The new president also benefited from the nature of the times. Although 1981 was hardly a repeat of 1933, there was a definite sense of the need for immediate action to meet urgent problems. In its first issue after Reagan's inauguration, the *Congressional Quarterly Weekly Report* declared that "one of Reagan's biggest advantages is the sense of both parties in Congress that the nation's problems are now very serious indeed."[55] Similarly, David Stockman, a principal architect and proponent of Reagan's budgeting and tax proposals, remembers that when the president announced his "Program for Economic Recovery" to a joint session of Congress in February 1981, "the plan already had momentum and few were standing in the way." Reagan was "speaking to an assembly of desperate politicians who . . . were predisposed to grant him extraordinary latitude in finding a new remedy for the nation's economic ills . . . not because they understood the plan or even accepted it, but because they had lost all faith in the remedies tried before."[56]

The president's advisers recognized immediately that the perceptions of a mandate and the dramatic elevation of Republicans to majority status in the Senate provided it with a window of opportunity to effect major changes in public policy. Like LBJ, the White House knew it had to move quickly before the environment became less favorable. Thus, the president was ready with legislation, even though it was complex and hastily written.[57] Moreover, within a week of the March 30, 1981, assassination attempt on Reagan, Michael Deaver convened a meeting of other high-ranking aides at the White House to determine how best to take advantage of the new political capital the shooting had created.

The Reagan administration also knew it lacked the political capital to pass a broad program. Thus, it enforced a rigorous focus on the president's economic plan and defense spending—its priority legislation—and essentially ignored divisive social issues and tried to keep Central America on the back burner.[58] According to Max Friedersdorf, the head of Reagan's legislative liaison office, "In '81, during the whole course of the year, we only had three major votes."[59] These votes took place at wide intervals. By focusing its political resources on its priorities, the administration succeeded in using the budget to pass sweeping changes in taxation and defense policy.

CONCLUSION

Presidents are increasingly dependent on their parties for support for their initiatives, while the opposition is increasingly likely to oppose them. Although the default position of almost all contemporary members of the president's party in Congress is to support the White House, this reflexive backing is often not enough to pass legislation, especially major proposals. Thus, the president often finds that he needs to convince some members of his party to support his initiatives. Nevertheless, there is little evidence that presidents have much success in doing so, and those chief executives with the strongest legislative skills do not obtain more support from their party's cohort than do those less proficient in the legislative arts. Moreover, presidents cannot rely on increasing the size of their party's cohort in either presidential or midterm elections—although it is worth the effort if they are high in the polls.

Presidential party legislative leadership operates in an environment largely beyond the president's control and must compete with other, more stable factors that affect voting in Congress in addition to party. These include ideology, personal views and commitments on specific policies, and the interests of constituencies. By the time a president tries to exercise influence on a vote, most members of Congress have made up their minds on the basis of these other factors. Thus, a president's partisan appeals are likely to be critical only for those few members of Congress who remain open to conversion after other influences have had their impact.

The best evidence is that the presidential mobilization of his party in Congress is at the margins of congressional decision making. Even presidents who appeared to dominate Congress were actually facilitators rather than directors of change. They understood their own limitations and overtly took advantage of opportunities in their environments. Working at the margins, they successfully guided legislation through Congress. When these resources diminished, they reverted to the more typical stalemate that usually characterizes presidential-congressional relations.[60]

PART III

Conclusion

CHAPTER 10

Leadership, Opportunity, and Strategic Assessments

THE CHALLENGES OF governing have rarely been greater. The distance between the parties in Congress and between identifiers with the parties among the public is the greatest in a century. The public accords Congress the lowest approval ratings in modern history, but activists allow its members little leeway to compromise. The inability of Congress and the president to resolve critical problems results in constant crises in financing the government, endless debate over immigration, health care, environmental protection, and other crucial issues, and a failure to plan effectively for the future.

It is not surprising that presidents would choose a strategy for governing based on the premise of overcoming impediments to policy change by creating new opportunities through persuasion. Entering the White House with vigor and drive, they are eager to create a legacy. Unfortunately, they also begin their tenures with the arrogance of ignorance and thus infer from their success in reaching the highest office in the land that both citizens and elected officials will respond positively to themselves and their initiatives. As a result, modern presidents invest heavily in leading the public in the hope of leveraging public support to win backing in Congress.[1]

Although it may be appealing to explain major policy changes in terms of persuasive personalities, public opinion is too biased, the political system is too complicated, power is too decentralized, and interests are too diverse for one person, no matter how extraordinary, to dominate. Neither the public nor Congress is likely to respond to the White House's efforts at persuasion. Presidents cannot create opportunities for change. There is overwhelming evidence that presidents, even "great communicators," rarely move the public in their direction. Indeed, the public often moves *against* the position the president favors. Similarly, there is no systematic evidence that presidents can reliably move members of Congress to support them through persuasion.

The context in which the president operates is the key element in presidential leadership. Making strategic assessments by asking a few key questions about the president's political environment provides us crucial leverage for evaluating a president's likely success in obtaining the support of the public and Congress for his initiatives. Understanding the nature and possibilities of leadership puts us in a better position to evaluate both the performance of presidents and the opportunities for change and to set our expectations accordingly.

Successful leadership, then, is not the result of the dominant chief executive of political folklore who reshapes the contours of the political landscape, altering his strategic position to pave the way for change. Rather than creating the conditions for important shifts in public policy, effective leaders are facilitators who work at the margins of coalition-building to recognize and exploit opportunities in their environments. When the various streams of political resources converge to create opportunities for major change, presidents can be critical facilitators in engendering significant alterations in public policy.

Recognizing and exploiting opportunities for change—rather than creating opportunities through persuasion—are the essential presidential leadership skills. As Edgar declared in *King Lear*, "Ripeness is all." To succeed, presidents have to evaluate the opportunities for change in their environments carefully and orchestrate existing and potential support skillfully. Successful leadership requires that the president have the commitment, resolution, and adaptability to take full advantage of opportunities that arise.

Barack Obama was no exception. Working closely with congressional leaders, he exploited the advantage provided by the large Democratic majorities in Congress in 2009 and 2010 to enact a number of major changes in public policy, including an historic fiscal stimulus, health care reform, and financial regulation. Moreover, he kept up the pressure in the lame-duck session at the end of 2010, pushing through the repeal of "don't ask, don't tell," ratification of the New START treaty, and a compromise on taxes and unemployment insurance. Obama helped to transform policy without performing transformational leadership.[2]

The president displayed the analytical insight necessary to identify opportunities for change and many of the skills and characteristics necessary to take advantage of them, including energy, perseverance, and resiliency.

What he lacked was a framework for evaluating his ability to expand or even maintain his coalition and avoid long-term strategic failure.

COALITIONS OF THE WILLING

Presidents are not without some ability to influence the context in which they operate. Facilitating coalitions of the willing is at the heart of presidential leadership. Although presidents find it difficult or impossible to *change* opinion, the White House may benefit from the fact that motivated reasoning encourages co-partisans to follow the president's lead. At least in some instances, the president's association with a policy is an especially powerful signal to those predisposed to support his initiatives. Moreover, by reinforcing his partisans' predispositions, presidents can counter opposition party attacks and discourage his supporters from abandoning him. In addition, co-partisans appear to be resilient in returning to support after periods of bad news.

Signaling can only take the president so far, however. Many of the president's co-partisans may still oppose his initiatives. As with other tools of presidential leadership, signaling is at the margins of coalition-building. In addition, reinforcement is a two-edged sword. Motivated reasoning encourages the large number of people who are usually predisposed against the president to oppose his policies.

There is even less potential influence from cross-pressuring co-partisans. Although some partisans follow the president's signals, even when his views are contrary to their own policy preferences, such changes in opinion may be short-lived and provide the president a fragile base for coalition-building. Moreover, even though in such instances the president may be taking stances broadly consistent with the views of opposition party identifiers, he cannot depend on successfully garnering their support. Instead, he is more likely to antagonize them and thus increase the disapproval of his policy.

There are times when the White House finds public opinion diffuse but broadly supportive of where it wants to lead. The president may attempt to clarify the public's wishes and show how they are consistent with his policies, frame proposals to emphasize their consistency with the public's existing views, and increase the salience of White House initiatives that are popular with the public. However, it is difficult for the president to focus the public's attention and make his popular initiatives more salient.

Occasionally there is a White House initiative on which the public has not developed attitudes, seeming to offer the president especially favorable conditions for influencing opinion. Nevertheless, we have not found that the president can overcome the partisan predispositions that soon develop on such issues or the broad trends in public attitudes.

At first glance it may appear that technological advances in communication should make it easier for the president to reach the public, and to do so on his own terms. Yet audience fragmentation and ideological insulation actually make it more difficult to reach the majority of the population. Moreover, the opposition is able to exploit the same tools to challenge the White House and reinforce the tendencies of its adherents. Thus, the impact of the new media on the president's ability to govern appears to be marginal.

The ultimate goal of presidential persuasion is obtaining support in Congress. The sizes of the president's party cohorts in the House and Senate largely determine his prospects for success because of the dispositions of fellow partisans to support their leader and the proclivity of opposition party members to oppose him. Nevertheless, presidential mobilization of his party in Congress is at the margins of congressional decision making. Presidents have little success in changing the minds of members of Congress, even those in their own party. They can sometimes make side payments to obtain votes, but such actions often depend on resources over which they have little or no control, especially when the opposition controls one or both houses of the legislature. Moreover, there is little the president can do to increase the size of his party cohort. Indeed, it usually shrinks during his tenure.

Persuasion, even when it is aimed at those inclined to follow the president's lead, is a limited tool. Scholars and other analysts of the presidency need to understand the potential of persuasion and the role of strategic context as they seek to explain and predict the impact of presidential leadership. It is even more vital that presidents themselves recognize the nature of leadership in America.

The Importance of Making Strategic Assessments

Strategies for governing based on the premise of creating opportunities for change are prone to failure. Presidents—and the country—often endure self-inflicted wounds when they fail to appreciate the limits of their influence. The White House not only wastes the opportunities that do exist but sometimes—as in Franklin D. Roosevelt's Court-packing bill, Bill Clinton's health care reform proposal, and George W. Bush's effort to reform Social Security—presidents also create the conditions for political disaster and undermine their ability to govern in the long term.[3] The dangers of overreach and debilitating political losses alert us that it is critically important for presidents to assess accurately the potential for obtaining public and congressional support.

The Obama administration overestimated the opportunities for change in its environment and the president's ability to create new opportunities. When the president thought he could fashion opportunities for change by expanding his supporting coalition, promoting a large, liberal agenda appeared to pose little political risk. Yet the White House could not obtain public support for many of its most visible proposals, nor could it attract Republican votes in Congress. These failures were inevitable and demonstrate the importance of making clear-eyed strategic assessments of the opportunity structure of a new administration.[4]

In a nationally televised interview shortly after the 2010 midterm elections, the president acknowledged that one major contributor to the "big government Obama" narrative was the health care reform law. "At the time, we knew that it probably wasn't great politics," Obama reflected. "I made the decision to go ahead and do it. And it proved as costly politically, as we expected. Probably actually a little more costly than we expected, politically." The president added, "We thought that if we shaped a bill that wasn't that different from bills that had previously been introduced by Republicans, including a Republican Governor in Massachusetts who's now running for president, we would be able to find some common ground there. And we just couldn't." In addition, the debate over health care "created the kind of partisanship and bickering that really turn people off. Partly because the economy was still on the mend. And the entire focus on health care for so many months meant that people thought we were distracted and weren't paying attention to . . . the key thing that was on their minds." In the end, the president concluded, "There's no doubt that it hurt us politically."[5]

The president was correct. The administration's advocacy of unpopular policies, especially health care reform, alienated much of the public, especially those in the middle of the ideological and partisan spectrums.[6] The protracted focus on the Affordable Care Act, probably the least popular major piece of legislation passed since the advent of public opinion polling, helped energize the right and kept the administration from focusing on the economy, the public's highest priority.[7]

The Democratic losses in the 2010 midterm elections—63 seats in the House and 6 in the Senate—cost Obama his party's large majorities in Congress, gave Republicans control of the House, and undermined his potential to govern for the rest of his tenure. As Democratic senator Chuck Schumer later declared, by overreaching on health care reform in 2009–2010, the president squandered the opportunity presented by the Democratic majorities to pass legislation aimed at helping the middle class weather the recession.[8] He might have added immigration reform and climate change legislation as well. Moreover, the Republican gains in state legislatures, where in 2011 they held the most seats since the Great Depression, increased the probability of redistricting that would favor the GOP and thus increase the probability of Republican majorities in Congress for the next decade.

Losing the congressional seats put the president on the defensive. The new House Republican majority took the lead opposing the White House and displayed impressive unity on the big issues, including health care, environmental protection, reproductive rights, budgeting, and the debt ceiling. The 112th Congress was deeply polarized. The president could succeed in passing some important policy changes in a context of polarization when he had the votes in the 111th Congress, but there was little probability of success when the opposition was large and disdainful of compromise. Conditions did not improve in the president's second term, and following the 2014 midterm elections, Democrats had the smallest contingent in the House (and in state legislatures) since the 71st Congress (1929–1930). There was little possibility of Congress responding positively to major presidential initiatives. Interestingly, health care and the Affordable Care Act created the most widely used issue in Republican-sponsored commercials in U.S. Senate races.

We will never know if it would it have been prudent for the president to have moved more slowly and with a narrower focus, nurtured his electoral majority, built greater public confidence in his leadership, and emerged with a stronger mandate to pursue his postponed campaign agenda. It is possible that Democrats could not have passed an overhaul of health care at any other time[9] and that doing so was worth losing the ability to act on a range of other important issues. Perhaps.

What we know for certain is that it would have been useful for the White House to have made a rigorous and informed assessment of the potential of his leadership so that the president could have understood the trade-offs he was likely to face and choose accordingly. For example, understanding that he would not in the short term be able to change public opinion regarding health care reform or the fiscal stimulus, the two most visible issues of his first two years, might have cast a different light on his decisions regarding his agenda and the sequencing of initiatives.

Some in the Obama White House came to understand the limitations of persuasive leadership, of course. One presidential adviser complained, "There is this sense on Capitol Hill that somehow the president can go out and make a speech and everything just magically becomes better."[10] David Axelrod added, "I would love to live in a world where the president could snap his fingers or even twist arms and make change happen, but in this great democracy of ours, that's not the way it is."[11] Chastened by his experience, even the president became a fatalist regarding how his words would be received.[12] Yet this understanding of the nature of leadership came too late to influence strategic planning.

Undermining the Potential for Compromise

There is an additional danger to failing to understand the limits of persuasion. Presidents and their opponents may underestimate each other and eschew necessary compromises in the mistaken belief that they can persuade members of the public and Congress to change their minds.

The Framers created a deliberative democracy that requires and encourages reflection and refinement of the public's views through an elaborate decision-making process. Those opposed to change need only win at one point in the policymaking process—say in obtaining a presidential veto—whereas those who favor change must win every battle along the way. To win all these battles usually requires the support of a sizable majority of the country, not just a simple majority of 51 percent. As a result, the Madisonian system calls for moderation and compromise.

The principal mechanism for overcoming the purposefully inefficient form of government established by the Constitution is the extra-constitutional institution of political parties. Representatives and senators of the president's party are almost always the nucleus of coalitions supporting the president's programs. Thus, parties help overcome the fractures of shared powers. Yet, unless one party controls both the presidency and Congress and has very large majorities in both houses of Congress, little is likely to be accomplished without compromise.

When parties are broad, there is potential for compromise because there will be some ideological overlap among members of the two parties. When the parties are unified and polarized, however, they exacerbate conflict and immobilize the system. Critical issues such as immigration, environmental protection, taxation, and budgeting go unresolved.

We expect political parties in a parliamentary system to take clear stands and vigorously oppose each other. Such a system usually works because the executive comes from the legislature and can generally rely on a supportive majority to govern. Partisan polarization has given the United States parliamentary-style political parties operating in a system of shared powers, virtually guaranteeing gridlock. Moreover, minority interests that want to stop change are likely to win, raising troubling questions about the nature of our democracy.

For the U.S. system to work, then, requires a favorable orientation toward compromise. Such a temperament is found in the very roots of the nation. Recalling the events of the Philadelphia Constitutional Convention, James Madison observed that "the minds of the members were changing" throughout the convention, in part due to a "yielding and accommodating spirit" that prevailed among the delegates.[13]

A reliance on persuasive leadership may not only threaten the disposition to compromise but also undermine the context necessary for negotiation. Presidents' persistence in emphasizing persuasion may increase both elite and public polarization and thus decrease their chances of success in governing. When political leaders take their cases directly to the public, they have to accommodate the limited attention spans of the public and the availability of space on television. As a result, the president and his opponents often reduce choices to stark black and white terms. When leaders frame issues in such terms, they typically frustrate rather than facilitate building coalitions. Such positions are difficult to compromise, which hardens negotiating positions.

Too often persuasive discourse revolves around destroying enemies rather than producing legislative products broadly acceptable to the electorate. Frightening people about the evils of the opposition is often the most effective means of obtaining attention and inhibiting support for change. Such scare tactics encourage ideologically charged and harsh attacks on opponents while discouraging the comity necessary for building coalitions. When people are sorted into enclaves in which their views are constantly and stridently reaffirmed, as they often are today, neither the public nor members of Congress are likely to display a compromising attitude. How can you compromise with those holding views diametrically opposed to yours and whom your party leaders and other political activists relentlessly vilify?

When presidents launch aggressive public promotions for their policies and themselves, they invite opponents to challenge them. Business and professional associations use paid advertising, orchestrate events to attract press coverage, and finance think tanks to offer analyses that can serve as sources for reporters and editorial writers seeking to "balance" the administration's case.[14] Public campaigns to propel health reform into law by Bill Clinton and Barack Obama, for instance, provoked wide-ranging and expensive counter-mobilizations by business associations, the insurance industry, and others threatened by reform.[15] The effect was to trigger motivated reasoning and thus activate existing conservative attitudes and partisan beliefs among Republicans, which helped to produce and reinforce sharp partisan differences in support for the Affordable Care Act.[16]

More broadly, an emphasis on persuasion is at the core of the permanent campaign and is fundamentally anti-deliberative. Campaigning focuses on persuasion, mobilization, competition, conflict, and short-term victory. Leaders wage campaigns in either/or terms. Conversely, governing involves deliberation, cooperation, negotiation, and compromise over an extended period. Campaigns prosecute a cause among adversaries rather than deliberate courses of action among collaborators. Campaign communications by partisan officials are designed to win elections rather than to educate the public. Thus, the incentives for leaders are to stay on message rather than to engage with opponents and to frame issues rather than inform their audience about anything in detail.[17]

In the permanent campaign, political leaders do not look for ways to insulate controversial or difficult policy decisions from their vulnerability to demagoguery and oversimplification. Campaigning requires projecting self-assurance rather than admitting ignorance or uncertainty about complex issues and counterattacking and switching the subject rather than struggling with tough questions. It is better to have a campaign issue for the next election than deal with an issue by governing.

In sum, the tendencies in the permanent campaign are for civility to lose out to conflict, compromise to deadlock, deliberation to sound bites, and legislative product to campaign issues. None of these characteristics of contemporary politics promote the resolution of long-standing issues.

Staying Private

How, then, can the president encourage an "accommodating spirit" among opposition members of Congress? There is no silver bullet. However, it might be profitable to focus more on creating a context for compromise. While public efforts at persuasion are not helpful, quiet negotiations may be.

It is no secret that negotiations are best done in private. James Madison remembered that in writing the Constitution:

> It was . . . best for the convention for forming the Constitution to sit with closed doors, because opinions were so various and at first so crude that it was necessary they should be long debated before any uniform system of opinion could be formed. Meantime the minds of the members were changing. . . . Had the members committed themselves publicly at first, they would have afterwards supposed consistency required them to maintain their ground, whereas by secret discussion no man felt himself obliged to retain his opinions any longer than he was satisfied of their propriety and truth, and was open to the force of argument. Mr. Madison thinks no Constitution would ever have been adopted by the convention if the debates had been public.[18]

The same principles of successful negotiation hold more than two centuries later. Examples of the White House and Congress strategically engaging in quiet negotiations to produce important legislation include the

Clean Air Act Amendments of 1990, the budget agreement of 1990, and the No Child Left Behind Act of 2001. Polarization, of course, is even greater now than it was during the Bush presidencies, which should encourage the president to be all the more open to alternative strategies for governing.

The Balanced Budget Act of 1997 provides an especially telling illustration. The residue of first-term budget battles—and of the ensuing fall 1996 elections, in which Democrats tarred Republicans as Medicare killers—was a deep bitterness that seemed likely to poison the relationship between the Clinton White House and Congress indefinitely. Yet within a few months both sides reached an historic agreement on achieving a balanced budget within five years.

There was a dramatic shift from the rancorous partisan warfare that had dominated the consideration of the budget in the 104th Congress. Low-keyed, good faith negotiations began shortly after the president submitted his FY 1998 budget, and senior White House officials held a series of private meetings with members of Congress. Unlike the political posturing in late 1995 and early 1996, *neither side focused on moving the negotiations into the public arena.*

Staying private made it easier for both sides to compromise, and they each gained from doing so. For Republicans, the budget agreement capped a balanced-budget and tax-cutting drive that had consumed them since they took over Congress in 1995. They won tax and spending cuts, a balanced budget in five years, and a plan to keep Medicare solvent for another decade. Thus, although they did not win a radical overhaul of entitlement programs, they did make substantial progress toward their core goals.

For Clinton, the budget agreement represented perhaps his greatest legislative triumph. He left the bargaining table with much of what he wanted, including an increased scope for the child tax credit, a new children's health initiative, restoration of welfare benefits for disabled legal immigrants, increased spending for food stamps, and a host of other incremental increases in social spending.

These compromises did not satisfy everyone, of course. Clinton had to walk a fine line between compromising with Republicans and maintaining the support of Democratic liberals, who did not like budgetary constraints and did not want to hand the Republicans a positive accomplishment. Some Democrats were upset that they were not included in the negotiating process. Similarly, Republican leaders had to deal with die-hard conservatives, who did not want to compromise at all with the president.

The decision of President Clinton and the Republican congressional leaders to seize on the opportunity provided by the surging economy and the groundwork formed by the budgets of 1990 and 1993 and to quietly negotiate and compromise, letting everyone claim victory, made the budget agreement possible. In addition, the success of these executive-legislative negotiations paved the way for additional talks of a similar nature on Social Security and Medicare that may have ultimately proved fruitful if it were not for the confounding influence of the impeachment inquiry in 1998.

Why would the White House attempt to stay private in the face of inflammatory provocations from the opposition? There are three good reasons. First, going public does not work. Second, if elites can make deals, and the agreements result in successful outcomes, the public is likely to reward them for doing so. Although the polarization we see in Washington has its roots in local elections and constituency politics,[19] the public is less polarized than its elected representatives.[20] Moreover, it wants elected officials to compromise, as we saw in the 2013 government shutdown.[21]

Finally, keeping negotiations private may make it easier for each side to compromise in reaching a broader deal because each side can view the entire package more favorably than it views each of the component parts. The lack of transparency in the negotiating process—as opposed to in the results of the negotiations—allows leaders some freedom from the inevitable pressures not to compromise on any part of the deal.

"Staying private" will not change the electoral incentives to defeat opponents. Nor will it narrow the ideological differences between the parties or produce unified government. However, staying private *is* likely to contribute to reducing gridlock, incivility, and public cynicism and deserves a more prominent role in the president's strategic arsenal.

Caveats

The White House will not unilaterally disarm in the face of virulent criticism. Presidents will sometimes conclude that they must go public just to maintain the status quo. Maintaining preexisting support or activating those predisposed to back him can be crucial to a president's success. Consolidating core backers may require reassuring them as to his fundamental principles, strengthening their resolve to persist in a political battle, or encouraging them to become more active on behalf of a candidacy or policy proposal. When offered competing views, people are likely to respond according to their predispositions, so the White House will act to reinforce the predispositions of its supporters.

Nevertheless, promotion of policies and reaction to criticism can take a wide range of forms. It is possible to assert values and policies without incendiary rhetoric, and it is not necessary to begin negotiations with the other party by excoriating its elected officials in a cross-national speaking tour.

An additional complication to staying private is the willingness of both parties to make policy and to compromise to do it. Some members of Congress have adopted the approach to policymaking of relentless confrontation.[22] In addition, sometimes, especially for Republicans, the preferred position is to do nothing. Moreover, Republicans in the public, especially activist Tea Party Republicans, are much less likely than Democrats or Independents to support compromise on policy issues.[23]

When the default position of failure to negotiate is unacceptable, as in the fiscal cliff issue at the end of 2012, the parties are likely to negotiate. If the president offers the other party something it likes, as in George W. Bush's funding of community clinics and programs to combat AIDS in Africa, the opposition may well offer its support. Not always, however.

A president's willingness to make policy concessions to the opposition party will not alter the fact that the intense competition over control of the presidency and Congress has increased the incentives to engage in partisan warfare. The differences between the parties and the cohesion within them on floor votes are typically greater when the president takes a stand on issues. When the president adopts a position, members of his party have a stake in his success, while opposition party members have a stake in the president losing. Moreover, both parties take cues from the president that help define their policy views, especially when the lines of party cleavage are not clearly at stake or already well established.[24]

Further complicating the process of compromise is the lack of trust between the parties, a product of highly confrontational polarized politics. For years, officials on both sides of the aisle have known that one way to make a dent in the long-term problem of financing Social Security is adjusting the way we measure increases in the cost of living. Within hours of President Obama supporting such an adjustment in his budget, some Republicans, including the chair of the House Republican Campaign Committee, were claiming he wanted to balance the budget on the backs of seniors—the Democrat's worst nightmare.

In the end, there is no silver bullet. Nevertheless, we can increase both our understanding of presidential leadership and its impact on governing if scholars, journalists, pundits, and presidents alike grasp the essence of presidential leadership and act accordingly.

Notes

PREFACE

1. For my prediction of President Obama's first term, see George C. Edwards III, *Overreach: Leadership in the Obama Presidency* (Princeton, NJ: Princeton University Press, 2012), p. 7.

CHAPTER 1: ASKING THE RIGHT QUESTIONS

1. Richard E. Neustadt, *Presidential Power and the Modern Presidents* (New York: Free Press, 1990), p. 11.

2. Ibid., p. 10.

3. Ibid., p. 37. Italics in original.

4. Ibid., p. 4.

5. Ibid., p. 40.

6. Ibid., p. 32.

7. George C. Edwards III, *On Deaf Ears: The Limits of the Bully Pulpit* (New Haven, CT: Yale University Press, 2003).

8. Stephen Skowronek, *The Politics Presidents Make: Leadership from John Adams to Bill Clinton* (Cambridge, MA: Harvard University Press, 1997). See also his remarks at the Annual Meeting of the American Political Science Association, 2006.

9. Skowronek, *The Politics Presidents Make*.

10. Maureen Dowd, "No Bully Pulpit," *New York Times*, April 20, 2013.

11. Lawrence R. Jacobs and Robert Y. Shapiro, *Politicians Don't Pander* (Chicago: University of Chicago Press, 2000), pp. 45, 106, 136.

12. Barack Obama, Speech at the Democratic Party of Wisconsin Founders Day Gala, Milwaukee, Wisconsin, February 16, 2008.

13. David Axelrod, *Believer: My Forty Years in Politics* (New York: Penguin Press, 2015), pp. 371–377.

14. Quoted in Ronald Suskind, *Confidence Men: Wall Street, Washington, and the Education of a President* (New York: Harper, 2011), p. 370.

15. See, for example, Edwards, *On Deaf Ears*; B. Dan Wood, *The Politics of Economic Leadership* (Princeton, NJ: Princeton University Press, 2007); George C. Edwards IIII, *Governing by Campaigning: The Politics of the Bush Presidency*, 2nd ed. (New York: Long-

man, 2007); B. Dan Wood, *The Myth of Presidential Representation* (Cambridge, UK: Cambridge University Press, 2009); George C. Edwards III, *The Strategic President: Persuasion and Opportunity in Presidential Leadership* (Princeton, NJ: Princeton University Press, 2009), chaps. 2–3; George C. Edwards III, *Overreach: Leadership in the Obama Presidency* (Princeton, NJ: Princeton University Press, 2012), chap. 3; James N. Druckman and Lawrence R. Jacobs, *Who Governs? Presidents, Public Opinion, and Manipulation* (Chicago: University of Chicago Press, 2015), chap. 6.

16. See, for example, George C. Edwards III, *At the Margins: Presidential Leadership in Congress* (New Haven, CT: Yale University Press, 1989); Jon R. Bond and Richard Fleisher, *The President in the Legislative Arena* (Chicago: University of Chicago Press, 1980); Richard Fleisher, Jon R. Bond, and B. Dan Wood, "Which Presidents Are Uncommonly Successful in Congress?" in Bert Rockman and Richard W. Waterman, eds., *Presidential Leadership: The Vortex of Presidential Power* (New York: Oxford University Press, 2007); Edwards, *The Strategic President*, chaps. 4–5; Edwards, *Overreach*, chap. 6.

17. Edwards, *The Strategic President*.

18. James MacGregor Burns, *Leadership* (New York: Harper & Row, 1978), p. 2.

19. See Edwards, *Overreach*, pp. 183–185.

20. Skowronek, *The Politics Presidents Make*.

21. For critiques of Skowronek on this matter, see Douglas J. Hoekstra, "The Politics of Politics: Skowronek and Presidential Research," *Presidential Studies Quarterly* 29 (September 1999): 657–671; Andrew J. Polsky, "Partisan Regimes in American Politics," *Polity* 44 (January 2012): 51–80; Andrew J. Polsky, "Shifting Currents: Dwight Eisenhower and the Dynamic of Presidential Opportunity Structure," *Presidential Studies Quarterly* (March 2015): 91–109.

Chapter 2: Strategic Position with the Public

1. George C. Edwards III, *On Deaf Ears: The Limits of the Bully Pulpit* (New Haven, CT: Yale University Press, 2003); George C. Edwards III, *Overreach: Leadership in the Obama Presidency* (Princeton, NJ: Princeton University Press, 2012), chap. 3; George C. Edwards III, *The Strategic President: Persuasion and Opportunity in Presidential Leadership* (Princeton, NJ: Princeton University Press, 2009), chaps. 2–3; and *Governing by Campaigning: The Politics of the Bush Presidency*, 2nd ed. (New York: Longman, 2007).

2. See Edwards, *The Strategic President*, chaps. 2–3, 6.

3. Quoted in Ken Auletta, "Non-Stop News," *New Yorker*, January 25, 2010, p. 44. See also Jonathan Alter, *The Promise: President Obama, Year One* (New York: Simon & Schuster, 2010), p. 125.

4. Barack Obama, *Dreams from My Father* (New York: Crown Publishers, 1995), p. 106.

5. Peter Baker and Jonathan Weisman, "In Latest Campaign, Obama Takes Deficit Battle to the Public," *New York Times*, November 30, 2012; Alexis Simendinger, "To Strike Fiscal Deal, Obama Turns to the Public," *RealClearPolitics*, November 28, 2012; Peter Baker, "Obama Goes Back on the Trail Ahead of Debt Talks," *New York Times*, November 27, 2012; David Nakamura and Zachary A. Goldfarb, "Obama Public Relations Effort Aims to Avoid 'Fiscal Cliff,'" *Washington Post*, November 28, 2012; Carol E. Lee and Monica Langley, "A More Worried Obama Battles to Win Second Term," *Wall Street Journal*, August 31, 2012.

6. Ron Fournier, "From Guns to Immigration, Obama Circumventing GOP," *National Journal*, January 16, 2013.

7. Jonathan Alter, *The Center Holds: Obama and His Enemies* (New York: Simon & Schuster, 2013), p. 120.

8. Lee and Langley, "A More Worried Obama Battles to Win Second Term."

9. John Aloysius Farrell, Chris Frates, Nancy Cook, and Billy House, "The GOP's Failed 'Plan O': Inside the Fiscal-Cliff Saga," *National Journal*, January 2, 2013. Also see Ron Fournier, "From Guns to Immigration, Obama Circumventing GOP," *National Journal*, January 16, 2013.

10. Peter Baker and Jonathan Weisman, "In Latest Campaign, Obama Takes Deficit Battle to the Public," *New York Times*, November 30, 2012.

11. On the payroll tax cut, see NBC News/*Wall Street Journal* poll, October 6–10, 2011; CBS News/*New York Times* polls, September 10–15 and October 19–24, 2011. On student loans, see *Newsweek* poll conducted by Princeton Survey Research Associates International, November 9–10, 2006; CNN Poll conducted by Opinion Research Corporation, December 15–17, 2006; CNN/Opinion Research Corporation Poll. March 19–21, 2010; United Technologies/National Journal Congressional Connection Poll conducted by Princeton Survey Research Associates International, May 3–6, 2012.

12. Andrew Kohut, "Obama's 2010 Challenge: Wake Up Liberals, Calm Down Independents," Pew Research Center for the People and the Press, December 17, 2009.

13. Alter, *The Center Holds*, p. 111.

14. Press Briefing by Press Secretary Jay Carney, White House, July 10, 2013.

15. George C. Edwards III, *At the Margins: Presidential Leadership of Congress* (New Haven, CT: Yale University Press), chap. 8; Lawrence J. Grossback, David A. M. Peterson, and James A. Stimson, *Mandate Politics* (New York: Cambridge University Press, 2006).

16. Barack Obama, "Remarks by the President in a News Conference," White House, November 14, 2012.

17. *Washington Post*-ABC News poll, December 13–16, 2012.

18. 2012 National Exit Poll.

19. Quoted in Ben Terris, "A Presidential Mandate? How About 435 Congressional Ones?" *National Journal*, November 16, 2012.

20. Rebecca Kaplan, "Ryan: No Mandate for Obama in Election," *National Journal*, November 14, 2012. See also Alexis Simendinger and Caitlin Huey-Burns, "Amid 'Frank' Talks, Obama Uses Polls as Pry Bar," *RealClearPolitics*, December 14, 2012.

21. Obama, "Remarks by the President in a News Conference."

22. White House, "Transcript of News Conference by the President," January 14, 2013.

23. Gallup Poll, "Wyoming Residents Most Conservative, D.C. Most Liberal," January 31, 2014. The analysis is based on telephone interviews conducted as part of Gallup Daily tracking January 1–December 29, 2013. The sample includes 178,527 U.S. adults. The margin of sampling error for most states is ±3 percentage points, but is as high as ±6 percentage points for the District of Columbia.

24. Gallup Poll's annual Values and Beliefs Poll, May 2–7, 2013.

25. Pew Research Center, *2012 Values Survey*, April 4–15.

26. Christopher Ellis and James A. Stimson, *Ideology in America* (New York; Cambridge University Press, 2012); Shawn Treier and D. Sunshine Hillygus, "The Nature of

Political Ideology in the Contemporary Electorate," *Public Opinion Quarterly* 73 (Winter 2009): 679–703; Christopher Ellis and James A. Stimson, "Symbolic Ideology in the American Electorate," *Electoral Studies* 28 (September 2009): 388–402; William G. Jacoby, "Policy Attitudes, Ideology, and Voting Behavior in the 2008 Election," paper presented at the Annual Meeting of the American Political Science Association, 2009; James A. Stimson, *Tides of Consent: How Public Opinion Shapes American Politics* (New York: Cambridge University Press, 2004); Pamela J. Conover and Stanley Feldman, "The Origins and Meaning of Liberal/Conservative Identifications," *American Journal of Political Science* 25 (October 1981): 617–645; David O. Sears, Richard L. Lau, Tom R. Tyler, and Harris M. Allen, "Self-Interest vs. Symbolic Politics in Policy Attitudes and Presidential Voting," *American Political Science Review* 74 (September 1980): 670–684."

27. Philip E. Converse, "The Nature of Belief Systems in Mass Publics," in *Ideology and Discontent*, ed. David E. Apter (New York: Free Press, 1964), pp. 206–261.

28. Pew Research Center, *Political Polarization in the American Public*, June 12, 2014; Teresa E. Levitin and Warren E. Miller, "Ideological Interpretations of Presidential Elections," *American Political Science Review* 73 (September 1979): 751–771.

29. Robert Huckfeldt, Jeffrey Levine, William Morgan, and John Sprague, "Accessibility and the Political Utility of Partisan and Ideological Orientations," *American Journal of Political Science* 43 (July 1999): 888–911; Kathleen Knight, "Ideology in the 1980 Election: Ideological Sophistication Does Matter," *Journal of Politics* 47 (July 1985): 828–853; Levitin and Miller, "Ideological Interpretations of Presidential Elections"; James A. Stimson, "Belief Systems: Constraint, Complexity, and the 1972 Election," *American Journal of Political Science* 19 (July 1975): 393–417.

30. Paul Goren, Christopher M. Federico, and Miki Caul Kittilson, "Source Cues, Partisan Identities, and Political Value Expression," *American Journal of Political Science* 53 (October 2009): 805–820; Christopher M. Federico and Monica C. Schneider, "Political Expertise and the Use of Ideology: Moderating the Effects of Evaluative Motivation," *Public Opinion Quarterly* 71(Summer 2007): 221–252; William G. Jacoby, "Value Choices and American Public Opinion," *American Journal of Political Science* 50 (July 2006): 706–723; Paul Goren, "Political Sophistication and Policy Reasoning: A Reconsideration," *American Journal of Political Science* 48 (July 2004): 462–478; Paul Goren, "Core Principles and Policy Reasoning in Mass Publics: A Test of Two Theories," *British Journal of Political Science* 31(January 2001): 159–177; Huckfeldt, Levine, Morgan, and Sprague, "Accessibility and the Political Utility of Partisan and Ideological Orientations"; William G. Jacoby, "The Structure of Ideological Thinking in the American Electorate," *American Journal of Political Science* 39 (April 1995): 314–335; William G. Jacoby, "Ideological Identification and Issue Attitudes," *American Journal of Political Science* 35 (January 1991): 178–205; Stanley Feldman, "Structure and Consistency in Public Opinion: The Role of Core Beliefs and Attitudes," *American Journal of Political Science* 32 (May 1988): 416–440; Sears, Lau, Tyler, and Allen, "Self-Interest vs. Symbolic Politics in Policy Attitudes and Presidential Voting."

31. Thomas J. Rudolph and Jillian Evans, "Political Trust, Ideology, and Public Support for Government Spending," *American Journal of Political Science* 49 (July 2005): 660–671; William G. Jacoby, "Issue Framing and Government Spending," *American Journal of Political Science* 44 (October 2000): 750–767; William G. Jacoby, "Public

Attitudes toward Government Spending," *American Journal of Political Science* 38 (April 1994)): 336–361.

32. 2012 National Exit Polls.

33. Robert S. Erikson, Michael B. MacKuen, and James A. Stimson, *The Macro Polity* (New York: Cambridge University Press, 2002), pp. xxi, 289–291; John W. Kingdon, *Agendas, Alternatives, and Public Policies* (Boston: Little, Brown, 1984), pp. 68–69, 153.

34. Accessed at http://stimson.web.unc.edu/data/.

35. Peter K. Enns and Julianna Koch, "Public Opinion in the U.S. States: 1956–2010," *State Politics & Policy Quarterly* 13, no. 3 (2013): 349–372.

36. Kaiser Health Tracking Poll, March 5–10, 2013.

37. Kaiser Health Tracking Poll Omnibus Supplement, April 18–21, 2013.

38. Kaiser Health Tracking Poll, March 5–10, 2013.

39. Gallup polls, November 15–18, 2012; November 7–10, 2013; and November 6–9, 2014.

40. Gallup poll, September 6–9, 2012.

41. Gallup poll, September 5–8, 2013.

42. Erikson, MacKuen, and Stimson, *The Macro Polity*, chap. 9.

43. Ibid., pp. 344, 374.

44. Stuart N. Soroka and Christopher Wlezien, *Degrees of Democracy* (New York: Cambridge University Press, 2010).

45. Pew Research Center, *Political Polarization in the American Public*, 2014; Alan I. Abramowitz, *The Disappearing Center* (New Haven, CT: Yale University Press, 2010); Logan Dancey and Paul Goren, "Party Identification, Issue Attitudes, and the Dynamics of Political Debate," *American Journal of Political Science* 54 (July 2010): 686–699; Michael Bang Petersen, Rune Slothuus, and Lise Togeby, "Political Parties and Value Consistency in Public Opinion Formation," *Public Opinion Quarterly* 74 (Fall 2010): 530–550; Matthew Levendusky, *The Partisan Sort* (Chicago: University of Chicago Press, 2009); Adam J. Berinsky, *In Time of War: Understanding American Public Opinion from World War II to Iraq* (Chicago: University of Chicago Press, 2009). See also Morris P. Fiorina, with Samuel J. Abrams and Jeremy C. Pope, *Culture Wars? The Myth of Polarized America*, 3rd ed. (New York: Pearson Longman, 2011); Joseph Bafumi and Robert Y. Shapiro, "A New Partisan Voter," *Journal of Politics* 71 (January 2009): 1–24; Geoffrey C. Layman, Thomas M. Carsey, and Juliana Menasce Horowitz, "Party Polarization in American Politics: Characteristics, Causes, and Consequences," *Annual Review of Political Science* 9 (2006): 83–110; Gary C. Jacobson, *A Divider, Not a Uniter: George W. Bush and the American Public*, 3rd ed. (New York: Longman, 2011).

46. Pew Research Center, *Political Polarization in the American Public*, 2014; Andrew Garner and Harvey Palmer, "Polarization and Issue Consistency Over Time," *Political Behavior* 33 (June 2011): 225–246.

47. Nolan McCarty, Keith T. Poole, and Howard Rosenthal, *Polarized America: The Dance of Ideology and Unequal Riches* (Cambridge, MA: MIT Press, 2006).

48. Pew Research Center, *Political Polarization in the American Public*, 2014.

49. Pew Research Center, *2012 Values Survey*. Results are based on a national sample of 3,008 adults in the period April 4–15, 2012; Pew Research Center, *Political Polarization in the American Public*, 2014.

50. Pew Research Center, *Political Polarization in the American Public*, 2014.

51. Gallup polls, August 17, 2013–March 2, 2014.

52. Gallup poll, March 1–26, 2014.

53. Gary C. Jacobson, "Legislative Success and Political Failure: The Public's Reaction to Barack Obama's Early Presidency," *Presidential Studies Quarterly* 41 (June 2011): 221–222.

54. Kate Kenski, Bruce W. Hardy, and Kathleen Hall Jamieson, *The Obama Victory: How Media, Money, and Message Shaped the 2008 Election* (New York: Oxford University Press, 2010).

55. Spencer Piston, "How Explicit Racial Prejudice Hurt Obama in the 2008 Election," *Political Behavior* 32 (December 2010): 431–451; Michael Lewis-Beck, Charles Tien, and Richard Nadeau, "Obama's Missed Landslide: A Racial Cost?" *PS: Political Science and Politics* 43 (January 2010): 69–76; Benjamin Highton, "Prejudice Rivals Partisanship and Ideology When Explaining the 2008 Presidential Vote across the States," *PS: Political Science and Politics* 44 (July 2011): 6530–6535; Michael Tesler, "The Return of Old-Fashioned Racism to White Americans' Partisan Preferences in the Early Obama Era," *Journal of Politics* 75 (January 2013): 110–123.

56. Edwards, *Overreach*, chap. 1; Pew Research Center, *2012 Values Survey*, April 4–15, 2012; Alan I. Abramowitz, *The Polarized Public: Why Our Government Is So Dysfunctional* (New York: Pearson, 2012); Gary C. Jacobson, "Partisan Polarization in American Politics: A Background Paper," *Presidential Studies Quarterly* 43 (December 2013): 688–708. See also William G. Jacoby, "Is There a Culture War? Conflicting Value Structures in American Public Opinion," *American Political Science Review* 108 (November 2014): 754–771.

57. Charlie Cook, "Intensity Matters," *National Journal*, October 24, 2009.

58. *Newsweek* poll, August 25–26, 2010.

59. Calculations by Gary C. Jacobson from CCES data.

60. See Keith T. Poole and Howard Rosenthal's DW-Nominate Common Space First Dimension scores for presidents at voteview.com/blog/?p=1195

61. Nate Silver, "As Swing Districts Dwindle, Can a Divided House Stand?" *New York Times*, December 27, 2012. Only 14 of these are Republican seats.

62. American National Election Study. The 2012 National Exit Poll found that 92 percent of Democrats voted for Obama and 93 percent of Republicans voted for Romney.

63. Jacobson, "Partisan Polarization in American Politics," pp. 696–697.

64. See Brendan Nyhan, "New Surveys Show the Persistence of Misperceptions," HUFFPOST POLLSTER, July 30, 2012; Pew Research Center for the People & the Press, Pew Forum on Religion & Public Life, conducted by Princeton Survey Research Associates International, June 28–July 9, 2012. Nearly a third of Republicans said Obama was a Muslim.

65. HuffPost/YouGov poll, January 30–February 2, 2013.

66. For previous presidents, see Jacobson, *A Divider, Not a Uniter*, p. 151. The poll for Obama is from the Gallup tracking poll, January 21–27, 2013.

67. Pew Research Center, *Political Polarization in the American Public*, 2014. See also Shanto Iyengar, Guarav Sood, and Yphtach Lelkes, "Affect, Not Ideology: A Social Identity Perspective on Socialization," *Public Opinion Quarterly* 76 (Fall 2012): 405–431; Alan I. Abramowitz, "Americans Are Politically Divided and Our Feelings toward the Parties Show It," *Sabato's Crystal Ball*, July 10, 2014.

68. Bruce A. Desmarais, Raymond J. La Raja, and Michael S. Kowal, "The Fates of Challengers in U.S. House Elections: The Role of Extended Party Networks in Supporting Candidates and Shaping Electoral Outcomes," *American Journal of Political Science* 59 (January 2015): 194–211; Hans Noel, *Political Ideologies and Political Parties in America* (New York: Cambridge University Press, 2013); Gregory Koger, Seth Masket, and Hans Noel, "Partisan Webs: Information Exchange and Party Networks," *British Journal of Political Science* 39 (July 2009): 633–653; Paul S. Herrnson, "The Roles of Party Organizations, Party-Connected Committees, and Party Allies in Elections," *Journal of Politics* 71 (October 2009): 1207–1224; Seth Masket, *No Middle Ground: How Informal Party Organizations Control Nominations and Polarize Legislatures* (Ann Arbor: University of Michigan Press, 2009); Matt Grossmann and Casey B. Dominguez, "Party Coalitions and Interest Group Networks," *American Politics Research* 37 (September 2009): 767–800.

69. Alter, *The Center Hold*, p. 19.

70. Pew Research Center, *Political Polarization in the American Public*, 2014.

71. Piston, "How Explicit Racial Prejudice Hurt Obama in the 2008 Election"; Lewis-Back, Tien, and Nadeau, "Obama's Missed Landslide: A Racial Cost?"; Highton, "Prejudice Rivals Partisanship and Ideology When Explaining the 2008 Presidential Vote across the States."

72. Spee Kosloff, Jeff Greenberg, Toni Schmader, Mark Dechesne, and David Weise, "Smearing the Opposition: Implicit and Explicit Stigmatization of the 2008 U.S. Presidential Candidates and the Current U.S. President," *Journal of Experimental Psychology* 139 (August 2010): 383–398.

73. Piston, "How Explicit Racial Prejudice Hurt Obama in the 2008 Election."

74. Alan I. Abramowitz, "The Race Factor: White Racial Attitudes and Opinions of Obama," *Sabato's Crystal Ball*, May 12, 2011.

75. Michael Tesler, "The Return of Old-Fashioned Racism to White Americans' Partisan Preferences in the Early Obama Era," *Journal of Politics* 75 (January 2013): 110–123.

76. Michael Tesler, "The Spillover of Racialization into Health Care: How President Obama Polarized Public Opinion by Racial Attitudes and Race," *American Journal of Political Science* 56 (July 2012): 690–704.

77. Kevin Arceneaux and Martin Johnson, *Changing Minds or Changing Channels?* (Chicago: University of Chicago Press, 2013); Matthew Levendusky, *How Partisan Media Polarize America* (Chicago: University of Chicago Press, 2013); Nathalie J. Stroud, *Niche News: The Politics of News Choice* (New York: Oxford University Press, 2011); Kathleen Hall Jamieson and Joseph N. Cappella, *Echo Chamber: Rush Limbaugh and the Conservative Media Establishment* (New York: Oxford University Press, 2008).

78. Pew Research Media Attitudes Survey, July 22–26, 2009.

79. Pew Research Center, News Consumption Survey, June 8–28, 2010.

80. This discussion is based on Edwards, *On Deaf Ears*, chaps. 4–9.

81. On the importance of repetition in strengthening and increasing confidence in attitudes, see James N. Druckman and Toby Bolsen, "Framing, Motivated Reasoning, and Opinions about Emergent Technologies," *Journal of Communication* 61 (August 2011): 659–688; Wesley G. Moons, Diane Mackie, and Teresa Garcia-Marques, "The Impact of Repetition-induced Familiarity on Agreement with Weak and Strong Arguments," *Journal of Personality and Social Psychology* 96 (January 2009): 32–44; Michele

P. Claibourn, "Making a Connection: Repetition and Priming in Presidential Campaigns," *Journal of Politics* 70 (October 2008): 1142–1159; Richard Johnston, Michael G. Hagen, and Kathleen Hall Jamieson, *The 2000 Presidential Election and the Foundations of Party Politics* (New York: Cambridge University Press, 2004); Daron R. Shaw, "The Effect of TV Ads and Candidate Appearances on Statewide Presidential Votes, 1988–96," *American Political Science Review* 93 (June 1999): 345–361; Prashant Malaviya and Brian Sternthal, "The Persuasive Impact of Message Spacing," *Journal of Consumer Psychology* 6, no. 3 (1997): 233–255; Ida E. Berger, "The Nature of Attitude Accessibility and Attitude Confidence," *Journal of Consumer Psychology* 1, no. 2 (1992): 103–123; John T. Cacioppo and Richard E. Petty, "Effects of Message Repetition on Argument Processing, Recall, and Persuasion," *Basic and Applied Social Psychology* 10, no. 1 (1989): 3–12.

82. David Gergen, *Eyewitness to Power: The Essence of Leadership* (New York: Simon & Schuster 2000), pp. 54, 186. Also see Martha Joynt Kumar, *Managing the President's Message: The White House Communications Operation* (Baltimore, MD: Johns Hopkins University Press, 2007), chaps. 2–3.

83. "Remarks by President Bush in a Conversation on Strengthening Social Security," Greece, New York, March 24, 2005.

84. Dennis Chong and James N. Druckman, "Dynamic Public Opinion: Communication Effects over Time," *American Political Science Review* 104 (November 2010): 663–680; Douglas A. Hibbs, Jr., "Implications of the 'Bread and Peace' Model for the 2008 Presidential Election," *Public Choice* 137 (October 2008): 1–10; Seth J. Hill, James Lo, Lynn Vavreck, and John Zaller, "The Duration of Advertising Effects in the 2000 Presidential Campaign," paper presented at the 2008 Annual Meeting of the American Political Science Association, Boston; Dennis Chong and James N. Druckman, "A Theory of Framing and Opinion Formation in Competitive Elite Environments," *Journal of Communication* 57 (February 2007): 99–118; Alan Gerber, James G. Gimpel, Donald P. Green, and Daron R. Shaw, "The Influence of Television and Radio Advertising on Candidate Evaluations: Results from a Large Scale Randomized Experiment," paper presented at the 2007 Annual Meeting of the Midwest Political Science Association, Chicago; Diana C. Mutz and Byron Reeves, "The New Videomalaise: Effects of Televised Incivility on Political Trust," *American Political Science Review* 99 (February 2005): 1–15; Claes H. de Vreese, "Primed by the Euro," *Scandinavian Political Studies* 27 (March 2004): 45–65; James N. Druckman and Kjersten R. Nelson, "Framing and Deliberation: How Citizens' Conversations Limit Elite Influence," *American Journal of Political Science* 47 (October 2003): 729–745; David Tewksbury, Jennifer Jones, Matthew W. Peske, Ashlea Raymond, and William Vig, "The Interaction of News and Advocate Frames: Manipulating Audience Perceptions of a Local Public Policy Issue," *Journalism and Mass Communication Quarterly* 77 (December 2000): 804–829.

85. John R. Zaller, *The Nature and Origins of Mass Opinion* (New York: Cambridge University Press, 1992), pp. 102–113; Danielle Shani, "Knowing Your Colors: Can Knowledge Correct for Partisan Bias in Political Perceptions?", paper presented at the annual meeting of the Midwest Political Science Association, Chicago, 2006.

86. Zaller, *The Nature and Origins of Mass Opinion*, p. 48; William G. Jacoby, "The Sources of Liberal–Conservative Thinking: Education and Conceptualization," *Political Behavior* 10 (December 1988): 316–332; Robert C. Luskin, "Measuring Political Sophistication," *American Journal of Political Science* 31 (November 1987): 856–899; W. Rus-

sell Neuman, *The Paradox of Mass Politics; Knowledge and Opinion in the American Electorate* (Cambridge, MA: Harvard University Press, 1986); Edward G. Carmines and James A. Stimson, "The Two Faces of Issue Voting," *American Political Science Review* 74 (March 1980): 78–91; Philip E. Converse, "The Nature of Belief Systems in Mass Publics," in David E. Apter, ed., *Ideology and Discontent*, (New York: Free Press, 1964).

87. James H. Kuklinski, Paul J. Quirk, Jennifer Jerit, David Schwieder, and Robert F. Rich, "Misinformation and the Currency of Democratic Citizenship," *Journal of Politics* 62 (August 2000): 790–816. See also Brendan Nyhan, "Why the 'Death Panel' Myth Wouldn't Die: Misinformation in the Health Care Reform Debate," *Forum* 8, no. 1 (2010). Accessed at www.bepress.com/forum/vol8/iss1/art5.

88. Brendan Nyhan and Jason Reifler, "When Corrections Fail: The Persistence of Political Misperceptions," *Political Behavior* 32 (June 2010): 303–330; David P. Redlawsk, Andrew J. W. Civettini, and Karen M. Emmerson, "The Affective Tipping Point: Do Motivated Reasoners Ever 'Get It'?" *Political Psychology* 31 (August 2010): 563–593.

89. Ruth Mayo, Yaacov Schul, and Eugene Burnstein, " 'I Am Not Guilty' vs 'I Am Innocent': Successful Negation May Depend on the Schema Used for Its Encoding," *Journal of Experimental Social Psychology* 40 (July 2004): 433–449.

90. Norbert Schwarz, Lawrence J. Sanna, Ian Skurnik, and Carolyn Yoon, "Metacognitive Experiences and the Intricacies of Setting People Straight: Implications for Debiasing and Public Information Campaigns," *Advances in Experimental Social Psychology* 39 (2007): 127–161; Ian Skurnik, Carolyn Yoon, Denise C. Park, and Norbert Schwarz, "How Warnings about False Claims Become Recommendations," *Journal of Consumer Research* 31 (March 2005): 713–724.

91. John Bullock, "Experiments on Partisanship and Public Opinion: Party Cues, False Beliefs, and Bayesian Updating," PhD dissertation, Stanford University, 2007.

92. David Kahneman and Amos Tversky, "Choices, Values, and Frames," *American Psychologist* 39 (April 1984): 341–350; David Kahneman and Amos Tversky, "Prospect Theory: An Analysis of Decision under Risk," *Econometrica* 47 (March 1979): 263–292.

93. Stuart N. Soroka, *Negativity in Democratic Politics* (New York: Cambridge University Press, 2014); Susan T. Fiske, "Attention and Weight in Person Perception: The Impact of Negative and Extreme Behavior," *Journal of Personality and Social Psychology* 38, no. 6 (1980): 889–906; David L. Hamilton and Mark P. Zanna, "Differential Weighting of Favorable and Unfavorable Attributes in Impressions of Personality," *Journal of Experimental Research in Personality* 6, nos. 2–3 (1972): 204–212.

94. Richard Lau, "Two Explanations for Negativity Effects in Political Behavior," *American Journal of Political Science* 29 (February 1985): 119–138.

95. See, for example, David W. Brady and Daniel P. Kessler, "Who Supports Health Reform?" *PS: Political Science and Politics* 43 (January 2010): 1–5.

96. Michael D. Cobb and James H. Kuklinski, "Changing Minds: Political Arguments and Political Persuasion," *American Journal of Political Science* 41 (January 1997): 88–121. On the role of emotion in political decision making, see Joanne M. Miller, "Examining the Mediators of Agenda Setting: A New Experimental Paradigm Reveals the Role of Emotions," *Political Psychology* 28 (December 2007): 689–717; George E. Marcus, W. Russell Neuman, and Michael MacKuen, *Affective Intelligence and Political Judgment* (Chicago: University of Chicago Press, 2000); George E. Marcus, *The Sentimental Citizen*

(University Park: Pennsylvania State University Press, 2002); Michael MacKuen, Jennifer Wolak, Luke Keele, and George E. Marcus, "Civic Engagements: Resolute Partisanship or Reflective Deliberation," *American Journal of Political Science* 54 (April 2010): 440–458.

97. Kevin Arceneaux, "Cognitive Biases and the Strength of Political Arguments," *American Journal of Political Science* 56 (April 2012): 271–285.

98. See, for example, Andrew Goldman, "Cornel West Flunks the President," *New York Times*, July 22, 2011; Robert Reich, "The Empty Bully Pulpit," *American Prospect*, July 27, 2011; Drew Westen, "What Happened to Obama?" *New York Times*, August 6, 2011; Maureen Dowd, "No Bully Pulpit," *New York Times*, April 20, 2013.

CHAPTER 3: STRATEGIC POSITION WITH CONGRESS

1. George C. Edwards III, *The Strategic President: Persuasion and Opportunity in Presidential Leadership* (Princeton, NJ: Princeton University Press, 2009), chaps. 4–5; George C. Edwards III, *At the Margins: Presidential Leadership of Congress* (New Haven, CT: Yale University Press), chaps. 9–10; Jon R. Bond and Richard Fleisher, *The President in the Legislative Arena* (Chicago: University of Chicago Press, 1990), chap. 8; Richard Fleisher, Jon R. Bond, and B. Dan Wood, "Which Presidents Are Uncommonly Successful in Congress?" in Bert Rockman and Richard W. Waterman, eds., *Presidential Leadership: The Vortex of Presidential Power*, (New York: Oxford University Press, 2007).

2. George C. Edwards III, Andrew Barrett, and Jeffrey Peake, "The Legislative Impact of Divided Government," *American Journal of Political Science* 41 (April 1997): 545–563.

3. See Keith Poole's analysis on his blog dated November 13, 2012, accessed at voteview.com/blog/?p=609.

4. See Keith Poole's blog dated November 8, 2012, accessed at voteview.com/blog/?p=602.

5. Geoffrey Kabaservice, *Rule and Ruin: The Downfall of Moderation and the Destruction of the Republican Party, From Eisenhower to the Tea Party* (New York: Oxford University Press, 2012); Soren Jordan, Clayton Webb, and B. Dan Wood, "Polarization and the Party Platforms, 1944–2012," paper prepared for delivery at the Annual Meeting of the Midwest Political Science Association, Chicago, Illinois, April 11–14, 2013; Thomas E. Mann and Norman J. Ornstein, *It's Even Worse Than It Looks* (New York: Basic Books, 2012); Gary C. Jacobson, "Partisan Polarization in American Politics," *Presidential Studies Quarterly* 43 (December 2013): 4; Joseph Daniel Ura and Christopher R. Ellis, "Partisan Moods: Polarization and the Dynamics of Mass Party Preferences," *Journal of Politics* 74 (January 2011): 1–15.

6. Mann and Ornstein, *It's Even Worse Than It Looks*, p. 103.

7. Carol E. Lee and Monica Langley, "A More Worried Obama Battles to Win Second Term," *Wall Street Journal*, August 31, 2012.

8. Tim Alberta, "Defenders of the Faith," *National Journal*, May 25, 2013.

9. Earle Black and Merle Black, *Politics and Society in the South* (Cambridge, MA: Harvard University Press, 1987); Paul Frymer, "The 1994 Aftershock: Dealignment or Realignment in the South," in Philip A. Klinkner, ed., *Midterm: The Elections of 1994 in Context* (Boulder, CO: Westview, 1995), 99–113; Richard Nadeau and Harold W. Stanley, "Class Polarization Among Native Southern Whites, 1952–90," *American Journal of*

Political Science 37 (August 1993): 900–919; M.V. Hood, III, Quentin Kidd, and Irwin L. Morris, "Of Byrd[s] and Bumpers: Using Democratic Senators to Analyze Political Change in the South, 1960–1995," *American Journal of Political Science* 43 (April 1999): 465–487; Martin P. Wattenberg, "The Building of a Republican Regional Base in the South: The Elephant Crosses the Mason-Dixon Line," *Public Opinion Quarterly* 55 (1991): 424–431; Charles S. Bullock III, Donna R. Hoffman, and Ronald Keith Gaddie, "The Consolidation of the White Southern Congressional Vote," *Political Research Quarterly* 58 (June 2005): 231–243; Seth C. McKee, *Republican Ascendancy in Southern U.S. House Elections* (Boulder, CO: Westview, 2010).

10. Jacobson, "Partisan Polarization in American Politics," p. 694. In the National Exit Polls, the respective figures were 86 percent and 84 percent.

11. Gary C. Jacobson, "How the Economy and Partisanship Shaped the 2012 Presidential and Congressional Elections," *Political Science Quarterly* 128, no. 1 (2013): 26–27. See also Gary C. Jacobson, "Barack Obama and the Nationalization of Electoral Politics in 2012," *Electoral Studies* (forthcoming).

12. Jacobson, "Barack Obama and the Nationalization of Electoral Politics in 2012"; Jacobson, "Partisan Polarization in American Politics," pp. 697, 700, 703.

13. Charlie Cook, "The Big Sort," *National Journal*, April 13, 2013.

14. Jacobson, "Partisan Polarization in American Politics," p. 702.

15. Calculations by Martin Wattenberg, University of California, Irvine.

16. ANES 2012.

17. Ronald Brownstein and Scott Bland, "Stairway to Nowhere," *National Journal*, January 12, 2013.

18. Pew Research Center poll, July 17–21, 2013, and November 6–9, 2014.

19. Theda T. Skocpol and Vanessa Williamson, *The Tea Party and the Remaking of Republican Conservatism* (New York: Oxford University Press, 2012); Jeffrey M. Berry, Sarah Sobieraj, and Suzanne Schlossberg, "Tea Party Mobilization," paper prepared for delivery at the Annual Meeting of the American Political Science Association, New Orleans, Louisiana, September 2012.

20. Pew Research Center poll, July 17–21. 2013.

21. Gallup poll, September 5–8, 2013; Pew Research Center for the People & the Press polls, January 9–13 and July 17–21, 2013 and November 6–9, 2014; Ronald B. Rapoport, Meredith Dost, Ani-Rae Lovell, and Walter J. Stone, "Republican Factionalism and Tea Party Activists," paper prepared for delivery at the Annual Meeting of the Midwest Political Science Association, April 11–14, Chicago. There is some reason to suspect preferences for compromise among other segments of the public. See Laurel Harbridge, Neil Malhotra, and Brian Harrison, "Public Preferences for Bipartisanship in the Policymaking Process," *Legislative Studies Quarterly* 39 (August 2014): 327–355; Laurel Harbridge and Neil Malhotra, "Electoral Incentives and Partisan Conflict in Congress: Evidence from Survey Experiments," *American Journal of Political Science* 55 (July 2011): 494–510.

22. Christopher S. Parker and Matt A. Barreto, *Change They Can't Believe In: The Tea Party and Reactionary Politics in America* (Princeton, NJ: Princeton University Press, 2011); Skocpol and Williamson, *The Tea Party and the Remaking of Republican Conservatism*, pp. 174, 178.

23. E. Scott Adler and John D. Wilkerson, *Congress and the Politics of Problem Solving* (New York: Cambridge University Press, 2013).

24. Nolan McCarty, Keith T. Poole, and Howard Rosenthal, *Polarized America: The Dance of Ideology and Unequal Riches* (Cambridge, MA: MIT Press, 2006); Skocpol and Williamson, *The Tea Party and the Remaking of Republican Conservatism*; Rapoport, Dost, Lovell, and Stone, "Republican Factionalism and Tea Party Activists."

25. *Washington Post*-ABC News poll September 12–15, 2013.

26. Pew Research Center poll, September 4–8, 2013.

27. Carl Hulse, " 'Vote No, Hope Yes' Defines Dysfunction in Congress," *New York Times*, February 12, 2014.

28. Gary C. Jacobson, "Partisan Polarization in Presidential Support: The Electoral Connection," *Congress and the Presidency* 30 (Spring 2003): 8–11.

29. Ryan Lizza, "Where the G.O.P.'s Suicide Caucus Lives," *New Yorker*, September 26, 2013; Charlie Cook, "The GOP Keeps Getting Whiter," *National Journal*, March 14, 2013.

30. Lizza, "Where the G.O.P.'s Suicide Caucus Lives"; Cook, "The GOP Keeps Getting Whiter."

31. Frances E. Lee, *Beyond Ideology: Politics, Principles, and Partisanship in the U.S. Senate* (Chicago: University of Chicago Press, 2009), chap. 4; Frances E. Lee, "Presidents and Party Teams: The Politics of Debt Limits and Executive Oversight, 2001–2013," *Presidential Studies Quarterly* 43 (December 2013): 775–791. See also Mann and Ornstein, *It's Even Worse Than It Looks*, pp. 18, 51.

32. Quoted in Jann S. Wenner, "Ready for the Fight: Rolling Stone Interview with Barack Obama," *Rolling Stone*, April 25, 2012.

33. Sean M. Theriault, *The Gingrich Senators: The Roots of Partisan Warfare in Congress* (New York: Oxford University Press, 2013); Sean M. Theriault, *Party Polarization in Congress* (New York: Cambridge University Press, 2008).

34. Sarah Binder, "The Senate's Partisan Fever (in 4 Charts)," *Washington Post*, July 22, 2014.

35. Karen DeYoung, "'President and Congress Play Waiting Game on Authorization for Islamic State Action," *Washington Post*, December 5, 2014.

36. David Wasserman, "House Overview: How House Democrats Beat the Point Spread," *Cook Political Report*, November 9, 2012.

37. Jacobson, "The Congressional Elections of 2012," p. 7.

38. ABC News/*Washington Post* polls, December 13–16, 2012, and April 11–14, 2013; CBS News poll, December 12–16, 2012; Pew Research Center for the People & the Press poll, December 5–9, 2012; McClatchy-Marist poll, December 4–6, 2012; AP-GfK poll, November 29–December 3, 2012; United Technologies/National Journal Congressional Connection Poll conducted by Princeton Survey Research Associates International, November 29–December 2, 2012.

39. Quoted in Alexis Simendinger and Caitlin Huey-Burns, "Amid 'Frank' Talks, Obama Uses Polls as Pry Bar," *RealClearPolitics*, December 14, 2012.

40. Lori Montgomery, "Democrats Challenge Obama on Medicare and Social Security Cuts," *Washington Post*, March 14, 2013. See also Felicia Sonmez, "Democrats Incensed with White House over Social Security, Medicare," *Washington Post*, July 8, 2011.

41. Ryan Grim and Sabrina Siddiqui, "Red-State Democrats Buck Obama On Social Security Cuts," *Huffington Post*, May 6, 2013.

42. George C. Edwards III and Andrew Barrett, "Presidential Agenda Setting in

Congress," in Jon R. Bond and Richard Fleisher, eds., *Polarized Politics: Congress and the President in a Partisan Era* (Washington, DC: Congressional Quarterly, 2000).

43. Carol E. Lee and Monica Langley, "A More Worried Obama Battles to Win Second Term," *Wall Street Journal*, August 31, 2012; Jonathan Alter, *The Center Holds: Obama and His Enemies* (New York: Simon & Schuster, 2013), pp. 2, 123–124.

44. Charlie Cook, "Advice to Obama: Make More Friends in Congress," *National Journal*, November 9, 2012.

45. Juliet Eilperin and Zachary A. Goldfarb, "After String of Setbacks, More Charm May Be the Last, Best Option for Obama," *Washington Post*, April 29, 2013.

46. David Remnick, "Going the Distance," *New Yorker*, January 27, 2014, p. 51.

47. Eilperin and Goldfarb, "After String of Setbacks, More Charm May Be the Last, Best Option for Obama."

48. Quoted in Lee and Langley, "A More Worried Obama Battles to Win Second Term."

49. Eilperin and Goldfarb, "After String of Setbacks, More Charm May Be the Last, Best Option for Obama."

50. Ibid.

51. Quoted in Lee and Langley, "A More Worried Obama Battles to Win Second Term."

52. Jackie Calmes, "Obama's G.O.P. Outreach Hits Barriers," *New York Times*, March 11, 2013; David Remnick, "Going the Distance," p. 41. Also see Alter, *The Center Holds*, p. 2.

53. Alter, *The Center Holds*, p. 124.

54. Quoted in Juliet Eilperin, "White House's Outreach Is Yielding Modest Benefits, Lawmakers Say," *Washington Post*, March 23, 2013. Also see Alter, *The Center Holds*, p 124.

55. Jackie Calmes, "Obama's G.O.P. Outreach Hits Barriers."

56. See, for example, Jackie Calmes and Jonathan Weisman, "Trying to Revive Talks, Obama Goes Around G.O.P. Leaders," *New York Times*, March 5, 2013; Rachel Weiner, "Obama Picked Up GOP Senators' Dinner Tab," *Washington Post*, March 6, 2013; Philip Rucker, "Obama Has 'Constructive' Lunch with Paul Ryan," *Washington Post*, March 7, 20, 2013; Jeremy Peters, " U.S. Budget Deal in Doubt; Obama's Trip to Hill Reveals Split," *New York Times*, March 13, 2013; Amie Parnes, "Obama: White House Dinner with GOP Senators 'Constructive,' " *The Hill*, April 10, 2013.

57. David M. Drucker, "Republicans Remain Skeptical of Obama's Charm Offensive," *Roll Call*, March 12, 2013.

58. Jeremy W. Peters and Michael D. Shear, "Obama Is Seen as Frustrating His Own Party," *New York Times*, August 18, 2014; Alter, *The Center Holds*, pp. 127, 143. See also Eilperin and Goldfarb, "After String of Setbacks, More Charm May Be the Last, Best Option for Obama."

59. See note 1 and sources cited therein.

60. This meeting is described in Robert Draper, *"Do Not Ask What Good We Do"* (New York: Free Press, 2012); and Alter, *The Center Holds*, p. 51.

61. Alter, *The Center Holds*, pp. 51–52.

62. Donna R. Hoffman and Alison D. Howard, *Addressing the State of the Union* (Boulder, CO: Lynne Rienner, 2006), 144; Donna R. Hoffman and Alison D. Howard,

"Obama in Words and Deeds," *Social Science Quarterly* 93 (2012): 1326; and updates by Donna R. Hoffman and Alison D. Howard.

CHAPTER 4: DIFFERENT QUESTIONS, DIFFERENT ANSWERS

1. Lawrence J. Grossback, David A. M. Peterson, and James A. Stimson, *Mandate Politics* (New York: Cambridge University Press, 2006).

2. Peter Baker, "Obama Goes Back on the Trail Ahead of Debt Talks, *New York Times*, November 27, 2012.

3. Ibid.

4. NBC News/*Wall Street Journal* poll, December 6–9, 2012; *Washington Post*-ABC News polls, November 21–25 and December 13–16, 2012; Fox News poll, December 9–11, 2012; Bloomberg National poll, December 7–10, 2012; CBS News poll, December 12–16, 2012; CBS News/*New York Times* polls, September 8–12, October 25–28, and December 12–16, 2012; Pew Research Center for the People & the Press polls, October 4–7 and December 5–9, 2012; McClatchy-Marist polls, July 9–11 and December 4–6, 2012; United Technologies/*National Journal* Congressional Connection polls conducted by Princeton Survey Research Associates International, October 12–14 and November 17–20, 2012; Dan Friedman, "Axelrod: Obama Has Tax Mandate," *New York Times*, November 12, 2012.

5. See Pew Research Center for the People & the Press polls, October 4–7 and December 5–9, 2012.

6. Gallup poll, January 3, 2013. See also Pew Research Center poll, January 3–6, 2013. The ABC News/*Washington Post* poll of January 2–6, 2013, found 45 percent approval of the agreement, but only 38 percent disapproval with 17 percent unsure.

7. Brandice Canes-Wrone, *Who Leads Whom? Presidents, Policy, and the Public* (Princeton, NJ: Princeton University Press, 2006), p. 80, chaps. 3–4.

8. Pew Research Center/*Washington Post* poll, November 29–December 2, 2012; Fox News poll, December 9–11, 2012; Gallup polls of December 1–2, 8–9, and 15–16, 2012; CBS News poll, December 12–16, 2012.

9. Pew Research Center/*Washington Post* poll, November 8–11, 2012; Pew Research Center for the People & the Press poll, November 29–December 2, 2012; Fox News poll, December 9–11, 2012; Gallup polls of December 1–2, 8–9, and 15–16, 2012; NBC News/*Wall Street Journal* poll, December 6–9, 2012; CBS News poll, December 12–16, 2012; CNN/ORC poll, November 16–18, 2012.

10. Gallup polls of December 1–2, 8–9, 15–16, and 21–22, 2012; *Washington Post*-ABC News poll December 13–16, 2012; NBC News/*Wall Street Journal* poll, December 6–9, 2012; CBS News poll, December 12–16, 2012.

11. NBC News/*Wall Street Journal* poll, December 6–9, 2012; *Washington Post*-ABC News polls, November 21–25 and December 13–16, 2012; Fox News poll, December 9–11, 2012; Bloomberg National Poll, December 7–10, 2012; CBS News poll, December 12–16, 2012; CBS News/*New York Times* polls, September 8–12, October 25–28, and December 12–16, 2012; Pew Research Center for the People & the Press polls, October 4–7 and December 5–9, 2012; McClatchy-Marist polls, July 9–11 and December 4–6, 2012; United Technologies/*National Journal* Congressional Connection polls conducted by Princeton Survey Research Associates International, October 12–14 and

November 17–20, 2012; Dan Friedman, "Axelrod: Obama Has Tax Mandate," *New York Times*, November 12, 2012.

12. Nelson D. Schwartz and Jonathan Weisman, "Unlikely Backers in a Battle Over Taxes," *New York Times*, December 11, 2012.

13. *Washington Post*-ABC News poll December 13–16, 2012; NBC News/*Wall Street Journal* poll, December 6–9, 2012; Pew Research Center for the People & the Press poll, November 8–11, 2012; Pew Research Center for the People & the Press poll, November 29–December 2, 2012; McClatchy-Marist poll, December 4–6, 2012.

14. ABC News/*Washington Post* poll, December 13–16, 2012; CBS News poll, December 12–16, 2012; NBC News/*Wall Street Journal* poll, December 6–9, 2012; Gallup poll, December 21–22, 2012.

15. ABC News/*Washington Post* polls, December 13–16, 2012, and April 11–14, 2013; CBS News poll, December 12–16, 2012; Pew Research Center for the People & the Press poll, December 5–9, 2012; McClatchy-Marist poll, December 4–6, 2012; AP-GfK poll, November 29–December 3, 2012; United Technologies/National Journal Congressional Connection Poll conducted by Princeton Survey Research Associates International, November 29–December 2, 2012.

16. Gallup tracking polls, February 25–26, 2013; Pew Research Center/*USA Today* poll, February 13–18, 2013.

17. Transcript, "Statement by the President on the Sequester," White House, March 1, 2013.

18. Gallup polls, March 2–3, March 11–12, April 6–7, April 29–30, and July 27–28, 2013.

19. Transcript, "Statement by the President on the Sequester," White House, March 1, 2013.

20. Jonathan Weisman, "G.O.P. Claims Victory as Bill to Curb Flight Delays Passes," *New York Times*, April 26, 2013.

21. Steven T. Dennis and Daniel Newhauser, "Obama's Lost Leverage," *Roll Call*, March 1, 2013.

22. Jennifer Steinhauer, "For Gun Bill Born in Tragedy, a Tangled Path to Defeat," *New York Times*, April 18, 2013.

23. Ron Fournier, "From Guns to Immigration, Obama Circumventing GOP," *National Journal*, January 16, 2013.

24. Peter Baker and Michael D. Shear, "Obama to 'Put Everything I've Got' Into Gun Control," *New York Times*, January 16, 2013. Also see Scott Wilson and Zachary A. Goldfarb, "With Domestic Legacy in Lawmakers' Hands, Obama Considers His Options," *New York Times*, April 13, 2013.

25. Gallup poll, January 7–10, 2013.

26. Gallup poll, January 17, 2013. See also Pew Research Center poll, January 9–13, 2013.

27. Pew Research Center poll, May 1–5, 2013.

28. Pew Research Center/*Washington Post* poll, April 18–21, 2013.

29. Ibid.

30. Gallup poll, May 4–5, 2013.

31. Jonathan Weisman, "Senate Blocks Drive for Gun Control," *New York Times*, April 17, 2013.

32. Nate Silver, "In Gun Ownership Statistics, Partisan Divide Is Sharp," *New York Times*, December 18, 2012.

33. Pew Research Center poll, January 9–13, 2013.

34. Pew Research Center poll, May 1–5, 2013.

35. See, for example, Maureen Dowd, "No Bully Pulpit," *New York Times*, April 20, 2013.

36. Pew Research Center poll, September 19–22, 2013. See also *New York Times/CBS News* poll, September 19–23; and *Washington Post*-ABC News poll, September 12–15, 2013.

37. CBS News poll, October 1–2, 2013.

38. ABC News/*Washington Post* poll, October 17–20, 2013.

39. CBS News poll, October 18–21, 2013.

40. Gallup poll, October 14–15, 2013.

41. CNN/ORC International poll, September 6–8, 2013; and *Washington Post*-ABC News poll, September 12–15, 2013; United Technologies/*National Journal* Congressional Connection Poll, conducted by Princeton Survey Research Associates International, September 25–29, 2013; CBS News/*New York Times* poll, September 19–23, 2013; and Pew Research Center poll, September 19–22, 2013.

42. Fox News poll, October 1–2, 2013; Pew Research Center poll, October 9–13, 2013; CBS News polls, October 1–2 and October 18–21, 2013; NBC News/*Wall Street Journal* poll, October 7–9, 2013; Gallup polls, September 27–28 and October 14–15, 2013; ABC News/*Washington Post* poll, October 17–20, 2013.

43. Gallup poll, October 3–6, 2013. See also ABC News/*Washington Post* poll, October 17–20, 2013.

44. Gallup poll, October 14–15, 2013.

45. George C. Edwards III and Andrew Barrett, "Presidential Agenda Setting in Congress," in Jon R. Bond and Richard Fleisher, eds., *Polarized Politics: Congress and the President in a Partisan Era* (Washington, DC: Congressional Quarterly, 2000).

46. George C. Edwards III and B. Dan Wood, "Who Influences Whom? The President, Congress, and the Media," *American Political Science Review* 93 (June 1999): 327–344.

CHAPTER 5: REINFORCING OPINION

1. George C. Edwards III, *On Deaf Ears: The Limits of the Bully Pulpit* (New Haven, CT: Yale University Press, 2003).

2. George C. Edwards III, *Governing by Campaigning: The Politics of the Bush Presidency*, 2nd ed. (New York: Longman, 2007).

3. George C. Edwards III, *Overreach: Leadership in the Obama Presidency* (Princeton, NJ: Princeton University Press, 2012).

4. George C. Edwards III, *The Strategic President: Persuasion and Opportunity in Presidential Leadership* (Princeton, NJ: Princeton University Press, 2009); Edwards, *On Deaf Ears*.

5. See Edwards, *On Deaf Ears*, chap. 5.

6. A good example is Kent Tedin, Brandon Rottinghaus, and Harrell Rodgers, "When the President Goes Public: The Consequences of Communication Mode for Opinion

Change across Issue Types and Groups," *Political Research Quarterly* 64 (September 2011): 506–519.

7. John R. Zaller, *The Nature and Origins of Mass Opinion* (New York: Cambridge University Press, 1992), p. 99, chap. 9. See also Adam J. Berinsky, "Assuming the Costs of War: Events, Elites, and American Public Support for Military Conflict," *Journal of Politics* 69 (November 2007): 975–997; and John R. Zaller, "Elite Leadership of Mass Opinion: New Evidence from the Gulf War," in W. Lance Bennett and David L. Paletz, eds., *Taken by Storm: The Media, Public Opinion, and U.S. Foreign Policy in the Gulf War* (Chicago: University of Chicago Press, 1994), pp. 186–209.

8. See Paul M. Sniderman and Sean M. Theriault, "The Structure of Political Argument and the Logic of Issue Framing," in Willem E. Saris and Paul M. Sniderman, eds., *Studies in Public Opinion: Attitudes, Nonattitudes, Measurement Error and Change* (Princeton, NJ: Princeton University Press, 2004). Also see Paul M. Sniderman, "Taking Sides: A Fixed Choice Theory of Political Reasoning," in Arthur Lupia, Mathew D. McCubbins, and Samuel L. Popkin, eds., *Elements of Reason: Understanding and Expanding the Limits of Political Rationality* (New York: Cambridge University Press, 2000); James N. Druckman, "Political Preference Formation: Competition, Deliberation, and the (Ir)relevance of Framing Effects," *American Political Science Review* 98 (November 2004): 671–686.

9. James N. Druckman, Jordan Fein, and Thomas J. Leeper, "A Source of Bias in Public Opinion Stability," *American Political Science Review* 106 (May 2012): 430–454.

10. Zaller, "Elite Leadership of Mass Opinion: New Evidence from the Gulf War."

11. James N. Druckman, Jordan Fein, and Thomas J. Leeper, "A Source of Bias in Public Opinion Stability," *American Political Science Review* 106 (May 2012): 430–454; Rune Slothuus and Claes H. de Vreese, "Political Parties, Motivated Reasoning, and Issue Framing Effects," *Journal of Politics* (July 2010): 630–645; Charles S. Taber, Damon Cann, and Simona Kucsova, "The Motivated Processing of Political Arguments," *Political Behavior* 31 (June 2009): 137–155; Charles S. Taber and Milton Lodge, "Motivated Skepticism in the Evaluation of Political Beliefs," *American Journal of Political Science* 50 (July 2006): 755–769; John T. Jost, "The End of the End of Ideology," *American Psychologist* 61, no. 7 (2006): 651–670; Richard R. Lau and David P. Redlawsk, *How Voters Decide: Information Processing in Election Campaigns* (New York: Cambridge University Press, 2006); Milton Lodge and Charles S. Taber, "The Automaticity of Affect for Political Leaders, Groups, and Issues: An Experimental Test of the Hot Cognition Hypothesis," *Political Psychology* 26 (June 2005): 455–482; David P. Redlawsk, "Hot Cognition or Cool Consideration: Testing the Effects of Motivated Reasoning on Political Decision Making," *Journal of Politics* 64 (November 2002): 1021–1044; Milton Lodge and Ruth Hamill, "A Partisan Schema for Political Information Processing," *American Political Science Review* 80 (June 1986): 505–519; Charles Lord, Lee Ross, and Mark R. Lepper, "Biased Assimilation and Attitude Polarization: The Effects of Prior Theories on Subsequently Considered Evidence," *Journal of Personality and Social Psychology* 37 (November 1979): 2098–2109.

12. Donald P. Green, Bradley Palmquist, and Eric Schickler, *Partisan Hearts and Minds* (New Haven, CT: Yale University Press, 2002); Alan S. Gerber, Gregory A. Huber, and Ebonya Washington, "Party Affiliation, Partisanship, and Political Beliefs: A Field Experiment," *American Political Science Review* 104 (November 20120): 720–744.

13. Jennifer Jerit and Jason Barabas, "Partisan Perceptual Bias and the Information Environment," *Journal of Politics* 74 (July 2012): 672–684.

14. See Howard Lavine, Christopher Johnston, and Marco Steenbergen, *The Ambivalent Partisan* (Oxford, UK: Oxford University Press 2012); Brendan Nyhan and Jason Reifler, *Misinformation and Fact-Checking: Research Findings from Social Science* (Washington, DC: New America Foundation, 2012); Alan S. Gerber and Gregory A. Huber, "Partisanship, Political Control, and Economic Assessments," *American Journal of Political Science* 54 (January 2010): 153–173; Paul Goren, Christopher M. Federico, and Miki Caul Kittilson, "Source Cues, Partisan Identities, and Political Value Expression," *American Journal of Political Science* 55 (October 2009): 805–820; Brian J. Gaines, James H. Kuklinski, Paul J. Quirk, Buddy Peyton, and Jay Verkuilen, "Same Facts, Different Interpretations: Partisan Motivation and Opinion on Iraq," *Journal of Politics* 69 (November 2007): 957–974; Edwards, *On Deaf Ears*, chap. 9; Larry Bartels, "Beyond the Running Tally: Partisan Bias in Political Perceptions," *Political Behavior* 24 (June 2002): 117–150; Christopher H. Achen and Larry M. Bartels, "It Feels Like We're Thinking: The Rationalizing Voter and Electoral Democracy," paper delivered at the Annual Meeting of the American Political Science Association, Philadelphia, 2006; Larry M. Bartels, *Unequal Democracy* (Princeton, NJ: Princeton University Press, 2008), chap. 5; Mathew J. Lebo and Daniel Cassino, "The Aggregated Consequences of Motivated Reasoning and the Dynamics of Partisan Presidential Approval," *Political Psychology* 28 (December 2007): 719–746; Gary C. Jacobson, *A Divider, Not a Uniter: George W. Bush and the American Public*, 3rd ed. (New York: Longman, 2011); Suzanna DeBoef and Paul M. Kellstedt, "The Political (and Economic) Origins of Consumer Confidence," *American Journal of Political Science* 48 (October 2004): 633–649; Steven Kull, Clay Ramsay, and Evan Lewis, "Misperceptions, the Media, and the Iraq War," *Political Science Quarterly* 118 (Winter 2003–2004): 569–598; Edwards, *Governing by Campaigning*, chap. 3; Paul D. Sweeney and Kathy L. Gruber, "Selective Exposure: Voter Information Preferences and the Watergate Affair," *Journal of Personality and Social Psychology* 46, no. 6 (1984): 1208–1221; Mark Fischle, "Mass Response to the Lewinsky Scandal: Motivated Reasoning or Bayesian Updating?" *Political Psychology* 21 (March 2000): 135–159.

15. YouGov.com poll, April 18–20, 2015.

16. Steven P. Nawara, "Who Is Responsible, the Incumbent or the Former President? Motivated Reasoning in Responsibility Attributions," *Presidential Studies Quarterly* 45 (March 2015): 110–131.

17. Adam J. Berinsky, *In Time of War: Understanding American Public Opinion from World War II to Iraq* (Chicago: University of Chicago Press, 2009), p. 124.

18. See also Logan Dancey and Geoffrey Sheagley, "Heuristics Behaving Badly: Party Cues and Voter Knowledge," *American Journal of Political Science* 57 (April 2013): 312–325.

19. James N. Druckman, Erik Peterson, and Rune Slothuus, "How Elite Partisan Polarization Affects Public Opinion Formation," *American Political Science Review* 107 (February 2013): 57–79; Geoffrey C. Layman, Thomas M. Carsey, John C. Green, Richard Herrera, and Rosalyn Cooperman, "Activists and Conflict Extension in American Party Politics," *American Political Science Review* 107 (June 2013): 324–346; Matthew Levendusky, *The Partisan Sort* (Chicago: University of Chicago Press, 2009). See also

Joshua Dyck and Shanna Pearson-Merkowitz, "To Know You Is Not Necessarily to Love You: The Partisan Mediators of Intergroup Contact," *Political Behavior* 36 (September 2014): 553–580.

20. Logan Dancey and Paul Goren, "Party Identification, Issue Attitudes, and the Dynamics of Political Debate," *American Journal of Political Science* 54 (July 2010): 686–699.

21. Stephen P. Nicholson, "Polarizing Cues," *American Journal of Political Science* 56 (January 2012): 52–66; Joanne R. Smith, Deborah J. Terry, Timothy R. Crosier, and Julie M. Duck, "The Importance of the Relevance of the Issue to the Group in Voting Intentions," *Basic and Applied Social Psychology* 27 no. 2 (2005): 163–170.

22. John G. Bullock, "Elite Influence on Public Opinion in an Informed Electorate," *American Political Science Review* 105 (August 2011): 496–515.

23. Druckman, Peterson, and Rune Slothuus, "How Elite Partisan Polarization Affects Public Opinion Formation." Party endorsements, particularly under conditions of polarization, do not appear to simply serve as cues people follow. Instead, cues seem to shape how the public views arguments put forth by different sides. See also Toby Bolsen, James N. Druckman, and Fay Lomax Cook, "The Influence of Partisan Motivated Reasoning on Public Opinion," *Political Behavior* 36 (June 2014): 235–262. But see Cheryl Boudreau and Scott A. MacKenzie, "Informing the Electorate? How Party Cues and Policy Information Affect Public Opinion about Initiatives," *American Journal of Political Science* 58 (January 2014): 48–62.

24. Penny S. Visser, George Y. Bizer, and Jon A. Krosnick, "Exploring the Latent Structure of Strength-Related Attitude Attributes," in Mark P. Zanna, ed., *Advances in Experimental Social Psychology*, vol. 38 (San Diego: Academic Press, 2006).

25. See Druckman, Peterson, and Slothuus, "How Elite Partisan Polarization Affects Public Opinion Formation."

26. Bolsen, Druckman, and Cook, "The Influence of Partisan Motivated Reasoning on Public Opinion"; Michael Bang Petersen, Martin Skov, Søren Serritzlew, and Thomas Ramsøy, "Motivated Reasoning and Political Parties: Evidence for Increased Processing in the Face of Party Cues," *Political Behavior* 35 (December 2013): 831–854.

27. James N. Druckman and Toby Bolsen, "Framing, Motivated Reasoning, and Opinions about Emergent Technologies," *Journal of Communication* 61 (August 2011): 659–688.

28. Jeffrey J. Mondak, "Source Cues and Public Approval: The Cognitive Dynamics of Public Support for the Reagan Administration," *American Journal of Political Science* 37 (February 1993): 186–212.

29. On the importance of source credibility, see James N. Druckman, "Using Credible Advice to Overcome Framing Effects," *Journal of Law, Economics, and Organization* 17, no. 1 (2001): 62–82; James N. Druckman, "On the Limits of Framing Effects: Who Can Frame?" *Journal of Politics* 63 (November 2001): 1041–1066; Joanne M. Miller and Jon A. Krosnick, "News Media Impact on the Ingredients of Presidential Evaluations: Politically Knowledgeable Citizens Are Guided by a Trusted Source," *American Journal of Political Science* 44 (April 2000): 301–315; James H. Kuklinski and Norman Hurley, "On Hearing and Interpreting Messages: A Cautionary Tale of Citizen Cue-Taking," *Journal of Politics* 56 (August 1994): 729–751.

30. Lavine, Johnston, and Steenbergen, *The Ambivalent Partisan*.

31. Carrie Budoff Brown and Jonathan Allen, "White House Returns to Obamacare Sales Mode," *Politico.com*, December 2, 2013; Edward-Isaac Dovere and Jonathan Allen, "White House Turns to Bully Pulpit for ACA Turnaround," *Politico.com*, December 3, 2013.

32. Jonathan Weisman and Sheryl Gay Stolberg, "G.O.P. Maps Out Waves of Attacks Over Health Law," *New York Times*, November 20, 2013.

33. Elizabeth Wilner, "The Affordable Care Act: When Political and Product Advertising Collide," paper delivered at the Annual Conference of the American Association for Public Opinion Research, Anaheim, CA, May 15–18, 2014.

34. Quoted in Jim VandeHei and Mike Allen, "Bush Rejects Delay, Prepares Escalated Social Security Push," *Washington Post*, March 3, 2005, p. A4.

35. Mike Allen and Jim VandeHei, "Social Security Push to Tap the GOP Faithful: Campaign's Tactics Will Drive Appeal," *Washington Post*, January 14, 2005, p. A6.

36. Ibid.

37. Gallup/CNN/*USA Today* poll, April 29–May 1, 2005.

38. For another example of divergent partisan responses to the president, see ABC/*Washington Post* poll, March 10–13, 2005.

39. See also Stephen P. Nicholson, "Polarizing Cues," *American Journal of Political Science* 56 (January 2012): 52–66.

40. Jeffrey J. Mondak, "Source Cues and Public Approval: The Cognitive Dynamics of Public Support for the Reagan Administration," *American Journal of Political Science* 37 (February 1993): 186–212.

41. Lee Sigelman and Carol K. Sigelman, "Presidential Leadership of Public Opinion: From 'Benevolent Leader' to Kiss of Death?" *Experimental Study of Politics* 7, no. 3 (1981): 1–22.

42. Ronald Reagan, *An American Life* (New York: Simon & Schuster, 1990), pp. 471, 479; Edwards, *On Deaf Ears*, pp. 51–54; Richard Sobel, ed., *Public Opinion in U.S. Foreign Policy: The Controversy over Contra Aid* (Lanham, MD: Rowman and Littlefield, 1993); Benjamin I. Page and Robert Y. Shapiro, *The Rational Public (Chicago: University of Chicago Press, 1992)*, p. 276.

43. Reagan, *An American Life*, p. 479.

44. CNBC, All-America Economic Survey, September 16–19. The sample was 812.

45. Scott Wilson and Zachary A. Goldfarb, "With Domestic Legacy in Lawmakers' Hands, Obama Considers His Options," *New York Times*, April 13, 2013; Ryan Lizza, "Getting to Maybe: Inside the Gang of Eight's Immigration Deal," *New Yorker*, June 24, 2013, pp. 48–49. For a similar example, see Bob Woodward, *The Price of Politics* (New York: Simon & Schuster, 2012), pp. 255–256.

46. Michael D. Shear, "Difficult Spot for Obama on Immigration Push," *New York Times*, July 11, 2013.

47. Jackie Calmes, "Obama Must Walk Fine Line as Congress Takes Up Agenda," *New York Times*, April 7, 2013.

48. News Conference by the President, James S. Brady Press Briefing Room, The White House, April 30, 2013, www.whitehouse.gov/the-press-office/2013/04/30/news-conference-president.

49. See Manu Raju, "How Patty Murray Won Over Dems on Budget Fight," *Politico.com*, December 13, 2013.

CHAPTER 6: EXPLOITING EXISTING OPINION

1. Martha Joynt Kumar, *Managing the President's Message: The White House Communications Operation* (Baltimore, MD: Johns Hopkins University Press, 2007), p. 9.

2. A key source on these activities is Kumar, *Managing the President's Message*. See also Brendan J. Doherty, *The Rise of the President's Permanent Campaign* (Lawrence: University Press of Kansas, 2012); Matthew Eshbaugh-Soha and Jeffrey S. Peake, *Breaking through the Noise* (Palo Alto, CA: Stanford University Press, 2011).

3. See Jeffrey Tulis, "The Two Constitutional Presidencies," in Michael Nelson, ed., *The Presidency and the Political System* (Washington, DC: CQ Press, 1984), pp. 78–79.

4. John W. Kingdon, *Agendas, Alternatives, and Public Policies*, 2nd ed. (Boston: Little, Brown, 1995), pp. 146–150.

5. Frank Baumgartner and Bryan D. Jones, *Agendas and Instability in American Politics* (Chicago: University of Chicago Press, 1993), pp. 236–237.

6. Michael Nelson, "The President and the Court: Reinterpreting the Court-packing Episode of 1937," *Political Science Quarterly* 103 (Summer 1988): 272.

7. Richard J. Carwardine, *Lincoln* (Essex, UK: Longman 2003), pp. xiii, 304.

8. See, for example, Douglas L. Wilson, *Lincoln's Sword: The Presidency and the Power of Words* (New York: Knopf, 2006); Phillip Shaw Paludan, *"The Better Angels of our Nature": Lincoln, Propaganda and Public Opinion in the North During the American Civil War* (Fort Wayne, IN: Lincoln Museum, 1992); Garry Wills, *Lincoln at Gettysburg: The Words that Remade America* (New York: Simon & Schuster, 1992).

9. Michael Kempner, "Five Best Books on Public Relations," *Wall Street Journal*, November 25, 2006, p. P10. Kempner is the president and CEO of MWW Group public relations. The Lincoln book is Ronald C. White, Jr., *The Eloquent President* (New York: Random House, 2005).

10. Carwardine, *Lincoln*, pp. xiii, 47, 193–198, 218, 306.

11. Quoted in Michael Burlingame and John R. Turner Ettlinger, eds., *Inside Lincoln's White House: The Complete Civil War Diary of John Hay* (Carbondale: Southern Illinois University Press, 1997), p, 135.

12. Carwardine, *Lincoln*, p. 306.

13. Ibid., pp. xiii, 260, 273, 292, 306, 310.

14. Ibid., pp. 249, 261–262.

15. Ibid., pp. 86, 193, 205, 219, 249. See also Garry Wills, *Certain Trumpet: The Call of Leaders* (New York: Simon & Schuster, 1994), p. 16.

16. Paludan, *"The Better Angels of our Nature,"* pp. 13–15.

17. David Herbert Donald, *Lincoln* (New York: Simon & Schuster, 1995), pp. 14–15.

18. Abraham Lincoln, Letter to Albert G. Hodges, April 4, 1864, *The Collected Works of Abraham Lincoln*, Vol. 7, ed. Roy P. Basler (New Brunswick, NJ: Rutgers University Press, 1953), p. 281.

19. Quoted in Donald, *Lincoln*, p. 332.

20. See Paludan, *"The Better Angels of our Nature."*

21. Harold Holzer, *Lincoln and the Power of the Press* (New York: Simon & Schuster, 2014), p. 477.

22. Ibid.; Carwardine, *Lincoln*, pp. 249, 257–280; Paludan, *"The Better Angels of our Nature,"* pp. 6–9, 15–16.

23. Carwardine, *Lincoln*, pp. 249–250.

24. Ibid., pp. 202, 211–213, 291.

25. See George C. Edwards III, *The Strategic President* (Princeton, NJ: Princeton University Press, 2012), pp. 27–34.

26. Richard Hofstadter, *The American Political Tradition* (New York: Vintage, 1954), p. 316.

27. Quoted in Gerald M. Boyd, " 'General Contractor' of the White House Staff," *New York Times*, March 4, 1986, sec. A, p. 22.

28. See, for example, Arthur Lupia, "Shortcuts versus Encyclopedias: Information and Voting Behavior in California Insurance Reform Elections," *American Political Science Review* 88 (March 1994): 63–76; Samuel L. Popkin, *The Reasoning Voter* (Chicago: University of Chicago Press, 1991); Paul M. Sniderman, Richard Brody, and Philip E. Tetlock, *Reasoning and Choice* (New York: Cambridge University Press, 1991); Daniel Kahneman, Paul Slovic, and Amos Tversky, *Judgment Under Uncertainty: Heuristics and Biases* (New York: Cambridge University Press, 1982); Herbert A. Simon, "A Behavioral Model of Rational Choice," *Quarterly Journal of Economics* 69 (February 1955): 99–118.

29. Richard R. Lau, "Construct Accessibility and Electoral Choice," *Political Behavior* 11 (March 1989): 5–32; Thomas K. Srull and Robert S. Wyer, Jr., *Memory and Cognition in Their Social Context* (Hillsdale, NJ: Erlbaum, 1989); Robert S. Wyer, Jr., and Jon Hartwick, "The Recall and Use of Belief Statements as Bases for Judgments," *Journal of Experimental Social Psychology* 20 (January 1984): 65–85; E. Tory Higgins and Gary A. King, "Accessibility of Social Constructs: Information-Processing Consequences of Individual and Contextual Variation," in N. Cantor and J. F. Kihlstrom, eds., *Personality, Cognition, and Social Interaction* (Hillsdale, NJ: Erlbaum, 1981); Thomas K. Srull and Robert S. Wyer, Jr., "Category Accessibility and Social Perception: Some Implications for the Study of Person Memory and Interpersonal Judgments," *Journal of Personality and Social Psychology* 38, no. 6 (1980): 841–856; Thomas K. Srull and Robert S. Wyer, Jr., "The Role of Category Accessibility in the Interpretation of Information about Persons: Some Determinants and Implications," *Journal of Personality and Social Psychology* 37, no. 10 (1979): 1660–1672.

30. See, for example, Donald R. Kinder and Lynn M. Sanders, *Divided by Color: Racial Politics and Democratic Ideals* (Chicago: University of Chicago Press, 1996); Zhongdang Pan and Gerald M. Kosicki, "Framing Analysis: An Approach to News Discourse," *Political Communication* 10, no. 1 (1993): 55–75; William A. Gamson, *Talking Politics* (Cambridge, UK: Cambridge University Press, 1992); William A. Gamson and Andre Modigliani, "Media Discourse and Public Opinion on Nuclear Power: A Constructionist Approach," *American Journal of Sociology* 95 (July 1989): 1–37; William A. Gamson and Andre Modigliani, "The Changing Culture of Affirmative Action," in Richard D. Braungart, ed., *Research in Political Sociology*, vol. 3 (Greenwich, CT: JAI Press, 1987), p. 143.

31. There is some evidence that the president's rhetoric can prime the criteria on which the public evaluates him. See James N. Druckman and Justin W. Holmes, "Does Presidential Rhetoric Matter? Priming and Presidential Approval," *Presidential Studies Quarterly* 34 (December 2004): 755–778.

32. For the latter view that framing does not work by altering the accessibility to different considerations, see James N. Druckman, "On the Limits of Framing Effects:

Who Can Frame?" *Journal of Politics* 63 (November 2001): 1041–1066. See also Thomas E. Nelson, Rosalee A. Clawson, and Zoe M. Oxley, "Media Framing of a Civil Liberties Conflict and Its Effect on Tolerance," *American Political Science Review* 91 (September 1997): 567–584; and Joanne M. Miller and Jon A. Krosnick, "News Media Impact on the Ingredients of Presidential Evaluations: Politically Knowledgeable Citizens Are Guided by a Trusted Source," *American Journal of Political Science* 44 (April 2000): 301–315.

33. Over the past generation, the research on public opinion has produced a large number of studies showing the impact of priming and framing on people's opinions. For evidence of the impact of framing effects, see Samara Klar, "The Influence of Competing Identity Primes on Political Preferences," *Journal of Politics* 75 (October 2013): 1108–1124; Dan Cassino and Cengiz Erisen, "Priming Bush and Iraq in 2008: A Survey Experiment," *American Politics Research* 38 (March 2010): 372–394; Nicholas J. G. Winter, "Beyond Welfare: Framing and the Racialization of White Opinion on Social Security," *American Journal of Political Science* 50 (April 2006): 400–420; Nicholas A. Valentino, Vincent L. Hutchings, and Ismail K. White, "Cues that Matter: How Political Ads Prime Racial Attitudes During Campaigns," *American Political Science Review* 96 (March 2002): 75–90; Thomas E. Nelson, "Policy Goals, Public Rhetoric, and Political Attitudes," *Journal of Politics* 66 (May 2004): 581–605; Nicholas A. Valentino, Vincent L. Hutchings, and Ismail K. White, "Cues that Matter: How Political Ads Prime Racial Attitudes During Campaigns," *American Political Science Review* 96 (March 2002): 75–90; William G. Jacoby, "Issue Framing and Public Opinion on Government Spending," *American Journal of Political Science* 44 (October 2000): 750–767; Thomas E. Nelson and Zoe M. Oxley, "Issue Framing Effects on Belief Importance and Opinion," *Journal of Politics* 61 (November 1999): 1040–1067; Joseph N. Cappella and Kathleen Hall Jamieson, *Spiral of Cynicism: The Press and the Public Good* (New York: Oxford University Press, 1997); Thomas E. Nelson, Rosalee A. Clawson, and Zoe M. Oxley, "Toward a Psychology of Framing Effects," *Political Behavior* 19 (September 1997): 221–246; Nelson, Clawson, and Oxley, "Media Framing of a Civil Liberties Conflict and Its Effect on Tolerance"; Donald R. Kinder and Lynn M. Sanders, *Divided by Color: Racial Politics and Democratic Ideals* (Chicago: University of Chicago Press, 1996); Thomas E. Nelson and Donald R. Kinder, "Issue Frames and Group-Centrism in American Public Opinion," *Journal of Politics* 58 (November 1996): 1055–1078; Dennis Chong, "How People Think, Reason, and Feel about Rights and Liberties," *American Journal of Political Science* 37 (August 1993): 867–899; W. Russell Neuman, Marion K. Just, and Ann N. Crigler, *Common Knowledge: News and the Construction of Political Meaning* (Chicago: University of Chicago Press, 1992); John Zaller and Stanley Feldman, "A Simple Theory of the Survey Response: Answering Questions versus Revealing Preferences," *American Journal of Political Science* 36 (August 1992): 579–616; Stanley Feldman and John Zaller, "The Political Culture of Ambivalence: Ideological Responses to the Welfare State," *American Journal of Political Science* 36 (February 1992): 268–307; Donald R. Kinder and Lynn M. Sanders, "Mimicking Political Debate with Survey Questions: The Case of White Opinion on Affirmative Action for Blacks," *Social Cognition* 8, no. 1 (1990): 73–103; Jon A. Krosnick and Donald R. Kinder, "Altering the Foundations of Support for the President through Priming," *American Political Science Review* 84 (June 1990): 497–512; John H. Aldrich, John Sullivan, and Eugene Borgida, "Foreign Affairs and Issue Voting: Do Presidential Candidates Waltz Before a Blind Audience?" *Ameri-*

can Political Science Review 83 (March 1989): 123–141; Daniel Kahneman and Amos Tversky, "Rational Choice and the Framing of Decisions," in Hillel J. Einhorn and Robin M. Hogarth, eds., *Rational Choice: The Contrast between Economics and Psychology* (Chicago: University of Chicago Press, 1987); Daniel Kahneman and Amos Tversky, "Choices, Values, and Frames," *American Psychologist* 39 (April 1984): 341–350; Amos Tversky and Daniel Kahneman, "The Framing of Decisions and the Psychology of Choice," *Science* 211 (30 January 1981): 453–458.

34. James N. Druckman and Lawrence R. Jacobs, *Who Governs? Presidents, Public Opinion, and Manipulation* (Chicago: University of Chicago Press, 2015), chap. 5.

35. For a good discussion of this point, see Lawrence R. Jacobs and Robert Y. Shapiro, *Politicians Don't Pander* (Chicago: University of Chicago Press, 2000), pp. 49–52.

36. See Druckman and Jacobs, *Who Governs?*

37. "Remarks by the President on the Importance of Passing a Historic Energy Bill," White House Transcript, June 25, 2009.

38. See, for example, William B. Riker, *The Art of Political Manipulation* (New Haven, CT: Yale University Press, 1986); William B. Riker, *The Strategy of Rhetoric: Campaigning for the American Constitution* (New Haven, CT: Yale University Press, 1996); William B. Riker, "The Heresthetics of Constitution Making: The Presidency in 1787, with Comments on Determinism and Rational Choice," *American Political Science Review* 78 (March 1984): 1–16.

39. Byron E. Shafer and William J. M. Claggett, *The Two Majorities: The Issue Context of Modern American Politics* (Baltimore, MD: Johns Hopkins University Press, 1995). See also James N. Druckman, Lawrence R. Jacobs, and Eric Ostermeier, "Candidate Strategies to Prime Issues and Image," *Journal of Politics* 66 (November 2004): 1180–1202.

40. John R. Petrocik, "Divided Government: Is It All in the Campaigns," in Gary W. Cox and Samuel Kernell, eds., *The Politics of Divided Government* (Boulder, CO: Westview, 1991); John R. Petrocik, "Issue Ownership in Presidential Elections, with a 1980 Case Study," *American Journal of Political Science* (August 1996): 825–850.

41. Andrew Gelman and Gary King, "Why Are American Presidential Election Campaign Polls So Variable When Votes Are So Predictable?" *British Journal of Political Science* 23 (Part 4, 1993): 409–451.

42. See, for example, Carl Albert, interview by Dorothy Pierce McSweeny, April 13, 1969, interview 3, transcript, pp. 8–9, Lyndon Johnson Library, Austin, Texas.

43. See, for example, Richard P. Nathan et al., *Revenue Sharing: The Second Round* (Washington, DC: Brookings Institution, 1977).

44. David Gergen, *Eyewitness to Power: The Essence of Leadership* (New York: Simon & Schuster 2000), p. 348.

45. Quoted in Steven V. Roberts, "Return to the Land of the Gipper," *New York Times*, March 9, 1988, p. A28.

46. Ronald Reagan, *Where's the Rest of Me? The Autobiography of Ronald Reagan* (New York: Karz, 1965), p. 138.

47. Bob Woodward, *The Agenda: Inside the Clinton White House* (New York: Simon & Schuster, 1994), pp. 243, 247–248.

48. Quoted in Howard Goldberg, "Clinton Pollster Says Administration 'Lost' Control of Its Agenda," Associated Press, May 22, 2993.

49. "Democrats Look to Salvage Part of Stimulus Plan," *Congressional Quarterly Weekly Report*, April 24, 1993, p. 1002.

50. George C. Edwards III, *On Deaf Ears: The Limits of the Bully Pulpit* (New Haven, CT: Yale University Press, 2003), pp. 35–36.

51. Jann S. Wenner and William Greider, "President Clinton," *Rolling Stone*, December 9, 1993, p. 43.

52. Alter, *The Promise*, pp. 272–274.

53. Peter Baker, "Familiar Obama Phrase Being Groomed as a Slogan," *New York Times*, May 16, 2009.

54. Shear, "White House Revamps Communications Strategy."

55. White House Transcript, "Remarks by the President at GOP House Issues Conference," January 29, 2010.

56. Alessandra Stanley, "The News Conference: The Same, and Different," *New York Times*, February 10, 2009.

57. Quoted in Ronald Brownstein, "The Solvency Solution," *National Journal*, February 7, 2009.

58. Nate Silver, "The Proliferation of 'Pork,' " *FiveThirtyEight*, February 4, 2009.

59. Pew Research Center's News Index Survey, February 6–9, 2009.

60. Drew Armstrong, "Axelrod Fuels Democratic Message Machine for Health Care Overhaul," *CQ Today*, May 13, 2009; Robert Pear, "Democrats to Develop Plan to Sell Health Care," *New York Times*, May 13, 2009.

61. Peter Slevin, "Obama Turns to Grass Roots to Push Health Reform," *Washington Post*, June 24, 2009.

62. Michael D. Shear, "Poll Results Drive Rhetoric of Obama's Health-Care Message," *Washington Post*, July 30, 2009.

63. George C. Edwards III, *Overreach: Leadership in the Obama Presidency* (Princeton, NJ: Princeton University Press, 2012), pp. 89–99.

64. Jennifer Hopper, "Technical 'Glitches' or 'Obama's Katrina'? Presidential Framing, News Media Scandal Coverage, & the Politics of the HealthCare.Gov Rollout," paper presented at the Annual Meeting of the American Political Science Association, Washington, DC, August 27–31, 2014.

65. Mark Landler, "Obama Plans to Unveil His Agenda for Economy," *New York Times*, July 21, 2013; Annie Lowrey, "President Adopts Catchphrase to Describe Proposed Recipe for Economic Revival," *New York Times*, July 22, 2013.

66. An exception to the experimental nature of framing studies is Jacoby, "Issue Framing and Public Opinion on Government Spending." He employed NES data to present both frames to the same sample. Even here, however, the framing occurred in the context of an interview in which different frames were presented at different times.

67. See Hans Noel, "The Coalition Merchants: The Ideological Roots of the Civil Rights Realignment," *Journal of Politics* 74 (January 2012): 156–173; Mark A. Smith, *The Right Talk: How Conservatives Transformed the Great Society into the Economic Society* (Princeton, NJ: Princeton University Press, 2007); Edward G. Carmines and James A. Stimson, *Issue Evolution: Race and the Transformation of American Politics* (Princeton, NJ: Princeton University Press, 1989).

68. See Paul M. Sniderman and Sean M. Theriault, "The Structure of Political Argument and the Logic of Issue Framing," in Willem E. Saris and Paul M. Sniderman, eds.,

Studies in Public Opinion: Attitudes, Nonattitudes, Measurement Error and Change (Princeton, NJ: Princeton University Press, 2004). Also see Dennis Chong and James N. Druckman, "Counterframing Effects," *Journal of Politics* 75 (January 2013): 1–16; Dennis Chong and James N. Druckman, "Framing Public Opinion in Competitive Democracies," *American Political Science Review* 101 (November 2007): 637–655; James N. Druckman, "Political Preference Formation: Competition, Deliberation, and the (Ir)relevance of Framing Effects," *American Political Science Review* 98 (November 2004): 671–686; Paul M. Sniderman, "Taking Sides: A Fixed Choice Theory of Political Reasoning," in Arthur Lupia, Mathew D. McCubbins, and Samuel L. Popkin, eds., *Elements of Reason: Understanding and Expanding the Limits of Political Rationality* (New York: Cambridge University Press, 2000).

69. James N. Druckman, Jordan Fein, and Thomas J. Leeper, "A Source of Bias in Public Opinion Stability," *American Political Science Review* 106 (May 2012): 430–454.

70. James N. Druckman and Kjersten R. Nelson, "Framing and Deliberation: How Citizens' Conversations Limit Elite Influence," *American Journal of Political Science* 47 (October 2003): 729–745.

71. James N. Druckman, "Using Credible Advice to Overcome Framing Effects," *Journal of Law, Economics, and Organization* 17 (April 2001): 62–82.

72. Donald P. Haider-Markel and Mark R. Joslyn, "Gun Policy, Opinion, Tragedy, and Blame Attribution: The Conditional Influence of Issue Frames," *Journal of Politics* 63 (May 2001): 520–543.

73. Gregory A. Huber and John S. Lapinski, "The 'Race Card' Revisited: Assessing Racial Priming in Policy Contests," *American Journal of Political Science* 50 (April 2006): 421–40.

74. Druckman and Nelson, "Framing and Deliberation."

75. Gregory A. Huber and Celia Paris, "Assessing the Programmatic Equivalence Assumption in Question Wording Experiments: Understanding Why Americans Like Assistance to the Poor More Than Welfare," *Public Opinion Quarterly* 77 (January 2013): 385–397; Gabriel S. Lenz, "Learning and Opinion Change, Not Priming: Reconsidering the Priming Hypothesis," *American Journal of Political Science* 53 (October 2009): 821–837.

76. Daniel J. Hopkins, "The Exaggerated Life of Death Panels: The Limits of Framing Effects in the 2009–2012 Health Care Debate." Available at SSRN: http://ssrn.com/abstract=2163769.

77. Frank R. Baumgartner, Jeffrey M. Berry, Marie Hojnacki, Beth L. Leech, and David C. Kimball, *Lobbying and Policy Change: Who Wins, Who Loses, and Why* (Chicago: University of Chicago Press, 2009), chap. 9.

78. Quoted in Michael B. Grossman and Martha J. Kumar, *Portraying the President* (Baltimore, MD: Johns Hopkins University Press, 1981), p. 26.

79. Thomas E. Patterson, *Out of Order* (New York: Knopf, 1993), pp. 16–21, 113–115; Matthew Robert Kerbel, *Edited for Television* (Boulder, CO: Westview, 1994), pp. 111–112; Kevin G. Barnhurst and Catherine A. Steele, "Image-Bite News: The Visual Coverage of Elections on U.S. Television, 1968–1992," *Press/Politics* 1, no. 2 (Winter 1997): 40–58; S. Robert Lichter and Richard E. Noyes, *Good Intentions Make Bad News*, 2nd ed. (Lanham, MD: Rowman and Littlefield, 1996), pp. 116–126; Richard Nadeau, Richard G. Niemi, David P. Fah, and Timothy Amato, "Elite Economic Forecasts, Eco-

nomic News, Mass Economic Judgments, and Presidential Approval," *Journal of Politics* 61 (February 1999): 109–135; "Campaign 2000 Final: How TV News Covered the Election Campaign," *Media Monitor* 14 (November/December 2000).

80. Dwight F. Davis, Lynda Lee Kaid, and Donald L. Singleton, "Information Effects of Political Commentary," *Experimental Study of Politics* 6 (June 1977): 45–68; Lynda Lee Kaid, Donald L. Singleton, and Dwight F. Davis, "Instant Analysis of Televised Political Addresses: The Speaker versus the Commentator," in Brent D. Ruben, ed., *Communication Yearbook I* (New Brunswick, NJ: Transaction Books, 1977), pp. 453–464; John Havick, "The Impact of a Televised State of the Union Message and the Instant Analysis: An Experiment." Unpublished paper, Georgia Institute of Technology, 1980.

81. David L. Paletz and Robert M. Entman, *Media—Power—Politics* (New York: Free Press, 1981), p. 70.

82. Pew Research Center poll, January 17–19, 2014. N = 800.

83. Pew Research Center poll, January 15–19, 2014.

84. W. Russell Neuman, *The Paradox of Mass Politics; Knowledge and Opinion in the American Electorate* (Cambridge, MA: Harvard University Press, 1986), pp. 170, 172, 177–178, 186.

85. See, for example, Markus Prior, *Post–Broadcast Democracy: How Media Choice Increases Inequality in Political Involvement and Polarizes Elections* (New York: Cambridge University Press, 2007).

86. Ryan L. Claassen and Benjamin Highton, "Does Policy Debate Reduce Information Effects in Public Opinion? Analyzing the Evolution of Public Opinion on Health Care," *Journal of Politics* 68 (May, 2006): 410–420.

87. Philip E. Converse, "The Nature of Belief Systems in Mass Publics," in David Apter, ed., *Ideology and Discontent* (Glencoe, IL: Free Press, 1964); William G. Jacoby, "The Sources of Liberal-Conservative Thinking: Education and Conceptualization," *Political Behavior* 10 (Winter 1988): 316–332; Robert C. Luskin, "Measuring Political Sophistication," *American Journal of Political Science* 31 (November 1987): 856–899; Neuman, *The Paradox of Mass Politics*; Edward G. Carmines and James A. Stimson, "The Two Faces of Issue Voting," *American Political Science Review* 74 (March 1980): 78–91; John R. Zaller, *The Nature and Origins of Mass Opinion* (New York: Cambridge University Press, 1992), , p. 48.

88. James H. Kuklinski, Paul J. Quirk, Jennifer Jerit, David Schwieder, and Robert F. Rich, "Misinformation and the Currency of Democratic Citizenship," *Journal of Politics* 62 (August 2000): 790–816.

89. Zaller, *The Nature and Origins of Mass Opinion*, pp. 102–113.

90. John R. Zaller, "Elite Leadership of Mass Opinion: New Evidence from the Gulf War," in W. Lance Bennett and David L. Paletz, eds., *Taken by Storm: The Media, Public Opinion, and U.S. Foreign Policy in the Gulf War* (Chicago: University of Chicago Press, 1994), pp. 186–209; Zaller, *The Nature and Origins of Mass Opinion*.

91. See, for example, James H. Kuklinski and Norman L. Hurley, "On Hearing and Interpreting Political Messages: A Cautionary Tale of Citizen Cue-Taking," *Journal of Politics* 56 (August 1994): 729–751.

92. See Brian J. Gaines, James H. Kuklinski, Paul J. Quirk, Buddy Peyton, and Jay Verkuilen, "Same Facts, Different Interpretations: Partisan Motivation and Opinion on Iraq," *Journal of Politics* 69 (November 2007): 957–974; Edwards, *On Deaf Ears*, chap.

9; Larry Bartels, "Beyond the Running Tally: Partisan Bias in Political Perceptions," *Political Behavior* 24 (June 2002): 117–150.

93. Druckman, "On the Limits of Framing Effects: Who Can Frame?" See also Miller and Krosnick, "News Media Impact on the Ingredients of Presidential Evaluations"; and James N. Druckman, "Using Credible Advice to Overcome Framing Effects," *Journal of Law, Economics, and Organization* 17 (April 2001): 62–82.

94. "Reagan Loses Ground on 'Contra' Aid Program," *Congressional Quarterly Weekly Report,* March 8, 1986, pp. 535–536.

95. Steven V. Roberts, "Senate Upholds Arms for Saudis, Backing Reagan," *New York Times,* June 6, 1986, sec. A, pp. l, 10. The 34 votes did sustain the president's veto, however.

96. They may also direct public attention to popular policy stances to increase their general public support. See Druckman and Jacobs, *Who Governs?*

97. Brandice Canes-Wrone, *Who Leads Whom? Presidents, Policy, and the Public* (Princeton, NJ: Princeton University Press, 2006), p. 80, chaps. 3–4.

98. Christopher Olds, "Assessing Presidential Agenda-Setting Capacity: Dynamic Comparisons of Presidential, Mass Media, and Public Attention to Economic Issues," *Congress & the Presidency* 40 (September–December 2013): 255–284.

99. Jeffrey E. Cohen, *Presidential Responsiveness and Public Policy-Making* (Ann Arbor: University of Michigan Press, 1997).

100. Kim Quaile Hill, "The Policy Agendas of the President and the Mass Public: A Research Validation and Extension," *American Journal of Political Science* 42 (October 1998): 1328–1334.

101. B. Dan Wood, *The Politics of Economic Leadership* (Princeton, NJ: Princeton University Press, 2007), chap. 3.

102. Michael Waldman, *POTUS Speaks* (New York: Simon & Schuster, 2000), p. 216.

103. See E. E. Schattschneider, *The Semi-Sovereign People: A Realist's View of Democracy in America* (New York: Holt, Rinehart and Winston, 1960).

104. See Bryan D. Jones and Frank R. Baumgartner, *The Politics of Attention: How Government Prioritizes Problems* (Chicago: University of Chicago Press, 2005), chap. 3; Bryan D. Jones, *Reconceiving Decision-Making in Democratic Politics* (Chicago: University of Chicago Press, 1994), chap. 4.

105. Quoted in "MX Debate: It's Not Over," *New York Times,* March 30, 1985, pp. 1, 8. See also "Senate Hands Reagan Victory on MX Missile," *Congressional Quarterly Weekly Report,* March 23, 1985, pp. 515–523.

106. See, for example, William G. Howell, Saul P. Jackman, and Jon C. Rogowski, *The Wartime President: Executive Influence and the Nationalizing Politics of Threat* (Chicago: University of Chicago Press, 2014).

107. Lee Sigelman, "Gauging the Public Response to Presidential Leadership," *Presidential Studies Quarterly* 10 (Summer 1980): 427–433. See also Pamela Johnston Conover and Lee Sigelman, "Presidential Influence and Public Opinion: The Case of the Iranian Hostage Crisis," *Social Science Quarterly* 63 (June 1982): 249–264.

108. David Zarefsky, *President Johnson's War on Poverty: Rhetoric and History* (Tuscaloosa: University of Alabama Press, 1986), p. 24.

109. Jeffrey K. Tulis, *The Rhetorical Presidency* (Princeton, NJ: Princeton University

Press, 1987), pp. 161–172. See also Zarefsky, *President Johnson's War on Poverty* for a discussion of the administration's framing of the issue.

110. Druckman and Jacobs, *Who Governs?*, chap. 6.

111. Dan Thomas and Lee Sigelman, "Presidential Identification and Policy Leadership: Experimental Evidence on the Reagan Case," in George C. Edwards III, Norman C. Thomas, and Steven A. Shull, eds., *The Presidency and Public Policy Making* (Pittsburgh, PA: University of Pittsburgh Press, 1985), pp. 37–49. A poll of Utah residents found that although two-thirds of them opposed deploying MX missiles in Utah and Nevada, an equal number said they would either "definitely" or "probably" support President Reagan if he decided to go ahead and base the missiles in those states.

112. Gallup poll, September 24–27, 2007.

113. See Milton Lodge and Charles S. Taber, *The Rationalizing Voter* (New York: Cambridge University Press, 2013); and Edward G. Carmines and James A. Stimson, "The Two Faces of Issue Voting," *American Political Science Review* 74 (March 1980): 78–91.

114. NBC News/*Wall Street Journal* poll, November 22–23, 1985; Roper/*U.S. News & World Report* poll, October 15–16, 1986; NBC News/*Wall Street Journal* poll, November 30–December 1, 1987. See also SDI and US Defense Effort Survey, October 6–9, 1985.

115. Edwards, *On Deaf Ears*, pp. 57–59.

116. Kuklinski et al., "Misinformation and the Currency of Democratic Citizenship"; Robert C. Luskin, James S. Fishkin, and Roger Jowell, "Considered Opinions: Deliberative Polling in Britain," *British Journal of Political Science* 32 (July 2002): 455–487.

117. Gallup poll, July 10–11, 2001.

118. Gallup poll, August 3–5, 2001.

119. Ibid.

120. Gallup poll, August 10–12, 2001.

121. Gallup poll, July 21–21, 2006.

122. Gallup poll, April 13–15, 2007.

123. Quoted in Bob Woodward, *The Choice* (New York: Simon & Schuster, 1996), p. 315.

CHAPTER 7: CROSS-PRESSURING OPINION

1. Toby Bolsen, James N. Druckman, and Fay Lomax Cook, "The Influence of Partisan Motivated Reasoning on Public Opinion," *Political Behavior* 36 (June 2014): 235–262; James N. Druckman, Erik Peterson, and Rune Slothuus, "How Elite Partisan Polarization Affects Public Opinion Formation," *American Political Science Review* 107 (February 2013): 57–79.

2. See Dennis Chong and James N. Druckman, "Framing Public Opinion in Competitive Democracies," *American Political Science Review* 101 (December 2007): 637–655.

3. Pew Research Center poll, June 12–16, 2013. See also Pew Research Center poll, July 17–21, 2013.

4. Gallup poll, May 12–13, 2006.

5. Pew Research Center poll, June 12–16, 2013.

6. Barack Obama, "Remarks by the President to the White House Press Corps," White House transcript, August 20, 2013.

7. See also CBS News/*New York Times* poll, September 19–23, 2013; NBC News/*Wall Street Journal* poll, August 28–29 and September 5–8, 2013; United Technologies/*National Journal* Congressional Connection poll conducted by Princeton Survey Research Associates International, September 5–8, 2013; ABC News/*Washington Post* poll, September 12–15, 2013; Pew Research Center/*USA Today* poll, September 4–8 and 12–15, 2013; Gallup polls, September 3–4 and 11–12, 2013; McClatchy-Marist poll, September 7–8, 2013.

8. CNN/ORC poll, September 6–8, 2013.

9. ABC News/*Washington Post* poll, September 4–7, 2014. See also Pew Research Center poll, August 20–24, 2014.

10. Pew Research Center poll, September 2–9, 2014.

11. Dina Smeltz and Ivo Daadler, *Foreign Policy in the Age of Retrenchment* (Chicago: Chicago Council on Global Affairs, 2014), pp. 12–13, 28. Dian Smeltz and Craig Kafura, "Are Republicans Really the New Doves?" *The Monkey Cage, Washington Post*, October 6, 2014.

12. This opinion was remarkably stable and had changed little by July 2015. See Pew Research Center poll, July 14–20, 2015.

13. Gallup Poll tracking polls for September 1–7, 2014.

14. CBS News poll, February 13–17, 2015.

15. Edward G. Carmines and James A. Stimson, *Issue Evolution: Race and the Transformation of American Politics* (Princeton, NJ: Princeton University Press, 1989).

16. Mark Smith, *The Right Talk: How Conservatives Transformed the Great Society into the Economic Society* (Princeton, NJ: Princeton University Press, 2007).

17. Byron E. Shafer and Richard Johnston, *The End of Southern Exceptionalism* (Cambridge, MA: Harvard University Press, 2006).

18. Taeku Lee, *Mobilizing Public Opinion: Black Insurgency and Racial Attitudes in the Civil Rights Era* (Chicago: University of Chicago Press, 2002).

19. Gary C. Jacobson, *A Divider, Not a Uniter: George W. Bush and the American Public*, 2nd ed. (New York: Longman, 2007), p. 36. See also Bruce A. Desmarais, Raymond J. La Raja, and Michael S. Kowal, "The Fates of Challengers in U.S. House Elections: The Role of Extended Party Networks in Supporting Candidates and Shaping Electoral Outcomes," *American Journal of Political Science* 59 (January 2015): 194–211; Hans Noel, *Political Ideologies and Political Parties in America* (New York: Cambridge University Press, 2013); Gregory Koger, Seth Masket, and Hans Noel, "Partisan Webs: Information Exchange and Party Networks," *British Journal of Political Science* 39 (July 2009): 633–653; Paul S. Herrnson, "The Roles of Party Organizations, Party-Connected Committees, and Party Allies in Elections," *Journal of Politics* 71 (October 2009): 1207–1224; Seth Masket, *No Middle Ground: How Informal Party Organizations Control Nominations and Polarize Legislatures* (Ann Arbor: University of Michigan Press, 2009); Matt Grossmann and Casey B. Dominguez, "Party Coalitions and Interest Group Networks," *American Politics Research* 37 (September 2009): 767–800.

20. Morris P. Fiorina, *Culture War? The Myth of a Polarized America*, 3rd ed. (New York: Longman, 2010).

CHAPTER 8: REACHING THE BASE

1. Quoted in Reid Cherlin, "The Presidency and the Press," *Rolling Stone*, August 4, 2014.

2. Quoted in Ibid.

3. Quoted in Ibid.

4. Joe S. Foote, "Ratings Decline of Presidential Television," *Journal of Broadcasting and Electronic Media* 32 (Spring 1988): 225.

5. Matthew A. Baum and Samuel Kernell, "Has Cable Ended the Golden Age of Presidential Television?" *American Political Science Review* 93 (March 1999): 99–114; Jeffrey E. Cohen, *The Presidency in the Era of 24-Hour News* (Princeton, NJ: Princeton University Press, 2008).

6. *Washington Post*, March 1, 2001, p. C1.

7. Baum and Kernell, "Has Cable Ended the Golden Age of Presidential Television?"; Markus Prior, "News vs. Entertainment: How Increasing Media Choice Widens Gaps in Political Knowledge and Turnout," *American Journal of Political Science* 49 (July 2005): 577–592.

8. Nielsen Media Research.

9. Paul Brace and Barbara Hinckley, "Presidential Activities from Truman through Reagan: Timing and Impact," *Journal of Politics* 55 (May 1993): 387.

10. See Lori Cox Han, "New Strategies for an Old Medium: The Weekly Radio Addresses of Reagan and Clinton," *Congress & the Presidency* 33 (Spring 2006): 25–45.

11. Beverly Horvit, Adam J. Schiffer, and Mark Wright, "The Limits of Presidential Coverage of the Weekly Radio Address," *Press/Politics* 13, no. 1 (2008): 8–28.

12. Pew Research Center, *The State of the News Media 2015*.

13. Newspaper Association of America.

14. Pew Research Center, *The State of the News Media 2014*.

15. See blog.nielsen.com/nielsenwire/online_mobile/election-gives-online-news-sites-major-traffic-boost/; and Pew Research Center, *The State of the News Media 2014*.

16. Pew Research Center, *The State of the News Media 2014*; Pew Research Center, *News Use Across Social Media Platforms*, 2013; Pew Research Center, *In Changing News Landscape, Even Television Is Vulnerable*, 2012.

17. See Diane J. Heith, "The Virtual Primary Campaign: Connecting with Constituents in a Multimedia Age," in Meena Bose, ed., *The 2008 Road to the White House and Beyond* (College Station: Texas A&M University Press, 2011).

18. Reid Cherlin, "The Presidency and the Press," *Rolling Stone*, August 4, 2014.

19. Helene Cooper, "The Direct Approach," *New York Times*, December 18, 2008.

20. Quoted in Sheryl Gay Stolberg, "A Rewired Bully Pulpit: Big, Bold and Unproven," *New York Times*, November 22, 2008.

21. Stolberg, "A Rewired Bully Pulpit: Big, Bold and Unproven."

22. Chris Cillizza, "Obama Makes a Point of Speaking of the People, to the People," *Washington Post*, December 14, 2008, p. A05.

23. Virginia Heffernan, "The YouTube Presidency—Why the Obama Administration Uploads So Much Video," *New York Times*, April 12, 2009.

24. Brian Stelter, "Obama to Field Questions Posted by YouTube Users," *New York Times*, February 1, 2010.

25. Darren Samuelsohn, "Jon Stewart's Secret White House Visits," *Politico.com*, July 28, 2015.

26. Quoted in Zachary A. Goldfarb and Juliet Eilperin, "White House Looking for New Ways to Penetrate Polarized Media," *Washington Post*, May 6, 2014.

27. Quoted in Goldfarb and Eilperin, "White House Looking for New Ways to Penetrate Polarized Media."

28. Michael D. Shear, "Obama's Social Media Team Tries to Widen Audience for State of the Union Address," *New York Times*, January 19, 2015.

29. Kate Phillips, "Obama Rallies the Base on His Supreme Court Choice," *CQ Today*, May 27, 2009.

30. Oliver Knox, "When the White House Hates Your Tweet," *Yahoo! News*, May 1, 2014.

31. Mark Landler and Helene Cooper, "White House Eager to Project Image of Competence in Relief Efforts," *New York Times*, January 22, 2010.

32. See, for example, Ken Auletta, "Non-Stop News," *New Yorker*, January 25, 2010, p. 44.

33. Michael A. Fletcher and Jose Antonio Vargas, "The White House, Open for Questions," *Washington Post*, March 27, 2009, p. A02; Sheryl Gay Stolberg, "Obama Makes History in Live Internet Video Chat," *New York Times*, March 27, 2009.

34. Goldfarb and Eilperin, "White House Looking for New Ways to Penetrate Polarized Media."

35. Michael D. Shear, "White House Focuses on Reaching Latino Viewers," *New York Times*, July 16, 2013.

36. Pew Research Center, *The State of the News Media 2014*.

37. Carrie Budoff Brown and Reid J. Epstein, "White House Targets Local Media on Obamacare," *Politico*, November 26, 2013.

38. Quoted in Bob Woodward, *The Agenda: Inside the Clinton White House* (New York: Simon & Schuster, 1994), p. 313.

39. Pew Research Center, *The State of the News Media 2014*.

40. Cherlin, "The Presidency and the Press."

41. David Axelrod, *Believer: My Forty Years in Politics* (New York: Penguin Press, 2015), p. 347.

42. Quoted in Goldfarb and Eilperin, "White House Looking for New Ways to Penetrate Polarized Media."

43. Pew Research Center, *Mapping Twitter Topic Networks: From Polarized Crowds to Community Clusters*, February 20, 2014.

44. James Oliphant, "Progressive Bloggers Are Doing the White House's Job," *National Journal*, May 9, 2014.

45. Stolberg, "A Rewired Bully Pulpit."

46. Michael D. Shear, "Campaign Urges Reinstating Ban on Offshore Oil Drilling," *Washington Post*, April 30, 2010.

47. Elham Khatami, "Who Listens to Obama's Addresses?" *Congress.org*, November 8, 2010.

48. Burson-Marsteller, *Twiplomacy: Heads of State and Government and Foreign Ministers on Twitter*, July 2014, p. 4.

49. Quoted in Stolberg, "A Rewired Bully Pulpit."

50. Pew Internet & American Life Project 2008 Post-Election Survey, November 20–December 4, 2008.

51. Lois Romano, " '08 Campaign Guru Focuses on Grass Roots," *Washington Post*, January 13, 2009, p. A13.

52. Peter Wallsten, "Retooling Obama's Campaign Machine for the Long Haul," *Los Angeles Times*, January 14, 2009; Associated Press, "Obama Launches Grass-Roots Campaign," January 17, 2009.

53. Matt Bai, "Democrat in Chief?" *New York Times Sunday Magazine*, June 13, 2010.

54. Ceci Connolly, "Obama Policymakers Turn to Campaign Tools; Network of Supporters Tapped on Health-Care Issues," *Washington Post*, December 4, 2008, p. A1.

55. Quoted in ibid.

56. Quoted in Cillizza, "Obama Makes a Point of Speaking of the People, to the People."

57. Quoted in Wallsten, "Retooling Obama's Campaign Machine for the Long Haul." Italics added.

58. Chris Cillizza, "Obama Enlists Campaign Army in Budget Fight," *Washington Post*, March 16, 2009, p. A1.

59. Dan Eggen, "Obama's Machine Sputters in Effort to Push Budget; Grass-Roots Campaign Has Little Effect," *Washington Post*, April 6, 2009, p. A3.

60. Peter Slevin, "Obama Turns to Grass Roots to Push Health Reform," *Washington Post*, June 24, 2009.

61. Ibid.; and Eli Saslow, "Grass-Roots Battle Tests the Obama Movement," *Washington Post*, August 23, 2009.

62. Saslow, "Grass-Roots Battle Tests the Obama Movement."

63. Jeff Zeleny, "Health Debate Fails to Ignite Obama's Grass Roots," *New York Times*, August 15, 2009.

64. Jonathan Alter, *The Promise: President Obama, Year One* (New York: Simon & Schuster, 2010), pp. 252, 398.

65. Amy Gardner, "Midterms Pose Major Challenge for Obama's Grass-Roots Political Organization," *Washington Post*, March 28, 2010.

66. Philip Rucker, "Obama Mobilizes Volunteers to Urge Repeal of 'Don't Ask, Don't Tell,' " *Washington Post*, December 17, 2009.

67. Ibid.

68. Slevin, "Obama Turns to Grass Roots to Push Health Reform."

69. Adam Aigner-Treworgy, "OFA Collects 1.4 Million Signatures for Gun Control," *CNN politicalticker . . .* , May 7, 2013.

70. Jon Carson, "What Do You Have to Say to Congress?" *Organizing for Action*, April 18, 2013.

71. Reid J. Epstein, "OFA's First Foray Falls Short," *Politico*, May 3, 2013.

72. Juliet Eilperin, "Organizing for Action Struggles to Move the Needle on Obama's Agenda," *Washington Post*, May 11, 2013.

73. Philip Bump, "How Much Longer Will Organizing for Action Survive?" *Washington Post*, May 20, 2014.

74. Jonathan Kingler, "Going Private: Presidential Grassroots Lobbying Organizations, Targeted Appeals, and Neighborhood Persuasion Campaigns," paper presented

at the Annual Meeting of the American Political Science Association, Washington, DC, August 27–31, 2014.

75. Philip Bump, "Organizing For Action Wanted Us to Evaluate Them on Their Work. So We Did," *Washington Post*, July 30, 2014.

76. Epstein, "OFA's First Foray Falls Short."

77. Bump, "How Much Longer Will Organizing for Action Survive?"

78. Also see Diane J. Heith, "Obama and the Public Presidency: What Got You Here Won't Get You There," in Colin Campbell, Bert A. Rockman, and Andrew Rudalevige, eds., *The Barack Obama Presidency: Appraisals and Prospects* (Washington, DC: CQ Press, 2011).

CHAPTER 9: EXPLOITING PARTISANS IN CONGRESS

1. Lyndon Johnson quoted in Doris Kearns, *Lyndon Johnson and the American Dream* (New York: Harper & Row, 1976), p. 226.

2. See George C. Edwards III, *At the Margins: Presidential Leadership of Congress* (New Haven, CT: Yale University Press, 1989), chap. 4.

3. Ibid., p. 178.

4. Frances E. Lee, *Beyond Ideology: Politics, Principles, and Partisanship in the U.S. Senate* (Chicago: University of Chicago Press, 2009).

5. Jimmy Carter, *Keeping Faith* (New York: Bantam, 1982), p. 80.

6. John W. Kingdon, *Congressmen's Voting Decisions* (New York: Harper & Row, 1973), pp. 172–173.

7. Ibid., pp. 172, 175–176, 178, 180. See also Donald R. Matthews, *U.S. Senators and Their World* (New York: W.W. Norton, 1973), p. 140.

8. Quoted in Stephen J. Wayne, *The Legislative Presidency* (New York: Harper & Row, 1978), p. 151. See also Lawrence F. O'Brien, "Larry O'Brien discusses White House Contacts on Capitol Hill," in Aaron Wildavsky, ed., *The Presidency* (Boston, MA: Little Brown, 1969), p. 482.

9. Christopher R. Berry, Barry C. Burden, and William G. Howell, "The President and the Distribution of Federal Spending," *American Political Science Review* 104 (November 2010): 783–799; Adam M. Dynes and Gregory A. Huber, "Partisanship and the Allocation of Federal Spending: Do Same-Party Legislators or Voters Benefit from Shared Party Affiliation with the President and House Majority?" *American Political Science Review* 109 (February 2015): 172–186; Douglas L. Kriner and Andrew Reeves, "Presidential Particularism and Divide-the-Dollar Politics," *American Political Science Review* 109 (February 2015): 155–171; John Hudak, *Presidential Pork* (Washington, DC: Brookings Institution, 2014).

10. Lawrence O'Brien, in Robert L. Hardesty, ed., *The Johnson Years: The Difference He Made* (Austin, TX: Lyndon B. Johnson School of Public Affairs, 1993), p. 75.

11. Timothy P. Nokken, "Ideological Congruence Versus Electoral Success: Distribution of Party Organization Contributions in Senate Elections, 1990–2000," *American Politics Research* 31 (January 2003): 3–26; David F. Damore and Thomas G. Hansford, "The Allocation of Party Controlled Campaign Resources in the House of Representatives, 1989–1996," *Political Research Quarterly* 52 (June 1999): 371–385; David M. Cantor and Paul S. Herrnson, "Party Campaign Activity and Party Unity in the U.S.

House of Representatives," *Legislative Studies Quarterly* 22, no. 3 (August 1997): 393–415.

12. Jon R. Bond and Richard Fleisher, *The President in the Legislative Arena* (Chicago: University of Chicago Press, 1980), chap. 8; Richard Fleisher, Jon R. Bond, and B. Dan Wood, "Which Presidents Are Uncommonly Successful in Congress?" in Bert Rockman and Richard W. Waterman, eds., *Presidential Leadership: The Vortex of Presidential Power* (New York: Oxford University Press, 2007).

13. Keith Krehbiel, *Pivotal Politics: A Theory of U.S. Lawmaking* (Chicago: University of Chicago Press, 1998), chaps. 7–8.

14. For Carter's description of this process, see George C. Edwards III, "Interview with President Jimmy Carter," *Presidential Studies Quarterly* 38 (March 2008): 7–8, 12.

15. Calvin Mouw and Michael MacKuen, "The Strategic Configuration, Personal Influence, and Presidential Power in Congress," *Western Political Quarterly* 45 (September 1992): 598.

16. O'Brien, in Hardesty, *The Johnson Years*, p. 76. See also comments by Nicholas Katzenbach, p. 81.

17. See James L. Sundquist, *Politics and Policy: The Eisenhower, Kennedy, and Johnson Years* (Washington, DC: Brookings Institution, 1968).

18. Randall B. Woods, *LBJ: Architect of American Ambition* (New York: Free Press, 2006), p. 668.

19. Lawrence R. Jacobs, *The Health of Nations: Public Opinion and the Making of American and British Health Policy* (Ithaca, NY: Cornell University Press, 1993).

20. Quoted in Mark A. Peterson, *Legislating Together* (Cambridge, MA: Harvard University Press, 1990), pp. 69–70.

21. Carl Albert, interview by Dorothy Pierce McSweeny, July 9, 1969, interview 3, transcript, pp. 7, 11, Lyndon Baines Johnson Library, Austin, TX; Carl Albert, interview by Dorothy Pierce McSweeny, August 13, 1969, interview 4, transcript, pp. 22, 25, Lyndon Baines Johnson Library; Carl Albert, interview by Dorothy Pierce McSweeny, April 28, 1969, interview 1, transcript, pp. 22–23, Lyndon Baines Johnson Library; Carl Albert, interview by Dorothy Pierce McSweeny, June 10, 1969, interview 2, transcript, p. 14, Lyndon Baines Johnson Library.

22. Albert, interview 4, pp. 23–24. See also Joseph A. Califano, *A Presidential Nation* (New York: W. W. Norton, 1975), p. 155.

23. Quoted in Lawrence F. O'Brien, *No Final Victories* (New York: Ballantine, 1974), p. 180. See also p. 181.

24. O'Brien, in Hardesty, *The Johnson Years*, pp. 76–77. See also Nicholas Katzenbach, p. 81; Barefoot Sanders, p. 83; and Lee White, p. 84; and Russell Renka, "Comparing Presidents Kennedy and Johnson as Legislative Leaders," paper presented at the annual meeting of the Southern Political Science Association, Savannah, Georgia, November 1984, p. 10, table 4.

25. See, for example, Charles Halleck, interview by Stephen Hess, March 22, 1965, transcript, p. 28; Hale Boggs, interview by Charles T. Morrissey, May 10, 1964, transcript, p. 26, John F. Kennedy Library, Boston.

26. Henry Hall Wilson, interview by Joe B. Frantz, April 11, 1973, transcript, pp. 6–7, Lyndon Baines Johnson Library, Austin, TX.

27. Mike Manatos, interview by Joe B. Frantz, August 25, 1969, transcript, pp. 13–14, Lyndon Baines Johnson Library, Austin, TX.

28. John McCormack, interview by T. Harrison Baker, September 23, 1968, transcript, pp. 20, 39–40, Lyndon Baines Johnson Library; Carl Albert, interview by Dorothy Pierce McSweeny, July 9, 1969, interview 3, transcript, p. 4, Lyndon Baines Johnson Library; Goldman, *The Tragedy of Lyndon Johnson*, p. 68; Charles Halleck, interview by Stephen Hess, March 22, 1965, transcript, p. 27, John F. Kennedy Library, Boston; O'Brien, *No Final Victories*, pp. 106, 145–149, 188–189; Richard Bolling, *Power in the House* (New York: Capricorn, 1974), pp. 218, 229; Califano, *A Presidential Nation*, p. 155; Manatos, interview by Frantz, pp. 14, 29–30, 57–58 (see also p. 32); James L. Sundquist, *Politics and Policy* (Washington, DC: Brookings Institution, 1968), pp. 476–82; Joseph Cooper and Gary Bombardier, "Presidential Leadership and Party Success," *Journal of Politics* 30 (November 1968): 1012–1027; Aage R. Clausen, *How Congressmen Decide* (New York: St. Martin's, 1973), p. 146. See also Rowland Evans and Robert Novak, *Lyndon B. Johnson: The Exercise of Power* (New York: New American Library, 1966), p. 364.

29. Arthur M. Schlesinger, Jr., *Robert Kennedy and His Times* (New York: Ballantine, 1978), p. 742.

30. Quoted in William Greider, "The Education of David Stockman," *Atlantic*, December 1981, p. 52.

31. Renka, "Comparing Presidents Kennedy and Johnson as Legislative Leaders," p. 26. See also Albert, interview by McSweeny, interview 3, p. 3.

32. George C. Edwards III, *Presidential Influence in Congress* (San Francisco: W. H. Freeman, 1980), pp. 197–199.

33. Jon R. Bond and Richard Fleisher, *The President in the Legislative Arena* (Chicago: University of Chicago Press, 1990), pp. 215–218.

34. Manatos interview by Frantz, p. 18.

35. Quoted in Julian Zelizer, *The Fierce Urgency of Now* (New York: Penguin Press, 2015), p. 290.

36. Wilson, interview by Frantz, p. 9. See also Harold Barefoot Sanders, interview by Joe B. Frantz, March 24, 1969, tape 2, transcript, pp. 5, 8, Lyndon Baines Johnson Library, Austin, TX.

37. Michael R. Beschloss, *Taking Charge: The Johnson White House Tapes, 1963–1964* (New York: Simon & Schuster, 1997); Michael R. Beschloss, *Reaching for Glory: Lyndon Johnson's Secret White House Tapes, 1964–1965* (New York: Simon & Schuster, 2001).

38. Gary C. Jacobson, "The President's Effect on Partisan Attitudes," *Presidential Studies Quarterly* 42 (December 2012): 683–718.

39. ANES 2012. Both the 2012 National Exit Poll and the CCES found that 93 percent of partisans reported voting for their party's House candidates and 92 percent for their party's Senate candidate. The figures for split voting in the exit polls were 7 percent for the House and 9 percent for the Senate. A good review of this data can be found in Gary C. Jacobson, "Barack Obama and the Nationalization of Electoral Politics in 2012," *Electoral Studies* (forthcoming); and Gary C. Jacobson, "Partisan Polarization in American Politics," *Presidential Studies Quarterly* 43 (December 2013): 688–708.

40. James E. Campbell and Joe A. Sumners, "Presidential Coattails in Senate Elections," *American Political Science Review* 84 (June 1990): 513–524; and George C. Edwards III, *The Public Presidency* (New York: St. Martin's, 1983), pp. 83–93.

41. Paul Herrnson, Irwin Morris, and John McTague, "The Impact of Presidential

Campaigning for Congress on Presidential Support in the U.S. House of Representatives," *Legislative Studies Quarterly* 36 (February 2011): 99–122.

42. Edward-Isaac Dovere, "President Obama Plays the Campaign Calendar Blues," *Politico.com*, September 24, 2014.

43. For evidence of the impact of the president's campaigning in midterm elections, see Jeffrey E. Cohen, Michael A. Krassa, and John A. Hamman, "The Impact of Presidential Campaigning on Midterm U.S. Senate Elections," *American Political Science Review* 85 (March 1991): 165–178. On the president's effect on congressional elections more broadly, see James E. Campbell, *The Presidential Pulse of Congressional Elections* (Lexington: University Press of Kentucky, 1993).

44. Zelizer, *The Fierce Urgency of Now.*

45. Woods, *LBJ*, p. 560.

46. Lyndon B. Johnson, *The Vantage Point: Perspectives on the Presidency, 1963–1969* (New York: Popular Library, 1971), p. 323. See also Eric F. Goldman, *The Tragedy of Lyndon Johnson* (New York: Dell, 1974), pp. 306–307, Nicholas Katzenbach in Hardesty, ed., *The Johnson Years*, p. 81.

47. See Bill Moyers in Hardesty, ed., *The Johnson Years*, pp. 65–66.

48. Quoted in Harry McPherson, *A Political Education* (Boston: Little, Brown, 1972), p. 268.

49. See Paul C. Light, *The President's Agenda: Domestic Policy Choice from Kennedy to Carter* (Baltimore, MD: Johns Hopkins University Press, 1982), pp. 58–59, on the utility of this approach. Also see Lee White in Hardesty, ed., *The Johnson Years*, p. 84.

50. Quoted in Jack Valenti, *A Very Human President* (New York: W. W. Norton, 1975), p. 144. See also Kearns, *Lyndon Johnson and the American Dream*, pp. 216–217; Goldman, *The Tragedy of Lyndon Johnson*, pp. 306–307; McPherson, *A Political Education*, pp. 268, 428.

51. See Edwards, *At the Margins*, pp. 204–205; Joseph A. Califano, Jr., *The Triumph and Tragedy of Lyndon Johnson* (New York: Simon & Schuster, 1991), pp. 119–120.

52. Nevertheless, Johnson was always ready to exploit an opportunity. For example, he saw an opportunity to exploit the assassination of Martin Luther King, Jr., for a fair housing bill and the assassination of Robert Kennedy for a gun control measure. See Califano, *The Triumph and Tragedy of Lyndon Johnson*, pp. 276, 292.

53. Woods, *LBJ*, p. 805.

54. Zelizer, *The Fierce Urgency of Now*, p. 303.

55. "Numerous Factors Favoring Good Relationship Between Reagan and New Congress," *Congressional Quarterly Weekly Report*, January 24, 1981, p. 172.

56. David A. Stockman, *The Triumph of Politics* (New York: Harper & Row, 1986), pp. 79–80; see also p. 120.

57. See Greider, "The Education of David Stockman," pp. 38, 40, 43, 45, 54; Lawrence J. Korb, "Spending Without Strategy," *International Security* 12 (Summer 1987): 169.

58. James A. Baker III, *"Work Hard, Study . . . and Keep Out of Politics!"* (New York: G. P. Putnam's Sons, 2006), pp. 132–133, 136–137, 148, 171; Lou Cannon, *President Reagan: The Role of a Lifetime* (New York: Simon & Schuster, 1991), pp. 163, 344.

59. Quoted in Bernard Weinraub, "Back in the Legislative Strategist's Saddle Again," *New York Times*, May 28, 1985, p. A10.

60. George C. Edwards III, *The Strategic President: Persuasion and Opportunity in Presi-*

dential Leadership (Princeton, NJ: Princeton University Press), chaps. 4–5; Edwards, *At the Margins*, chaps. 9–10.

CHAPTER 10: LEADERSHIP, OPPORTUNITY, AND STRATEGIC ASSESSMENTS

1. George C. Edwards III, *On Deaf Ears: The Limits of the Bully Pulpit* (New Haven, CT: Yale University Press, 2004); Samuel Kernell, *Going Public: New Strategies of Presidential Leadership*, 4th ed. (Washington, DC: CQ Press, 2007); George C. Edwards III, *Governing by Campaigning: The Politics of the Bush Presidency*, 2nd ed. (New York: Longman, 2007); George C. Edwards III, *The Public Presidency* (New York: St. Martin's, 1983).

2. See George C. Edwards III, *Overreach: Leadership in the Obama Presidency* (Princeton, NJ: Princeton University Press, 2012), chaps. 4–6.

3. George C. Edwards III, *The Strategic President: Persuasion and Opportunity in Presidential Leadership* (Princeton, NJ: Princeton University Press, 2009), pp. 192–199.

4. Edwards, *Overreach*.

5. Transcript: "President Barack Obama," *60 Minutes*, Interview by Steve Kroft, November 4, 2010.

6. Brendan Nyhan, Eric McGhee, John Sides, Seth Masket, and Steven Greene, "One Vote Out of Step? The Effects of Salient Roll Call Votes in the 2010 Election," *American Politics Research* 40 (September 2012): 844–879; Gary C. Jacobson, "The Republican Resurgence in 2010," *Political Science Quarterly* 127 (Spring 2011): 35–66; Gary C. Jacobson, "Legislative Success and Political Failure: The Public's Reaction to Barack Obama's Early Presidency," *Presidential Studies Quarterly* 41 (June 2011): 231–232; David W. Brady, Morris P. Fiorina, and Arjun S. Wilkins, "The 2010 Elections: Why Did Political Science Forecasts Go Awry?" *PS: Political Science and Politics* 44 (April 2011): 247–250; Chris Cillizza, "What Effect Did Health-care Reform Have on Election?" *Washington Post*, November 7, 2010; Survey conducted jointly by Resurgent Republic and Democracy Corps on behalf of the Bipartisan Policy Center, November 2–3, 2010, among 886 voters in the midterm election; Kaiser Health Tracking Poll, November 3–6, 2010; Nate Silver, "Health Care and Bailout Votes May Have Hurt Democrats," *New York Times*, November 16, 2010; Eric McGhee, "Did Controversial Roll Call Votes Doom the Democrats?" *The Monkey Cage*, November 4, 2010; Eric McGhee, "Which Roll Call Votes Hurt the Democrats?" *The Monkey Cage*, November 9, 2010.

7. See, for example, Gallup poll of September 13–16, 2010.

8. Jeremy W. Peters, "Schumer Criticizes Timing of Affordable Care Act," *New York Times*, November 25, 2014.

9. This was the president's view. See David Axelrod, *Believer: My Forty Years in Politics* (New York: Penguin Press, 2015), pp. 372–373.

10. Quoted in Shailagh Murray, Michael D. Shear, and Paul Kane, "2009 Democratic Agenda Severely Weakened by Republicans' United Opposition," *Washington Post*, January 24, 2010.

11. Quoted in Sheryl Gay Stolberg, "White House Nudges Test the Power of Persuasion," *New York Times*, February 24, 2010. See also "Press Briefing by Press Secretary Jay Carney," White House, July 10, 2013.

12. Jonathan Alter, *The Center Holds: Obama and His Enemies* (New York: Simon & Schuster, 2013), p. 111.

13. Quoted in Max Farrand, ed., "CCCLXVII, Jared Sparks: Journal, April 19, 1830," *The Records of the Federal Convention of 1787*, vol. III, rev. ed. (New Haven, CT: Yale University Press, 1966), pp. 479.

14. Mark Smith, *American Business and Political Power: Public Opinion, Elections, and Democracy* (Chicago: University of Chicago Press, 2000).

15. Lawrence R. Jacobs and Theda Skocpol, *Health Care Reform and American Politics*, rev. ed. (New York: Oxford University Press, 2012); Lawrence R. Jacobs and Robert Y. Shapiro, *Politicians Don't Pander: Political Manipulation and the Loss of Democratic Responsiveness* (Chicago: Chicago University Press, 2000); Darrel West and Burdett Loomis, *The Sound of Money: How Political Interests Get What They Want* (New York: W.W. Norton, 1999).

16. Lawrence R. Jacobs and Suzanne Mettler, "Why Public Opinion Changes: The Implications for Health and Health Policy," *Journal of Health Policy, Politics and Law* 36, no. 6 (2011): 917–933; April A. Strickland, Charles S. Taber, and Milton Lodge, "Motivated Reasoning and Public Opinion," *Journal of Health Politics, Policy and Law* 36, no. 6 (2011): 935–944.

17. David Brady and Morris Fiorina, "Congress in the Era of the Permanent Campaign," in Norman Ornstein and Thomas Mann, eds., *The Permanent Campaign and Its Future* (Washington, DC: American Enterprise Institute and Brookings Institution, 2000); Hugh Heclo, "Campaigning and Governing: A Conspectus," in *The Permanent Campaign and Its Future*; Norman J. Ornstein and Thomas E. Mann, "Conclusion: The Permanent Campaign and the Future of American Democracy," in *The Permanent Campaign and Its Future*.

18. Quoted in Farrand, ed., "CCCLXVII, Jared Sparks: Journal, April 19, 1830," pp. 479.

19. Gary C. Jacobson, "Partisan Polarization in American Politics: A Background Paper," *Presidential Studies Quarterly* 43 (December 2013): 688–708.

20. Alan I. Abramowitz, *The Disappearing Center* (New Haven, CT: Yale University Press, 2010); Morris P. Fiorina, with Samuel J. Abrams and Jeremy C. Pope, *Culture Wars? The Myth of Polarized America*, 3rd ed. (New York: Pearson Longman, 2011).

21. Gallup poll, October 14–15, 2013; Pew Research Center poll, October 3–6, 2013; CBS News poll, October 1–2, 2013.

22. Sean M. Theriault, *The Gingrich Senators: The Roots of Partisan Warfare in Congress* (New York: Oxford University Press, 2013); Sean M. Theriault, *Party Polarization in Congress* (New York: Cambridge University Press, 2008).

23. Gallup poll, September 5–8, 2013; Pew Research Center poll, January 9–13, 2013, July 17–21, 2013, and November 6–9, 2014; Ronald B. Rapoport, Meredith Dost, Ani-Rae Lovell, and Walter J. Stone, "Republican Factionalism and Tea Party Activists," paper prepared for delivery at the Annual Meeting of the Midwest Political Science Association, Chicago, April 11–14, 2013.

24. Francis E. Lee, *Beyond Ideology: Politics, Principles, and Partisanship in the U.S. Senate* (Chicago: University of Chicago Press, 2009); Francis E. Lee, "Presidents and Party Teams: The Politics of Debt Limits and Executive Oversight, 2001–2013," *Presidential Studies Quarterly* 43 (December 2013): 775–791; Thomas E. Mann and Norman J. Ornstein, *It's Even Worse than It Looks* (New York: Basic Books, 2012).

Index